Environmental Policy and Administrative Change

Implementation of the National Environmental Policy Act

Richard N.L. Andrews
University of Michigan

Lexington Books
D.C. Heath and Company
Lexington, Massachusetts
Toronto

Library of Congress Cataloging in Publication Data

Andrews, Richard N L
  Environmental policy and administrative change.

  "The national environmental policy act of 1969": p.
  Includes index.
    1. Environmental law—United States. 2. United States. Laws,
statutes, etc. National environmental policy act of 1969. I. United
States. Laws, statutes, etc. National environmental policy act of 1969.
1976. II. Title
KF3775.A96   353.008'232   76-7265
ISBN 0-669-00682-3

Published simultaneously in Canada

Printed in the United States of America

International Standard Book Number: 0-669-00682-3

Library of Congress Catalog Card Number: 76-7265

Environmental Policy and Administrative Change

**To Maynard
and
to Hannah**

Contents

List of Tables and Figure

Figure

Foreword

When in 1789 a truly national government was first established for the United States, great care was taken to restrict and control its use of Executive power. The government was based upon a written constitution that specified powers and functions delegated to it *by* the people *from* the states—"We the people," the Preamble begins. All powers *not* so delegated were retained by the states or by the people, who were the only legitimate authors of government. These powers, categorized as legislative, executive, and judicial, were divided among three branches of the government so that none could be wholly independent of the others and none could control the others. By this constitutional mechanism it was hoped that people could exercise effective control over the actions of their federal officials.

The National Environmental Policy Act (NEPA) was written because the constitutional mechanics of the founders proved inadequate to their purpose of popular control. They could not foresee the enormous growth of federal power in response to the needs of a populous, industrialized, and interdependent nation They could not foresee the enormous concentration of private economic power, the development of professionalism in the public service and of advanced technology throughout broad sectors of the economy. As the nation became more complex and diverse in values, goals, and economic activities, its government became more specialized, client-oriented, and self-directing. Correspondingly, its agencies became less responsive to the public generally as they directed their concerns primarily to their special clients or missions.

For example, the Department of Agriculture, the Bureau of Reclamation, the Corps of Engineers, and the Federal Highway Administration became locked into policies and client relationships that reinforced specialized mission objectives, but isolated and insulated them from changing public attitudes and values. Responding to special needs and interests, the Congress wrote laws that cumulatively conferred great powers upon these agencies, but were enacted with little foresight regarding their indirect consequences. And so when, in the nineteen sixties, public awareness of environmental deterioration reached a point of loud demand for corrective action, they and many other institutions, public and private, were slow to hear the message and slower yet to take it seriously.

The White House Conference on Natural Beauty in 1965 marked the beginning of a popular effort to redirect the priorities of the federal agencies— to force them in pursuit of their missions to take account of public concern for the quality of the environment. Failure of the Executive Branch to lead this movement after 1965 resulted in massive grass roots pressure upon the Congress. The National Environmental Policy Act is a rare and notable consequence of Congressional initiative in response to a widely-felt public need. The people led the Congress, and the Congress, acting on their behalf, sought to redirect a reluctant President and Executive Branch.

The National Environmental Policy Act is therefore an illustration of the politics of American self-government. It is a case of social control toward broad public objectives being applied to the bureaucratic and technical functions of government. The Act does not *establish* environmental policy, but it declares what that policy *ought to be* and, through the environmental impact assessment provision (Sec. 102.2C), requires the agencies to show that they have paid attention to these policy objectives.

Recognizing that the mandated policy goes against the grain of traditional agency policy and practice, and that environmental considerations may rank low among Presidential comprehension and priorities, the Congress opened the way to citizen enforcement through the impact statement review procedures. The courts, in liberalizing standing-to-sue provisions, and in giving a generally strict interpretation of the agency performance required by the Act, have further enlarged this opening toward a more effective role for the citizen in the shaping and administration of public policy.

The foregoing considerations point directly toward the two ways in which this book by Richard Andrews is important. It is obviously important as an examination of how the American people are dealing with a major social problem—their relationship to their environment. The book is important because of the critical nature of the environmental issues with which it, and NEPA, deals. But it is also important as political science—as a case study in how that abstract collectivity of real people called "the American public" attempts to clarify, modify, and direct the priorities of their national government. It is also a study in the problem of identifying "the public interest," because environmental priorities are obviously not the same for all people.

The NEPA activates value conflicts formerly repressed or latent in American society. But the distrubing potential of the Act is greater than its practical effect thus far because its possibilities have not been fully utilized. Presidents, with the exception of actions by Richard Nixon during the first months following enactment, have failed to give it vigorous support. The courts, moreover, have been ambivalent with respect to the practical significance of its substantive provisions (Sec. 101). The Congress has underfunded the Council on Environmental Quality (in deference to Presidential priorities) and no President, to date, has chosen to use the C.E.Q. as an instrument of policy, or permitted it to use fully its statutory powers.

This book is a perceptive and realistic assessment of this important exceptional and controversial piece of federal legislation. It focuses upon a moving target, as the Act continues to be interpreted, resisted, and modified by events.

NEPA is not well understood by a public whose anxieties produced it; and it is often confused with the regulatory legislation pertaining to the quality of air, water, and to specific environmental hazards. The large literature generated by NEPA is heavily concentrated in the law journals and is not conveniently accessible to readers generally. This volume is therefore additionally welcome as it brings an important issue to the public in a single comprehensible volume. It deserves a wide audience, not merely among persons with special environmental interests, but among the public generally.

Madrid, February 21, 1976   **Lynton K. Caldwell**

Preface

The National Environmental Policy Act, which became law on New Year's Day of 1970, seemed rather unremarkable at the time of its passage. It was a short law: it had only two titles and could be printed easily on four pages. It was a most uncontroversial proposal: it sailed through Congress in ten months, with only one to two days of hearings in each house; its drafts passed the Senate by unanimous consent and the House with only fifteen dissenting votes; and its final version passed both houses easily by voice vote. With all the controversy of the previous year over the Santa Barbara oil spill, and the nomination of Governor Walter Hickel as Secretary of the Interior, it must have looked to most observers and legislators like just one more rhetorical bandaid to mollify a concerned public—long on symbolism but short and cheap on substance.

Looking back from the perspective of six years later, however, we survey a rather extraordinary record of activities and changes in government that have been induced or compelled by this simple-looking piece of legislation. Most obviously, federal agencies have already prepared and released more than 6,000 of the "detailed statements" that NEPA required for any "major federal action that might significantly affect the quality of the human environment". This figure represents an average of over 1,000 per year, on everything from highway segments and new federal office buildings to dams, powerplant licenses, nuclear technology development, and coal and oil leases. Hundreds of federal proposals have been challenged in court, and many of these have been enjoined at least temporarily while further studies were completed. Many actions have been modified, and some have been abandoned, as a result of the considerations introduced by this law. More generally, on the basis of information on expected impacts provided by these documents, the spotlight of publicity has been focussed to an unprecedented degree upon federal action proposals across the land. Finally, while Congressmen may not have thought carefully about the possible implications of this law when they passed it, it has since been emulated by statute or executive order in twenty-two states and several foreign nations, who can claim no such ignorance; and despite grumbling and threats of a "backlash," the Congress itself has amended the law only in a few minor respects. Clearly, this statute has created a major innovation in the administration of public programs, and one that has struck responsive chords with other governments as well.

In view of this record, it is rather surprising that no detailed analysis has yet been published concerning the effects of NEPA on the agencies charged with its implementation. An extensive legal literature has emerged, especially comments on the many judicial decisions that have been issued, and there has been a broad smattering of general evaluations as well as case studies of individual controversies. It appears, however, that extremely few people have attempted to look carefully at the overall *patterns* of response to this law exhibited by the various federal agencies—despite the fact that it was these patterns of administrative behavior, not merely the outcome of one or another project, that NEPA's originators sought most deliberately to modify.

This book is an effort to fill part of the gap that has thereby emerged and to illuminate some of the important lessons that can be learned from the study of agencies' responses to a new mandate such as NEPA. Its approach is to compare two federal programs that are lodged in very different organizational environments—the water resource development programs of the Army Corps of Engineers and the Soil Conservation Service—but that consist in large part of actions such as the impoundment of reservoirs and the excavation of river and stream channels that are very similar in their environmental impacts. The value of such a comparison is at least twofold: it can tell us a great deal about the variance among administrative responses to a common legislative mandate, especially if significant differences can be shown even between agencies taking similar actions, and it can also suggest broader propositions about the influence of organizational and political environment upon the adaptive behavior of administrative agencies. If these propositions are correct, they suggest important conclusions not only about the efficacy of NEPA, but about the efficacy of any legislative attempt to modify the behavior patterns of administrative bureaucracies that seeks to use instruments such as those created in NEPA.

Two cautionary notes are in order concerning the extent to which the conclusions of this study can be generalized. First, water resource development programs share certain features with other government programs, but they are only one sector of government activity and do have certain idiosyncracies as well. Other sorts of programs have experienced some different sorts of problems; revenue-sharing, regulatory, and land-management programs are examples. Second, the agencies' responses to NEPA are still evolving, though at a slower rate than in the early years that are the subject of this study. Generally accepted interpretations have been developed for many of the early questions that arose, and despite important remaining differences, NEPA's procedural requirements have generally been assimilated into agency practice. Yet many lawsuits are still being filed and often won against the agencies, and the threat of controversy continues to exert a pervasive cautionary force on agencies contemplating environmentally significant actions; and as long as this force exists, continued evolution may be expected in agency efforts to cope with it and adapt to it.

With these mild cautions in mind, I believe that this study may provide fruitful insights concerning the effects of NEPA on federal agencies, both for the many citizens and administrators who have become participants in environmental management controversies, and for students with a more general interest in law and government, public administration and public policy studies, and water resource planning and management.

Richard N.L. Andrews

Acknowledgments

Information and ideas shared with me by a diverse collection of persons have materially contributed to this research, and I should like to take this opportunity to express my appreciation to these persons, individually and collectively, for their assistance. Many staff members of the agencies took time to respond to questionnaires concerning the effects of NEPA in their jurisdictions, and others provided me with documentary data, interviews, and other information that helped to form the basis for this study. In the latter category, thanks are also due to staff members of the Council on Environmental Quality, the Office of Management and Budget, the Library of Congress, and several congressional committees whose jurisdictions include the agencies and the subjects discussed. Particular thanks are also due the Natural Resource Programs Division of the Office of Management and Budget, which provided me with the opportunity to carry out staff research on topics related to the subject of this study. Some of these officials may disagree with my interpretations of the evidence or with the conclusions drawn from it, and they bear no responsibility for either. I am grateful for their contributions, however, and I welcome their further comments and suggestions.

Portions of this work appeared previously in 16 *Natural Resources Journal*, published by the University of New Mexico School of Law and are reprinted by permission. Also, portions herein appeared in the *Environmental Law Reporter*, © 1976 by the Environmental Law Institute, reprinted by permission. I wish to acknowledge both of these publishers.

I owe a special debt of gratitude to Maynard M. Hufschmidt and Blair T. Bower, both of whom have been unstinting sources of ideas, criticisms, experienced judgement, and other assistance to me. I acknowledge their contributions, both to this study and to my understanding of environmental issues generally, with sincere thanks. Milton S. Heath, Jonathan B. Howes, Deil S. Wright, Robert T. Daland, Philip Soper, Lynton K. Caldwell, and William W. Hill also commented upon drafts of this manuscript at various stages of completion; many of their comments have been incorporated, and all have been appreciated.

Particular thanks are also due to the staff of the School of Natural Resources Service Center of the University of Michigan, who shared the prodigious task of typing drafts of the manuscript: particularly Myrtle Kreie, Joan Greear, L. Jean Honey, and Donna M. Kraetzer.

Finally, I should like to express personal thanks to Hannah Wheeler Andrews, whose ideas as well as her patience have been helpful to me throughout this research, and to Sarah Huntington Andrews, whose arrival enlivened some stages of it.

This study was supported in part by a fellowship granted by Resources for the Future, Inc., and its support is gratefully acknowledged. The conclusions, opinions, and other statements contained in the study, however, are those of the author, and not necessarily those of Resources for the Future, Inc.

1 Federal Agencies and Environmental Policy

The most important feature of the [National Environmental Policy] Act, . . . and probably the least recognized, is that it established new decision-making procedures for all agencies of the Federal government. Some of these procedures are designed to establish checks and balances to ensure that potential environmental problems will be identified and considered early in the decision-making process and not after irrevocable commitments have been made.*

—Senator Henry M. Jackson,
Author of the National Environmental Policy Act

The National Environmental Policy Act—now known as NEPA—was an attempt by members of the Congress to change the processes by which the agencies of the federal government planned their activities. Its proximate origin was a growing congressional concern, during the late 1960s, over the disjointed and inconsistent manner in which federal agencies made decisions affecting the human environment. Its purpose, as stated by its principal author, was to ensure that federal plans and decisions reflected fair consideration of all conflicting demands for the uses of such resources; in the words of this author, Senator Henry M. Jackson of Washington, in introducing the bill:

The responsibilities and functions of government institutions as presently organized are extremely fractionated. We have, for example, separate agencies and separate policies on shipping, fisheries, mines, forests, and water resource development. At some point in our history we felt it was wise to organize Government around these concepts. This organization reflects our early national goals of resources exploitation, economic development, and conquest.

Our national goals have, however, changed a great deal in recent years. Today Government organization does not reflect this change in objectives and the new demands which are being placed on the environment . . . New approaches are required if we are to be successful in the management of our future environment.[1]

The new approach to environmental management sponsored by Senator Jackson included three central elements: first, a general statement of congressional policy declaring a federal responsibility "to create and maintain . . .

---

*Henry M. Jackson, "Environmental Quality, the Courts, and Congress," *Michigan Law Review* LXVIII (May 1970), p. 1079.

productive harmony [between] man and nature";[2] second, the establishment of new procedural requirements, including one which required federal agencies to consider, and make public, the impacts of their actions on the human environment; and finally, the creation of a Council on Environmental Quality in the Executive Office of the President.

The first of these three elements, the general policy statement, was not a new or unusual sort of action for the Congress to take, though its substance affirmed principles that had not previously been stated as general policies of the federal government. The third, similarly, was not without precedent, though it was somewhat more unusual—the Council of Economic Advisors, for instance, is similar in its general structure and in many of its powers. The second element, however, established a new and unique mechanism for the achievement of change in the activities of administrative agencies. For the first time, agencies were required to file public statements describing the "environmental impacts" of their proposed actions and explicitly identifying alternatives to those proposals; and they were required to circulate these statements for comment by the full range of agencies whose activities might be affected by the proposal, and to make them public. They were further required to use the perspectives of diverse disciplines in developing their proposals, to give new consideration to intangible values, and to develop alternative proposals wherever significant conflicts were evident. These new mandates posed an unprecedented challenge not only to the goals of some agencies, but also to the accepted norms of behavior and planning in all of them.

This book is an attempt to chronicle the first few years of NEPA's implementation in two federal agencies; and by doing so, to shed light on the behavior of administrative agencies when confronted with new directives from the legislature. It does not pretend to capture the complete story, in part because other agencies may have responded in different ways during the same period, and in part because the record of NEPA's implementation is still being written. The interpretation of the law, both in practice and in the courts, will probably continue for years until it becomes indistinguishable from later directives and intervening events. In spite of this incompleteness, however, or perhaps especially for this reason, it is fruitful to study the law's history in illustrative agencies during the initial period when its direct effects were most clearly discernible.

The Environmental Policy Problem

The problem to which NEPA was addressed was actually two-fold. The underlying substantive problem was the apparent necessity for better maintenance of the human environment, and especially of those natural systems that undergird human life and various components of human well-being. As Senator Jackson pointed out, a shift in the mixture of national goals had taken place—partly due to increased knowledge of the workings of natural systems, partly due to changes in popular preferences—as clean air and water, open space, and the amenities of nature began to appear increasingly scarce compared to the fruits of economic development. Where previously there had been sufficient "slack" in development that demands for resources in their undeveloped condition could be satisfied without government action, as that slack disappeared it became more and more necessary to allocate these resources consciously among conflicting demands. Since divergences frequently existed between the values of these resources to their owners or economic users, and the values of them to other potential users or to society at large, some governmental action was necessary in order to protect these intangible and collective values against extinction by market processes that took inadequate account of them.[3] The demand for governmental regulation of air and water quality is illustrative of this problem.

This demand for pollution control was a forerunner and catalyst of the demand for a national environmental policy, but it was in several respects a different issue.[4] Pollution was a more manageable problem than "national environmental policy": it could be conceptualized in economic terms, its most significant costs and benefits and their distribution could be measured (though not always commensurably), and its apparent perpetrators were predominantly industries and municipalities rather than the federal government itself. It was the sort of problem that could be approached in traditional ways: for example, by setting up a new mission agency armed with standards, grants and enforcement authority, and directing the agency to "do something about it."

Recognition of the necessity for air and water quality management had a symbolic importance broader than its implications for those two resources, however. If even the air and the water were threatened by the effects of human development, then it was no longer possible to leave fulfillment of man's intangible and collective needs for environmental resources to "slack" in development, for that slack was the very frontier, like the nineteenth-century frontier in western lands, that was now disappearing.[a] It was necessary to *plan* to meet these needs, in conjunction with planning for development.

Such planning, however, required more than a new mission agency concerned with air and water quality management: it required a basic change in policy and priorities on the part of all the existing agencies. The symbolic "closing of the frontiers" in air and water resources thus helped to set the stage for a broader conflict, between new public preferences and needs in the utilization of

---

[a]The closing of America's western frontier in the 1890s provided part of the impetus for the earlier conservation movement, by forcing public recognition of the fact that the nation's territory was not limitless. This recognition was then transferred to other natural resources such as timber, minerals, and water. In much the same sense, recognition of the need for air and water quality management marked a "closing of the frontier" on two other resources that had previously been treated as limitless, and as in the earlier case, this recognition of finitude, along with other changes in the social environment, then catalysed a broader recognition of the finitude of other environmental resources.

environmental resources—as articulated by an increasingly urban Congress, no longer quite so strongly dominated by resource production interests—and the federal resource development agencies, which remained committed, whether because of their statutory missions, their professional and organizational values, or what they perceived as the realities of political power, to the priorities of an earlier period.

The second and more specific problem to which NEPA was addressed, then, was the increasingly evident fact that many federal agencies were part of the first problem rather than part of its solution. Most federal agencies had been established to carry out particular missions, and none had a mandate for comprehensive planning or coordination of governmental activities.[b] The Highway Administration was expected to provide highways, the National Park Service to provide national parks; the water resource development agencies were expected to provide navigation channels, flood control, and other specific services. The agencies' budgets and reward systems were based upon these missions, and their professional staffs normally included only the range of disciplines necessary to the fulfillment of these particular purposes. Each was expected to plan for the maximum fulfillment of a different and sometimes conflicting subset of public purposes, at the least possible fiscal cost; and even though the ranges of some of these subsets had been broadened in the past (for instance, to include such purposes as recreation and fish and wildlife enhancement in water resource projects), they fell far short of a mandate to plan for the full range of purposes that might require use of the resources affected by the agency's actions. They fell even farther short of considering the impact of each action on the future human environment.

Not only was the range of purposes considered by each agency limited, but the criteria by which proposed federal actions were evaluated frequently reflected primarily economic objectives, rather than the fuller and more heterogeneous range of objectives that comprise social value and well being. Economic growth or cost minimization by themselves say nothing about equity in the distribution of benefits of public action, about aesthetic preferences, or about

---

[b]The Congress rejected the concept of a comprehensive planning agency for the federal government in the early 1940s, when it denied funds to Franklin Roosevelt's National Resources Planning Board. To the extent that such overview is exercised anywhere in the federal government, it is exercised by the Office of Management and Budget, since only OMB has authority (in the name of the President) to allocate resources among the full range of conflicting federal activities and purposes. However, OMB's concern tends to be limited to federal *financial* resources, its planning capability is limited, and its authority is closely circumscribed by the prerogatives both of the Congress and of the President's personal staff.

In the absence of comprehensive planning or oversight, a variety of *coordinative* mechanisms have evolved to assist in the management of conflicts over competing uses of resources: for instance, interdepartmental committees, "lead agency" arrangements, coordination by Presidential aides or Executive Office agencies (such as OMB), and review by state and regional agencies. (Cf. Stephen K. Bailey, "Managing the Federal Government," in *Agenda for the Nation* (Washington, D.C.: The Brookings Institution, 1968), pp. 301-21.

numerous other less tangible, less quantifiable, but equally important dimensions of social value.

Charles Reich noted in 1966 that "In a society in which government supports and subsidizes so much, it is necessary that the intangible values be supported too."[5] Many such values, however, either were not provided for at all in federal agencies' plans and budgets—unless they could be added on to already-chosen plans as "fringe benefits," with minimal cost to the plan's more tangible purposes—or if they were provided for, it was by different and equally specialized agencies that in turn had no incentive to consider purposes other than their own. These latter agencies too frequently had far less power than the economic development agencies to insure consideration of their purposes, especially in cases where conflicts arose among government agencies concerning alternative proposals for use of particular resource systems.[6]

In short, the fragmentation of public purposes and values among disparate, mission-oriented agencies created the problem of *jurisdictional externalities*: values that were neglected in administrative decisions because they fell outside the jurisdiction of the agency responsible for an action. Such "externalities" were similar in their consequences to market externalities—an economic phenomenon for which the usual prescription of economists is government intervention—but they differed significantly in their causes. Problems caused by deficiencies in governmental processes could not be as straightforwardly solved by the prescription of government intervention. *Quis custodiet custodies*? who regulates the regulators? This was the central environmental policy problem in the federal government of 1970, the problem to which NEPA was addressed. The question that now arises, of course, is how effective is NEPA as a solution to that problem?

The chapters that follow will trace some of the principal effects of NEPA during the first few years following its enactment by using as comparative case studies the civil works program of the U.S. Army Corps of Engineers and the small watersheds program of the Soil Conservation Service. Both these programs regularly bring about significant modifications of the human environment towards the fulfillment of particular missions; and their traditional activities are sufficiently similar in some respects to make comparison of their responses to NEPA particularly enlightening.

Developing a National Environmental Policy

Legislation to establish some sort of "national environmental policy" was introduced in the Congress as early as 1959 and several times thereafter during the decade of the 1960s; but the real momentum leading to enactment of such a policy did not begin to gather until 1968. A bill proposed in 1959 would have established a "unified statement of conservation, resource and environmental policy" and would have created a high-level "Council of Conservation, Resource, or Environmental Advisors," and bills introduced in 1966 and 1967 were intended to fulfill similar purposes.[1] Several Committees of the House of Representatives, as well as Senator Jackson's Committee on Interior and Insular Affairs, took an interest in this issue.

Two reports issued in the summer of 1968 appear in retrospect to mark the beginning of "national environmental policy" as a major congressional legislative initiative. The first, published by Congressman Emilio Q. Daddario's Subcommittee on Science, Research and Development, was entitled *Managing the Environment*; and unlike most previous reports on environmental quality, it examined closely the relationship between the objective of environmental quality and the management structure of the federal government. It noted that the activities of the federal government that have major impacts on environmental resources were divided among no less than nine major agencies and concluded that:

There are conflicts when environmental quality is managed by different policies, originating in conservation, agriculture, esthetics, recreation, economic development, human health, and so on . . . . The operational engineering programs which may affect the quality of the environment are not coordinated through a single group, but are handled through individual interagency liaisons (if they are coordinated at all).

. . . Existing institutions can do the job if they operate (1) under a coherent national policy for the environment, and (2) with an expanded understanding of ecological facts and processes.[2]

During the same month, a second report was published as a committee print by Senator Jackson's Interior and Insular Affairs Committee. Entitled *A National Policy for the Environment*, it had been prepared at the request of the Committee by Lynton K. Caldwell, Professor of Government at Indiana University, with

7

assistance from staff members of the committee and of the Library of Congress.[3] This report laid out a wide range of considerations and issues that must underlie any attempt to formulate a "national environmental policy," but perhaps the most important—and one that we shall see was later seriously neglected—was its definition of environmental policy in terms of the *total human environment*, not merely in terms of biological systems or aesthetic preservation. This crucial principle is worth quoting at length:

> Environmental policy, broadly construed, is concerned with the maintenance and management of those life-support systems—natural and manmade—upon which the health, happiness, economic welfare, and physical survival of human beings depend . . . .
>
> Environmental policy should not be confused with efforts to preserve natural or historical aspects of the environment in a perpetually unaltered state. Environmental quality does not mean indiscriminate preservationism, but it does imply a careful examination of alternative means of meeting human needs before sacrificing natural species or environments to other competing demands.
>
> Environmental quality is not identical with any of the several schools of natural resources conservation. A national environmental policy would, however, necessarily be concerned with natural resource issues. But the total environmental needs of man—ethical, esthetic, physical, and intellectual, as well as economic—must also be taken into account . . . .
>
> The science of ecology can provide many of the principal ingredients for the foundation of a national policy for the environment. But national policy for the environment involves more than applied ecology, it embraces more than any one science and more than science in the general sense.[4]

Publication of these reports was followed closely by an unusual "Joint Senate-House Colloquium to discuss a national policy on the environment" that was sponsored by the House Committee on Science and Astronautics (the parent committee of Daddario's subcommittee) and Jackson's Senate Committee on Interior and Insular Affairs. This Colloquium, held in July of 1968, produced a bipartisan "Congressional White Paper" containing possible elements of a national policy on the environment.[5] Finally, in February of 1969, Senator Jackson introduced the bill (S.1075) that would be enacted ten months later in revised form as the National Environmental Policy Act of 1969.

Legislative Action

Senate

The original bill introduced by Senator Jackson contained neither a declaration of national environmental policy nor any "action-forcing provisions" for the implementation of such a policy. It was a bill to authorize ecological research by the Secretary of the Interior and to establish a Council on Environmental Quality.[6] The bill was introduced in February 1969 and referred to Senator Jackson's Committee on Interior and Insular Affairs; a hearing was held in April; and in July an amended version was reported unanimously by the Committee, approved unanimously by the Senate, and referred to the House of Representatives.[7]

The principal amendment to the bill was a lengthy one added by Senator Jackson in May, which incorporated three new elements: (1) a "declaration of national environmental policy" in a new Title I; (2) a statement that "each person has a fundamental and inalienable right to a healthful environment"; and (3) a series of "action-forcing provisions" including the requirement of a "finding" by the responsible official concerning the probable environmental impacts of any major action.[8] It did not require a "detailed statement" by the official, nor did it require prior consultation and publication of comments on the findings. Otherwise, however, these "action-forcing provisions" were in most respects identical to the requirements enacted as Sections 102 (A), (B), (C), (D), and (E).[9]

The Senate committee report on this bill stated five purposes that it was intended to serve.[10] First, the law was to provide "a mandate, a body of law, a set of policies" to all federal agencies to guide their actions that might impact upon the environment. The report noted the committee's concern both for areas in which no policies had been established and for "those areas in which conflicting operational policies of different agencies are frustrating . . . the achievement of environmental quality objectives."

Many older operating agencies . . . do not at present have a mandate within the body of their enabling laws to allow them to give adequate attention to environmental values. In other agencies . . . an official's latitude to deviate from narrow policies or the "most economical alternative" to achieve an environmental goal may be strictly circumscribed by congressional authorizations . . . . S.1075, as reported by the committee, would provide all agencies and all Federal officials with a legislative mandate and a responsibility to consider the consequences of their actions on the environment. This would be true of the licensing functions of the independent agencies as well as the ongoing activities of regular Federal agencies.[11]

Second, the specific procedures and actions required of the agencies under Section 102 were intended to compel implementation of the new policy. As the committee report put it:

A statement of national policy for the environment—like other major policy declarations—is in large measure concerned with principle rather than detail; with an expression of broad national goals rather than narrow and specific procedures for implementation. But, if goals and principles are to be effective, they must be capable of being applied in action. S.1075 thus incorporates certain "action-forcing" provisions and procedures which are designed to assure that all Federal agencies plan and work toward meeting the challenge of a better environment.[12]

Third, the committee wanted to insure that federal agencies would have adequate knowledge and consideration of the environmental consequences of their actions. The bill extended authority to all agencies (under Section 201) to conduct research, studies, and surveys of such effects in conjunction with their ongoing programs; it authorized annual funding of up to one million dollars for an agency designated by the President to monitor environmental quality and impacts of natural resource development projects; and it strengthened the Office of Science and Technology.[13]

Fourth, the committee intended to establish an institutional focal point for environmental policy making in the federal government, with the functions of strengthening the Executive Office of the President in environmental matters, monitoring environmental trends, and serving an "early warning function" on emerging environmental problems; and to this end it created a three-member Board of Environmental Quality Advisors to the President, to be located in the Executive Office and patterned closely upon the Council of Economic Advisors established by the Full Employment Act of 1946.[14]

Finally, the Committee created the requirement of an annual environmental quality report in order to "provide a baseline and a periodic objective statement of national progress in achieving a quality environment."[15]

House of Representatives

S.1075 was passed by the Senate and sent to the House on July 10, 1969; but rather than being referred to a Committee of the House, it was held at the Speaker's desk until a similar bill originating in the House could be brought to the Floor for debate.[16] Congressman John Dingell had introduced a bill in February "to amend the Fish and Wildlife Coordination Act to provide for the establishment of a Council on Environmental Quality, and for other purposes."[a] This bill contained language similar to Jackson's in establishing the size and functions of a Council on Environmental Quality, but limited itself in that it contained only a brief and general statement of policy and none of the "action-forcing" provisions created by the Senate bill to compel implementation of policy by the operating agencies.

Seven days of hearings were held on H.R. 6750 during May and June 1969, and on July 11 the committee unanimously reported out a "clean bill," H.R. 12549, which was in most respects identical to H.R. 6750. The committee report on this bill reiterated in somewhat greater detail than had the Senate

---

[a]The purpose of proposing the law in this way appears, like Jackson's proposal of S. 1075 as a law to add to the powers of the Secretary of the Interior, to have been a parliamentary subterfuge to retain committee jurisdiction over the bill's development in Dingell's own Fish and Wildlife Subcommittee.

committee report the arguments in favor of a new and independent body in the Executive office that would be specifically concerned full-time with the environment:

The interdepartmental Council fills a clear and observed need today as a means of coordinating and resolving internal policy disputes between different executive agencies of the government . . . . This is not the principal purpose of this bill.

That purpose is rather to create, by legislative action, standing outside the programs that can be done and undone by unilateral executive action, a Council which can provide a consistent and expert source of review of national policies, environmental problems and trends, both long term and short term. Such a Council would act entirely independently of the executive, mission-oriented agencies . . . .

No organization, in existence or contemplated, except as provided for in this and similar bills, shows any sign of meeting that need. It is for this reason that your committee unanimously recommends the creation of such a Council through enactment of H.R. 12549.[17]

On September 23, H.R. 12549 was debated, amended from the Floor, and passed by the House by a vote of 372-15.[18]

Two important amendments were adopted during Floor debate by prior agreement between Congressman Dingell and their author, Congressman Wayne Aspinall.[19] The first of these amendments removed the bill from under the wing of the Fish and Wildlife Coordination Act and proposed it be a separate act applying to all classes of environmental impact rather than particularly to fish and wildlife. This appears to have been a straightforward remedy for the procedure by which Congressman Dingell had managed to keep control of the bill throughout its development. The other amendment, however, served to complicate later interpretation of the intent of Congress in passing the law. It consisted of one sentence:

Sec. 9. Nothing in this Act shall increase, decrease, or change any responsibility or authority of any Federal official or agency created by other provision of law.[20]

The effect of such a clause was to limit the Act—as passed by the House—to an unenforceable statement of general policy and thereby to make meaningless the "action-forcing" provisions contained in the Senate version. As Congressman Aspinall said in explaining the amendment:

I do want the *Record* to show that what we propose in the language is to make clear that nothing in this Act changes the authority and responsibility of existing agencies created by other provision of law. In my opinion, if additional authority is needed and direction to existing agencies is needed, they should be provided by separate legislation.[21]

Immediately after passage of H.R. 12549 with these amendments, its language was substituted in full into Senate bill S.1075, and that bill was then returned to the Senate with a request for a conference to resolve the differences between the versions.

The Muskie-Jackson Compromise

In the normal course of legislative events, the only further changes in the language of the bill would have been the compromises hammered out by the conference committee. In the case of NEPA, however, one further event intervened in the Senate before the bill went to conference. Throughout the development of S.1075, Senator Jackson had been engaged in a battle for committee jurisdiction and environmental prestige with Senator Edmund S. Muskie, whose subcommittee of the Public Works Committee had traditionally developed all legislation dealing with air and water pollution.[22] Senator Muskie's Water Quality Improvement Act proposal, S.7, had been undergoing extensive hearings in Muskie's subcommittee concurrently with Jackson's development of S.1075; and it included provisions for a national environmental policy of sorts, an Office of Environmental Quality in the Executive Office of the President, and an additional clause, section 16(c), which stated as an "action-forcing mechanism" that no federal agency might grant any license or permit until the applicant had presented certification from the appropriate state agency of compliance with applicable water quality standards. In order to rationalize the apparent conflict between the two bills, therefore, Jackson and Muskie negotiated compromise language while the bill was before the House.

On October 8, after Senator Jackson had presented the House's conference request to the Senate, he introduced an amendment to the Senate-passed language of S.1075 that amounted to the compromise language agreed to by himself and Muskie and requested that the Senate conferees be instructed to insist upon it. Both Jackson and Muskie gave speeches in which they indicated their agreement to the compromise language; the Senate adopted the amendment and instructed its conferees to insist upon it; and the bill was sent to conference.[23]

The new language included three major changes. First, the requirement of Section 102 (C) for a "finding" by the responsible official was changed to the requirement of a "detailed statement"; and an additional point covering "alternatives to the proposed action" was included in the required content of this statement. Each responsible official was directed to consult with and obtain the comments of other affected agencies before preparing this statement, to circulate it with the recommendation throughout the agency review process, and to make these comments and the statement itself available to the President, the Congress, and the public.

Second, a new section 103 was added, "to insure that the provisions of law such as section 16 (c) of S.7 are not affected by the requirements of section 102 of S.1075." In the words of their statement:

Section 16 (c) of S.7 would have the effect of exempting the Corps of Engineers and the Atomic Energy Commission and some other agencies from the requirement for a detailed statement on the environmental impact of proposed actions involving any discharge into the navigable waters of the United States.[24]

Finally, the functions included in Title II of S.1075 were rearranged among the proposed Board (Council) and the agencies, and some functions were deleted entirely in recognition that they were covered by provisions of S.7.[b]

Interestingly, the first of these changes turned out to have far greater consequences than its authors apparently anticipated. Their stated intent was to *weaken* the legal force of the required document, by requiring only a "detailed statement" subject to interagency review rather than a formal "finding"—thus forcing the development agencies to consult with those responsible for environmental protection rather than merely issuing their own determinations.[25] A consequence of the change, however, was to *strengthen* the "action-forcing provisions" as a whole, by substituting mechanisms for *external* review and challenge in place of the administrative requirements that had been crippled by the Aspinall amendment.[26] Whether or not the significance of this change was foreseen at the time, it was the public availability of the "detailed statements" and of the other agencies' comments on them that shaped the pattern of this law's implementation more than any other during its first several years.

Conference and Approval

The conference committee met three times, and submitted its report on December 17; the compromise language contained in this report was agreed to by the Senate on December 20 and by the House on December 23, and was enacted by President Richard M. Nixon on January 1, 1970, as the National Environmental Policy Act of 1969. Four significant changes were made in the bills by the conference committee before the report was agreed to, however.

First, the clause which became Section 101(c) was weakened from "each person has a fundamental and inalienable right to a healthful environment" to "each person should enjoy . . . ."[27] This change suggested Congress' unwillingness to declare a "right" that might be enforceable in court against governmental failure to provide such an environment. The explanatory report of the House conferees stated that the change was adopted "because of doubt on the part of

---

[b]One function that appears to have been simply dropped was the authority to develop and maintain an inventory of existing and proposed natural resource development projects and other works that might significantly modify the environment.

the House conferees with respect to the legal scope of the original Senate provision."[28]

Second, language requiring "review and approval" of agencies' methods for considering unquantified factors by the Council was weakened to require only "consultation." The effect of this change was to eliminate a suggestion, which had been introduced in the Muskie–Jackson amendment, that might give the Council direct authority over procedures of other government agencies.[c]

Third, Title II of the conference-passed bill established the Council on Environmental Quality proposed in the House version (as well as in the original S.1075), with the original three members rather than the five recommended by the House; it restored the requirement of Senate confirmation of the members; and it added new language to minimize duplication by the Council of activities performed by established agencies.

Finally, the qualifying phrase "to the fullest extent possible" was made to modify all of the "action-forcing provisions" of Section 102.[d] This change reflected a compromise between Senator Jackson's desire to force action and Congressman Aspinall's insistence that substantive changes in the agencies' goals and missions be made only by separate changes in the organic legislation of each individual agency. The significance of this change was mitigated, however, by an "explanation" of the phrase signed by all members of the conference committee except Aspinall, which defined it in the most compelling terms possible:

The House conferees are of the view that the new language does not in any way limit the Congressional authorization and directive to all agencies of the Federal Government set out in . . . Section 102. The purpose of the language is to make it clear that each agency . . . shall comply with the directives set out in subparagraphs (A) through (H) *unless the existing law* applicable to such agency's operations *expressly prohibits* or makes full compliance . . . impossible [emphasis added].[29]

Provisions of the National Environmental Policy Act

NEPA,[30] as it was enacted, had three principal thrusts. The first thrust, which followed the enacting clause and a brief statement of purpose, was the declaration of a national policy on the environment: in general to promote the general welfare, foster productive harmony between man and nature and fulfill the so-

---

[c]This change suggests that the Congress considered and rejected the proposal to give the Council broader veto powers. The Muskie–Jackson language had introduced a provision authorizing *review and approval* by the Council of the agencies' "methods and procedures for giving appropriate consideration to presently unquantified environmental values." See *Congressional Record*, October 8, 1969, pp. S 12117–18.

[d]One provision, requiring all agencies to review and propose changes in their statutory authorities to bring them into conformance with NEPA, was removed from the scope of this qualifier and made a separate requirement (Section 103 of the law as enacted).

cial, economic and other needs of present and future Americans, and specifically to:

1. Fulfill the responsibilities of each generation as trustee of the environment for succeeding generations;
2. Assure for all Americans safe, healthful, productive, and esthetically and culturally pleasing surroundings;
3. Attain the widest range of beneficial uses of the environment without degradation, risk to health or safety, or other undesirable and unintended consequences;
4. Preserve important historic, cultural, and natural aspects of our national heritage, and maintain, wherever possible, an environment that supports diversity, and variety of individual choice;
5. Achieve a balance between population and resource use that will permit high standards of living and a wide sharing of life's amenities;
6. Enhance the quality of renewable resources and approach the maximum attainable recycling of depletable resources.

A final clause of this section stated "that the Congress recognizes that each person should enjoy a healthful environment and that each person has a responsibility to contribute to the preservation and enhancement of the environment.[31]

The second thrust of the law, contained in Sections 102-105, was the establishment of a series of mandates and procedures binding on all agencies of the federal government, to compel them to implement the policy declared in Section 101. Among the most important of these were the following:

Sec. 102. The Congress authorizes and directs that, to the fullest extent possible: (1) the policies, regulations, and public laws of the United States shall be interpreted and administered in accordance with the policies set forth in this act, and (2) all agencies of the Federal Government shall—

A. utilize a systematic, interdisciplinary approach . . . in planning and in decision-making which may have an impact on man's environment;
B. identify and develop methods and procedures, in consultation with the Council on Environmental Quality . . . which will insure that presently unquantified environmental amenities and values may be given appropriate consideration in decision-making;
C. include in every recommendation or report on proposals for legislation and other major Federal actions significantly affecting the quality of the human environment, a detailed statement by the responsible official on—(i) the environmental impact of the proposed action, (ii) any adverse environmental effects which cannot be avoided should the proposal be implemented, (iii) alternatives to the proposed action, (iv) the relationship between local short-term uses of man's environment and the maintenance and enhancement of long-term productivity, and (v) any irreversible and irretrievable commitments of resources which would be involved in the proposed action should

it be implemented. Prior to making any detailed statement, the responsible Federal official shall consult with and obtain the comments of any Federal agency which has jurisdiction by law or special expertise with respect to any environmental impact involved. Copies of such statement and of the comments and views of the appropriate Federal, State, and local agencies . . . shall be made available to the President, the Council on Environmental Quality and to the public . . . and shall accompany the proposal through the existing agency review processes;

D. study, develop and describe appropriate alternatives to recommended courses of action in any proposal which involves unresolved conflicts conerning alternative uses of available resources; . . .

G. initiate and utilize ecological information in the planning and development of resource-oriented projects; and

H. assist the Council on Environmental Quality . . . .

Sec. 103. All agencies of the Federal Government shall review their present statutory authority, administrative regulations, and current policies and procedures for the purpose of determining whether there are any deficiencies or inconsistencies therein which prohibit full compliance with the purposes and provisions of this Act and shall propose to the President not later than July 1, 1971, such measures as may be necessary to bring their authority and policies into conformity with the intent, purposes, and procedures set forth in the Act.

Sec. 104. Nothing in section 102 or 103 shall in any way affect the specific statutory obligations of any Federal agency (1) to comply with criteria or standards of environmental quality, (2) to coordinate or consult with any other Federal or State agency, or (3) to act, or refrain from acting contingent upon the recommendations or certification of any other Federal or State agency.

Sec. 105. The policies and goals set forth in this Act are supplementary to those set forth in existing authorizations of Federal agencies.[32]

Finally, the third thrust of the law, which comprised Title II, was to establish a statutory three-member Council on Environmental Quality in the Executive Office of the President, with responsibilities to assist and advise the President; to gather information on conditions and trends in environmental quality; to "review and appraise the various programs and activities of the Federal Government in the light of the policy set forth in Title I of this Act . . . and to make recommendations to the President with respect thereto"; to develop and recommend national environmental policies to the President; to conduct investigations and analyses relating to environmental quality; to document and define environmental changes; to report annually to the President on the state and condition of the environment; and to furnish such other studies, reports, and recommendations as the President might request.[33]

Conclusion

The enactment of the National Environmental Policy Act marked a major departure by the Congress from traditional policies and implementation tools. The policy statement itself was not unusual: the direction of federal agencies toward lofty goals subject to their usual constraints ("consistent with other essential considerations") is a standard ingredient of congressional policy declarations. Likewise, establishment of the Council on Environmental Quality, while new, was not unprecedented: its powers, modeled on those of the Council of Economic Advisors, and stopped short of any authority to control or veto the activities of other agencies. The inclusion of "action-forcing provisions" to insure implementation of the law's purposes, however, was a radical and unprecedented innovation. Drafted at the suggestion of a professor of government, they represented an attempt to achieve, by changes in procedures, goals that might be difficult if not impossible to achieve by proposing direct changes in the legislation governing the activities of each federal agency.

It is probable that few Congressmen, in the rush to close legislative business before Christmas, even recognized the significance of the innovation that was being enacted. Congressman Aspinall clearly did and sought almost singlehandedly to block it; but even the bill's authors reportedly did not comprehend the full potential of the "action-forcing" provisions.[34]

The history of the bill's development appears to have been crucially important, in two respects, to the fact that such an innovation was enacted at all. Adroit use of committee jurisdiction was mentioned already, but equally significant was the fact that one potent action-forcer—requirement of a detailed, public statement on each action—was not added until the bill was sent to conference. The original bill passed the Senate by unanimous consent, but its teeth were not fully evident at the time. The House bill likewise passed by an overwhelming vote, but only after the Aspinall amendment was added to remove any teeth whatsoever. Not until the final vote, less than a week before Christmas, did the Congress finally consider the bill as it would be enacted—without the Aspinall amendment and with even stronger action-forcing provisions than it had previously included. Since amendment of conference reports is prohibited, the bill had then to be accepted or rejected in toto; and under the circumstances, only a controversy of the greatest magnitude could have resulted in rejection of the conference report. The bill was thus enacted with overwhelming support, though not without statements of misgivings by a handful of Congressmen.[35]

There is no doubt that NEPA was a broad and general, rather than a narrow and specific law: a "statesman's law rather than a lawyer's law," as Caldwell describes it.[36] To that extent, it was also an ambiguous law that required interpretation rather than mechanical implementation by the executive. In view of its intent—to adjust the priorities of all federal agencies—it probably could not have been otherwise. But despite its ambiguities, it was a coherent law, whose elements were clearly intended to reinforce one another in the achievement of the common purpose stated in its declaration of policy. The detailed statement, the other "action-forcing procedures," the creation of the Council on Environmental Quality—all of these were *means* intended to insure the attainment of the policy goals and not ends in themselves. NEPA was a policy law, not a procedural law, though it did incorporate procedures in order to achieve the desired policy changes.

From the point of view of the agencies, however, the procedures provided the starting point. These procedures were the "action-forcing" mechanism—as they were intended—that placed tangible and immediate demands upon them. The policy statement was less tangible and more threatening to the accepted, mission-oriented ways of doing business and thus less pressing to the agencies. *Some* change was clearly demanded, both by the content of the law and by the fact that new procedures and institutions—rather than merely a nonoperational statement of policy—had been created at all.[e] The *direction* of the desired change was also clear: the agencies were to give more thorough consideration to the impacts of their actions on "environmental values," however defined.[f] The *magnitude* of change required in each decision, however, was not clear, nor were the indicators for measuring it specified. What was "appropriate" consideration of "environmental amenities and values"? What was a "major federal action significantly affecting the quality of the human environment"? Did it include policies, permits, grants, and rules as well as projects? Which of these were "major"? Which of their effects were "significant," and by what measures? What was the operational meaning of the "human environment"? And what were "appropriate" alternatives?[g]

---

[e]Not only the specific content of the law is important in drawing this conclusion, but also the facts, first, that it was enacted at all; second, that it passed with bipartisan and overwhelming support (unanimously in the Senate, and 372–15 in the House); and third, that it contained not only a policy statement, but also specific procedural requirements for implementation, and a new institution—the Council on Environmental Quality—in which the Act's objectives were to be focussed and maintained on an ongoing basis. Establishment of a statutory council over the objections of the Administration was particularly significant, since it indicated legislative insistence that environmental considerations (however defined) be institutionalized on an ongoing basis in the executive branch.

[f]At the least, a mandate to *consider* environmental impacts had been given to all federal agencies, whatever their ultimate decisions. This was important in itself, especially in mission agencies such as the Corps of Engineers, the Federal Highway Administration, and others that were previously constrained to follow rigorous benefit-cost and least-dollar-cost criteria in the fulfillment of their statutory missions.

[g]Lest the impression be formed that all such laws are as ambiguous or undefined as NEPA, compare it with subsections 2(g) and 2(h) of the Fish and Wildlife Coordination Act (16 U.S.C. 661–666c), which provide clear definitions of both the size and types of projects covered and of the extent to which the law is retroactively applicable:

> The provisions of this section shall be applicable with respect to any project for the control and use of water as prescribed herein . . . but shall not be applicable . . . if the construction of the particular project or unit thereof . . . has been substantially completed. A project or unit thereof shall be considered substantially completed when sixty percent or more of the estimated construction cost has been obligated for expenditure.

NEPA itself could not and did not provide answers to these questions; and the agency it established to provide guidance in answering them had only just been created. In the meantime, the agencies were faced with the necessity of learning for themselves, by trial and error if not by authoritative definition, what their activities had to do with "national environmental policy."

The provisions of this Act shall not be applicable to those projects for the impoundment of water where the maximum surface area of such impoundments is less than 10 acres . . . .

NEPA differed from this previous law, of course, in the diversity of activities that the Congress intended it to cover, which complicated the problem of definition; but whatever reason may be given for such ambiguities, the difficulties of interpretation were real.

3 Executive Environmental Policy

The language and legislative history of the National Environmental Policy Act provide the initial context for the study of agencies' responses to the new law, but one further context must also be sketched to provide a fair understanding of those responses. This second context is the environmental policy of the Administration in power, in this case the Nixon Administration, since under the Constitution the agencies are expected to carry out the policies of the chief executive within the limits of the law.

The environmental policy of the Administration is transmitted to the agencies through several channels, and these channels do not necessarily transmit mutually consistent signals. The most direct channel is the statements and actions of the President himself; but while these indicate the President's policies concerning many issues, they do not necessarily provide guidance concerning the priorities and daily actions of the multitude of federal agencies charged with implementing national environmental policy. To understand executive environmental policy, therefore, we must examine not only Presidential statements and actions but also those of the *Executive Office*—that is, the agencies that oversee government activities in the name of the President. In particular, we must examine two agencies of the Executive Office: the new Council on Environmental Quality created by NEPA to coordinate environmental policy, and the Office of Management and Budget, which routinely oversees not only the expenditures of the agencies but also their implementation of the policies of the Administration in power.

Presidential Policy

In the Nixon Administration, as in the Congress, the enactment of the National Environmental Policy Act marked a watershed in commitment to the environment as a focus for policy action. No significant Presidential policy on environmental quality had been established by previous administrations,[1] nor had President Nixon taken more than a passing interest in it until several political storms—over the appointment of Walter Hickel as Interior Secretary, the Santa Barbara oil spill, and Defense Department plans for nerve gas dumping[2]—and the enactment of NEPA over his objections had demonstrated its political importance.[3]

Beginning with his signing of NEPA, however, in a symbolic and highly

21

publicized ritual on New Year's Day of a new decade, President Nixon embarked upon an unprecedented series of initiatives in the field of environmental protection, the combined effect of which was to make environmental quality a major symbolic commitment of his first administration.[a] By a major symbolic commitment to NEPA and an outpouring of well-publicized symbolic actions, Nixon clearly sought to convey the message that he as well as the Congress was committed to incorporating environmental considerations into federal administrative processes.

The Politics of Consensus

It is important to recognize, however, that NEPA was a political threat to the Nixon Administration and not an initiative of it. NEPA was a congressional initiative and one whose enactment Nixon had initially opposed; he had not shared in the development of it, nor had he demonstrated any previous commitment to the policy it declared.[b] He could hardly ignore it, however. It was a matter of great public concern; its enactment had demonstrated the bipartisan popularity of the environmental issue; and its author was one of two Democratic Senators, both clearly identified with the environmental issue, who might well run against him in the 1972 Presidential election. It was essential, therefore, that he at least build a credible record on the environmental issue.

On the other hand, NEPA also presented Nixon with political opportunities if he chose to seize leadership of the law's implementation. Its lofty, consensual policy declaration offered him the stance of "President of all the people," by which he might transcend the partisanship surrounding his Vietnam policy. Its procedure for review of agency actions offered him a new instrument for controlling the activities of the federal bureaucracy, which had been one of his goals ever since he took office. And its creation of a council within the Executive Office gave him his own staff with which to build a record of environmental initiatives prior to the 1972 Presidential elections.[c]

---

[a]Among these actions were special emphasis on environmental initiatives in the State of the Union Message, the Budget Message, and a special Environmental Message; appointment of three distinguished environmentalists as the first members of the Council on Environmental Quality; Executive orders directing implementation of NEPA and abatement of pollution from federal facilities; signing of two proposed treaties relating to environmental protection; cancellation of oil leases that threatened spillage and issuance of a contingency plan for the control of oil spills; and Executive orders creating the Environmental Protection Agency and National Oceanic and Atmospheric Administration.

[b]With the exception of a single radio-television address delivered on October 16, 1968. For a reference to the text of this address, see Lynton K. Caldwell, *Environment: A Challenge For Modern Society* (Garden City, N.Y.: Natural History Press, 1970), page 280, note 12.

[c]This may sound cynical, but it must be considered at least an element of the President's political calculus. Shelton also points out that 1970 was a congressional election year and that in this context Nixon's sudden advocacy of 37 new environmental proposals, 23 of

Nixon used the enactment of NEPA, therefore, as a springboard to regain the initiative in environmental policy making from the Congress; and his actions during the following one and a half to two years served, with a few exceptions, to try to demonstrate his leadership and commitment in this area.[d] In view of the circumstances surrounding his conversion to it, however, as well as later events, it is fair to suspect that his leadership was based upon the issue's proven political popularity and upon his desire to advocate the "politics of consensus" in 1970, rather than upon a personal commitment to its principles.

The Politics of Compromise

The Nixon Administration's emphasis upon environmental policy initiatives continued through the first half of 1971,[e] and as late as August 1971 President Nixon asserted his continuing support for the implementation of the National Environmental Policy Act.[4] During the summer of 1971, however, subtle changes in emphasis began to be evident, particularly an undercurrent of suggestions that the costs of achieving environmental quality—in terms both of money and of the achievement of other goals—needed to be considered more carefully in conjunction with the environmental impacts of proposed actions.[5] In the same message in which he reaffirmed his support of NEPA, Nixon went on to say that:

It is simplistic to seek ecological perfection at the cost of bankrupting the very tax-paying enterprises which must pay for the social advance the nation seeks .... We must develop a realistic sense of what it costs to achieve our national environmental goals and choose a specific level of goal with an understanding of its costs and benefits .... It is essential that we have both ... a healthy economy ... [and] a healthy environment.[6]

which would require congressional approval, could be interpreted as a blatant attempt to "seize the environment vote" by blaming the Democratically controlled Congress for failure to enact them. See Ronald L. Shelton, *The Environmental Era*, Dissertation, Cornell University, Ithaca, N.Y., 1973, p. 369.

[d]The most significant exceptions were commitments to early development of the supersonic transport (SST) and the Liquid Metal Fast Breeder Reactor (LMFBR), and creation of the "National Industrial Pollution Control Council" (NIPCC) in the Department of Commerce. Established by Executive order in April 1970 (Executive Order No. 11523, April 9, 1970), this Council consisted solely of industrial executives, met in secrecy, and in effect provided a privileged channel of access to government policy making for the industries that were most likely to be the targets of environmental regulations.

[e]Among its actions during this period were a directive to the Corps of Engineers halting construction of the Cross-Florida Barge Canal (which was declared illegal by a court of appeals in 1974); emphasis again in the State of the Union, Budget, and Special Environmental Messages; Executive orders giving increased protection to historically and culturally important sites and banning federal contracts, grants, or loans to businesses convicted of Clean Air Act violations; and appointment of two new Atomic Energy Commissioners who were reputedly sensitive to environmental concerns.

And in a speech the following month, a new tone in the Administration's policy came through clearly:

We are not going to allow the environment issue to be used sometimes falsely and sometimes in a demagogic way basically to destroy the (industrial) system.[7]

Such statements suggest that business and industrial interests had begun to reassert their traditional political power in persuading the Administration to back off from its vigorous symbolic leadership of environmental initiatives to a more moderate, compromising, "yes, but . . ." stance. As the distribution of the costs of environmental protection became more evident, the politics of consensus gave way to the politics of compromise.

The de-emphasis on environmental policy that had become evident during 1971 became even more pronounced in 1972, the year of the Presidential elections, as the rhetoric of environmental quality was succeeded by the rhetoric of energy and the economy.[8] The most plausible explanation for this phenomenon is that Nixon purposely changed his posture in preparation for the election campaign. The environment was a popular issue, but not a lucrative one; it was an issue upon which he must show solid achievements, especially when running against Senators Jackson and Muskie, but one on which a strong campaign emphasis might jeopardize the financial support of big business. Nixon probably decided that he had enough past initiatives on his record to appear credible (and to criticize the Congress for not enacting them all) and that he could now de-emphasize it in order to conciliate his campaign's financial supporters. In short, while environmental protection did not disappear from the Administration's agenda during 1972, it was treated as a *past* record to run on rather than a subject of new initiatives and priority attention.

The Politics of Highest Priority

An important implication of the election-year change of emphasis, from environment to energy and economy, was that the White House could no longer be expected to provide vigorous leadership on the environmental issue, since a second Nixon Administration would be obliged to fulfill the priorities espoused in its campaign promises. Nixon's 1973 State of the Union Message on Natural Resources and the Environment set the tone for the months ahead: its central thesis was that the environment was no longer a critical priority; it contained no new environmental protection initiatives; and the areas that it did list as high priorities for action were agriculture and energy resource development.

When we came to office in 1969, we tackled this problem [the environment] with all the power at our command. Now there is encouraging evidence that the United States has moved away from the environmental crisis that could have been and toward a new era of restoration and renewal. Today, in 1973, I can report to the Congress that we are well on the way to winning the war against environmental degradation—well on the way to making our peace with nature . . . .

One of the highest priorities of my Administration during the coming year will be a concern for energy supplies—a concern underscored this winter by occasional fuel shortages . . . . I shall soon submit a new and far more comprehensive energy message containing wide-ranging initiatives to ensure necessary supplies of energy at acceptable economic and environmental costs."[9]

The energy message, when it arrived, said little about energy conservation and a great deal in advocacy of at least six proposals whose potential consequences included major new hazards to environmental quality.[10]

If the election campaign of 1971-72 reflected the politics of compromise between environment and economy, the Nixon Administration's policies in 1973 and into 1974 could be termed the politics of highest priority; and the highest environment-related priority of the Administration was clearly the development of energy resources. This priority began to emerge as early as 1971 and 1972, in Presidential commitments to development of the Liquid Metal Fast Breeder Reactor and in a special message to the Congress regarding energy. It was stated explicitly in the President's Energy Message of April 1973,[11] and it was solidified beyond question by the Administration's responses to the "energy crisis" of winter 1974, which included the reallocation of vast sums of research funds to energy research and development, the creation of new energy policy institutions staffed with numerous industry personnel and exercising emergency powers, and the demonstrated willingness of the White House to support industry attacks on the environmental laws and regulations that had been created during recent years.[12] In his 1974 State of the Union Message, President Nixon unilaterally declared that the environmental movement had now entered a "second phase," in which

We must be concerned not only with clean air, clean water and wise land use, but also with the interaction of these environmental effects with our need to expand our energy supplies and to maintain general prosperity.[13]

Only the vigorous efforts of EPA Administrator Russell Train and Council on Environmental Quality Chairman Russell Peterson persuaded the White House not to seek major exemptions from environmental laws for energy development activities.[14]

The Politics of Survival

In 1974, however, an even higher priority came to dominate nearly all of the Nixon Administration's policies. This priority was political survival, in the face of the increasingly damaging allegations of political scandal and corruption associated with the word Watergate. The politics of consensus in 1970 had permitted a transcendence of narrow interests, in order to appeal to the broadest spectrum of constituencies. The politics of survival in 1974 dictated the opposite strategy; the sacrifice of nearly any policy, however popular, in the attempt to insure the support of thirty-four conservative members of the Senate who could block an impeachment conviction. The defeat of the National Land Use Policy bill in June 1974 by the House of Representatives symbolized this strategy. The bill, which had been conceived and developed as the logical sequel to NEPA and which the Administration less than six months before had hailed as its highest priority environmental initiative, was defeated by seven votes largely because of a withdrawal of Administration support under pressure from a conservative Arizona Congressman and Senator and right-wing lobby groups.[15]

By mid-1974, in short, environmental protection could no longer be considered a subject of deliberate, foresighted policy making by the White House; but neither had it ceased to be a major public political issue, as was demonstrated by the intensity of public pressures surrounding congressional debates over new legislation and by numerous other indications.[f] As a result, it became a form of political currency for the achievement of goals more important to the President, such as political survival. Noncontroversial programs were given increased support, to increase the President's credit with the Congress generally; and controversial proposals were treated in accordance with the wishes of the conservative minority who were Nixon's bedrock loyalists.[g] However rational such a strategy might be for the protection of President Nixon's incumbency, it was an abdication of the leadership necessary for the implementation of NEPA's

---

[f]For instance, the continued attention to environmental issues by the press, and by still-vigorous voluntary organizations at the local as well as the national level; the continued effectiveness of environmental lobbyists in preventing many weakening amendments to NEPA and to other environmental legislation; the unabated stream of environmental lawsuits and continuation of judicial decisions favoring environmentalist litigants (including both NEPA suits and actions against private parties, such as the widely publicized EPA suit against the Reserve Mining Company of Minnesota for asbestos pollution of Lake Superior); and the development of environmentally oriented land use control legislation, patterned on the federal bill, by numerous state legislatures.

[g]Interestingly, this "survival strategy" did not work entirely against the environment: one manifestation of it was an easing of budgetary control on a number of federal programs that were popular with the Congress as a whole, including the Land and Water Conservation Fund, solid waste management programs, and coastal zone management as well as the more traditional public works projects for water resource development. On less consensual issues, however, such as land use policy as well as strip mining control, where powerful conservative Congressmen opposed further progress in environmental policymaking, the Administration withdrew its support and even lobbied against enactment of the legislation. See sources noted previously and also *National Journal* VI (1974), pp. 206–07. Among President Nixon's last official acts before resigning his office in August 1974 were a a speech in which he stated that environmental regulations would have to be loosened in order to achieve economic goals and a veto of increased appropriations for environmental protection (which he denounced as "inflationary").

purposes and for solution of the tangible environmental problems that gave rise to NEPA's enactment. As subsequent events made clear, it was not a sufficient strategy for protection of President Nixon's incumbency either, and he found it necessary to resign his office in August 1974.

The Council on Environmental Quality

The policies of the Council on Environmental Quality during this same period reflected the predictable tension between its stated purposes and intentions, the political precariousness of its existence, and the growing pains experienced by any new agency. The powers given to it by the Congress left it severely dependent upon the support of the President, since it had no explicit authority to direct the actions of other agencies beyond its authority to appeal to the President, and this support was not unambiguous during this period, as the preceding pages indicate. It depended also upon the advice of intermediaries on the President's White House staff through whom the Council reported to him, many of whom had differing if not hostile views concerning the importance of environmental policy. [h]

Executive Order No. 11514

The Council's grant of authority from the President is contained in Executive Order No. 11514, which was published two months after the enactment of NEPA and which delegated to it the responsibilities given to the President by the Act.[16] This Executive order was in large part simply a recapitulation of the requirements of NEPA itself at the same level of generality. In two key respects, however, the Executive order went beyond the requirements of NEPA. First, the Executive order directed the heads of all federal agencies to:

. . . develop procedures to ensure the fullest practicable provision of timely public information and understanding of Federal plans and programs with environmental impact *in order to obtain the views of all interested parties. These procedures shall include, whenever appropriate, provisions for public hearings,* and shall provide the public with relevant information, including information on alternative courses of action [emphasis added].[17]

---

[h]Despite their statutory status as "advisors to the President," the members of the Council in fact met with the President only twice during their first three years in office, both times on the occasion of the presentation of the Council's annual report. Chairman Train met with him somewhat more frequently; but in its routine work the Council was fully three steps removed from the President—that is, it reported through a special assistant responsible for environmental matters, who in turn reported to the staff director of the Domestic Council (John Ehrlichman), and thence to the President. See Richard A. Liroff, "The Council on Environmental Quality," *Environmental Law Reporter* III (1973), pp. 50051–70, at p. 50062.

The Act itself, it will be recalled, required public availability of the "detailed statement" at an unspecified time in the process of review and approval, and development and discussion of appropriate alternatives when conflicts existed. The requirement of hearings, as well as the emphasis on timeliness, obtaining the views of interested parties, and providing information on alternatives, implied a further policy of increased public participation *before* the process of recommendation, review, and approval was completed.

Second, the Executive order created a broader role for the Council in overseeing certain aspects of NEPA's implementation. The Executive order authorized the Council to conduct public hearings on issues of environmental significance; to "coordinate" federal programs related to environmental quality rather than merely to "review and appraise" them; to issue guidelines to federal agencies concerning preparation of the "detailed statements" required by Section 102 (2) (C), and to issue other instructions to the agencies; and to request information from them that it needed in order to carry out its responsibilities.[18]

This expansion of the Council's oversight role is an important factor in understanding the Council's later behavior and the effects of its guidance on the agencies. First, it was delegated by the President, not by the Congress, and could as easily be withdrawn by him if he should choose to do so. The Council's oversight function was only generally stated in the law itself—indeed, comments by Senator Jackson and Professor Caldwell suggested that the Office of Management and Budget (then the Bureau of the Budget) might perform this function, thereby leaving the Council free to serve as expert policy advisors to the President.[19] OMB, however, had no interest in overseeing NEPA's implementation, and this oversight role was taken on by the Council.[20] One consequence of this decision was to place oversight of the law in the hands of the institution that was most apt to maintain a commitment to its purposes and that was in fact created by the same legislation. A corresponding weakness, however, was that this power of the Council existed only on sufferance from the Executive Office power structure, and it lacked both the authoritative force and the direct linkage with budget and management decisions that OMB possessed.

A second consequence of the expansion of the Council's oversight role was to intensify the inherent conflict between this and its other statutory role: the provision of confidential advice to the President. As a confidential advisor, the Council could be effective only by "team-playing"—that is, by supporting Presidential policy in public irrespective of what its private positions and recommendations might have been. As overseer of the implementation of NEPA, however, the Council's effectiveness depended upon advocacy of change in federal agency priorities (which might conflict with other Presidential policies), and upon visibility and credibility with its environmentalist constituency in the general public. Neither of these roles provided a solid base of political power or influence: the advisory role was directly dependent upon the favor of the President and risked diminishing the Council's external credibility, and the oversight role, while it promised a broader base of public support and constituency ties, was also dependent upon the President's continued favor (especially since it was derived principally from the Executive order rather than from the statute).[i] In cases where Presidential priorities differed significantly from those of environmentalist constituencies, therefore, the Council was left in a difficult position.

A final significant point about the Executive order was that it emphasized the "detailed statement" requirement, but said relatively little about the Act's other requirements.[21] This did not appear significant at the time, since the initial attention of nearly everyone focussed on the statement requirement and lawsuits had already been filed against several agencies to force the production of such statements. Perhaps in part because of this emphasis, however, both CEQ and the other agencies focussed from the outset almost exclusively upon the procedures for producing these statements and virtually ignored most of the law's other provisions (such as integrating the use of the social and natural sciences and environmental design arts, developing methods for appropriate consideration of unquantifiable values, preserving the national heritage, enhancing renewable resources, and approaching the maximum attainable recycling of depletable resources, etc.).

Interim Guidelines

The Council issued its first guidance to the agencies in April 1970 by providing "interim guidelines . . . for preparing environmental statements . . . as required by Section 102 (2) (C) of NEPA."[22] Consistent with the Executive order, these guidelines were directed solely to the production of the "detailed statements" and did not offer guidance on other provisions of the statute. In addition, they were not much more specific than the Act itself; they were almost wholly procedural rather than substantive;[j] and they left the responsibility for interpretation of most of the Act's requirements to the line agencies. They did establish a date by which the agencies must establish their own guidelines (June 1, 1970),

---

[i]An example of this latter risk was the fate of Secretary of the Interior Walter Hickel, who sought to build public support as an environmentalist independent of the White House and was promptly replaced. In the case of the Council, not only the career of one individual but the oversight authority of the agency itself would have been at stake. For an articulate summation of the former risk (the risks of direct dependence upon Presidential favor in the advisory role), see the comparison of the Council on Environmental Quality with the Council of Economic Advisors in Liroff, "The Council on Environmental Quality," pp. 50057–63, especially p. 50060.

[j]Although they did imply that substantive rather than merely procedural changes were intended.

but they gave little guidance concerning the appropriate content of those guidelines, even on matters that might affect many agencies with some uniformity.[k]

On four points, the Interim Guidelines did venture explicit interpretations.
First, Guideline 4 defined the "fullest extent possible" in the strict language of
the House managers (directing the agencies to comply unless prohibited by
statute), rather than in the permissive sense advocated by Congressman Aspinall;
and Guideline 13 reiterated the requirement of the Executive order that the
agencies review their statutory authorities and recommend any necessary
changes by September 1970.[l] Read together, these two guidelines clearly required the agencies either to comply immediately or to recommend specific
measures for overcoming the obstacles. Second, Guideline 7(b) required "mere
reference" to water quality certification rather than full discussion of water
quality impacts, thus indicating the Council's acceptance of Senator Muskie's
preferences concerning the relationship between environmental impact statements and water quality regulation.[23] Third, the Interim Guidelines specified
that the required agency comments on "detailed statements" must be in writing
and must be made public, though they left the timing of their publication to the
discretion of the agency;[m] and finally, the guidelines required that impact
statements be prepared for "highly controversial" actions regardless of other
measures of the significance of those impacts.[24]

An additional noteworthy point about the Interim Guidelines was their
creation of a new document not mentioned either in the Act or in the Executive
order: the so-called "draft statement" of environmental impacts, which has since
become a central element of the environmental review process. In the Interim
Guidelines, "draft statements" were mentioned as an optional means of state and
local review of proposed actions, subject to review by the Council *if* they were
prepared; they were not required for all actions that required final statements,
nor were they subject to public disclosure.[25] By February 1971, however, they
were being prepared for one-fourth to one-third of all projects for which final

---

[k]For instance, the applicability of the law to actions that were already underway; the meaning and scope of the "human environment"; the circumstances under which "project" or
"program" impact statements should be prepared; the levels of "significance" of impacts on
environmental conditions that would require preparation of a statement; the meaning of
"short-term" and "long-term" effects; and the definition of "irreversible" impacts.

[l]The fact that no agencies reported any significant needs for change in their statutory authorities may thus have deprived them of any legal excuse for failure to comply, even
though the reports may have been based upon conflicting or poorly thought out interpretations of ambiguous points. See testimony of CEQ Chairman Russell Train, in U.S. Congress, House Committee on Merchant Marine and Fisheries, *Administration of the National
Environmental Policy Act*, Hearings, Serial 91–41, Washington, D.C., 1971, Part 1, pp. 87–
88.

[m]NEPA did not explicitly require that the comments be in writing, and the Freedom of Information Act, which would otherwise apply, specifically exempts from public review
"working papers" and "interagency memoranda" (5 U.S.C. 552 *et. seq.*).

statements were submitted, and after the 1971 revision of the Council's guidelines, they became nearly universal.[26]

The lack of specificity in the Interim Guidelines may be attributed in part to the newness of the Council and to the newness of some of its members to the federal government. The fact that several of their deficiencies were remedied in the Council's 1971 revised guidelines lends support to this explanation.

Several of the positions taken by the Council in the Interim Guidelines, however, provided indications of a more fundamental policy strategy. This strategy was one of *accommodation* toward the other agencies of government rather than confrontation with them, of advice and assistance rather than aggressive coordination of their activities. With the exception of a few key points, for instance, such as strict interpretation of the "fullest extent possible," the Council left implementation of NEPA almost entirely to the line agencies within very general guidelines, rather than seeking to impose detailed and authoritative interpretations from above. It also played down the issue of public disclosure, thereby deferring to the traditional desires of the agencies to keep their decision processes closed to the public; and it deferred to the wishes of both Senator Muskie and the Atomic Energy Commission in requiring "mere certification" of water quality impacts, rather than waiting for judicial interpretation of this point. Most significantly, it focussed its oversight almost wholly upon the implementation of the "detailed statement" requirement of Section 102 (2) (C) and made no overt attempts to exercise its more general authority to issue "other instructions" to the agencies concerning implementation of other provisions of the Act.[n] As we shall see below, other actions and statements by the Council bear out these initial indications of a strategy of accommodation.

Congressional Oversight Hearings, 1970

The Council's policies, and particularly its "accommodation" approach, were further illuminated by its chairman's testimony during congressional oversight hearings by a subcommittee of the House Merchant Marine and Fisheries Committee in December 1970.[27] In his testimony, Chairman Train stressed what he called the generally cooperative responses of the agencies to NEPA and cited both the Corps of Engineers and the Atomic Energy Commission as examples

---

[n]It is easy to speculate, but difficult to predict retrospectively how effective the Council might have been had it been more "activist" in overseeing and advocating the implementation of the other provisions of NEPA from the start. The important point for what follows, however, is that the Council *did* center its own attention on the "detailed statement" requirement and that this emphasis may have been taken as a major cue by the other agencies in their implementation of the Act. Note that in the Council's first Annual Report, the discussion of NEPA's requirements did not even *mention* any provisions other than the "detailed statement." See Council on Environmental Quality, *Environmental Quality—1970* Washington, D.C., 1970, pp. 21-22.

of "exceedingly good support." However, he steadfastly refused to characterize any agencies as less cooperative or recalcitrant.[28] He also testified against the creation of more stringent requirements for public disclosure and argued that they would "create a monster" insofar as the administrative process was concerned.[29] He agreed to establish them only in response to direct threats that the committee would otherwise create them by legislation.[30] Finally, he urged that the Congressmen leave the implementation of NEPA to the stewardship of the Council, thus downplaying not only the conflict between the Council's two roles, but also the fact that it had already narrowed its oversight role to the "detailed statements" and embarked upon a policy of accommodation rather than confrontation with the other agencies.[o]

The Committee, however, used the hearings as an opportunity to challenge some of the emerging interpretations of the law, particularly the Council's policies concerning public disclosure of detailed statements and comments. Recent events (such as the supersonic transport proposal, and planned nerve gas dumping) provided examples of agencies' deliberate suppression of environmental impact information until controversial actions were accomplished facts:[31] and as Committee Chairman John Dingell pointed out, the Council had a mandate in the Executive order to "ensure the fullest practicable provision of timely public information" about actions with potential environmental impacts. The Committee therefore insisted upon the creation of an enforceable right to prior information—to public participation in the debate over alternatives, rather than merely public knowledge of the impacts of decisions after the fact—and it threatened to create this right by statute if the Council did not do so by its guidelines.[32]

The 1970 oversight hearings, then, may be credited with two achievements: first, with bringing into focus some of the problems of the first year's implementation of NEPA by the agencies, including the Council on Environmental

---

[o]Train's reasons for this position are not completely clear. One possible interpretation is that he genuinely believed that the Council had sufficient support from the President and influence with the agencies to fulfill this role, particularly if the committee were to endorse the broader oversight role specified in the Executive order. This interpretation is supported by his testimony both in 1970 and in the 1972 Joint Hearings, where he supported a proposed amendment to NEPA with the argument that "fundamentally what we need is basically a confirmation of the way this had been administered under our guidelines substantially from the beginning of the act." See U.S. Congress, Senate Committees on Public Works and on Interior and Insular Affairs, *National Environmental Policy Act*, Joint Hearings, Serial 92-H32, March 1972, Washington, D.C., 1972, pp. 33, 22-23.

However, his testimony also showed clearly the reliance of the Council upon the "underdog tactic" of accommodation and hence the necessity of effective pressures upon it from outside environmental advocates such as the committee in order to achieve administrative change. Another possible interpretation of Train's testimony, therefore, is that he was fully aware of this problem but adopted a posture of accommodation anyway, in order to appear to be an Administration "team-player" while letting a friendly committee "force" the Council to take stronger positions on some aspects of the agencies' implementation of the law.

Quality; and second, with forcing revision of the Council's guidelines to require disclosure of environmental impacts a reasonable length of time *before* taking administrative actions. Despite the fact that this latter requirement thus remained a matter of administrative guidelines rather than statutory requirement, it closed an important loophole that was being used by some agencies to thwart the "action-forcing" stimulus of public review and thus consolidated the innovation in the administrative process that was embodied in the concept of the "detailed statement."

1971 Revised Guidelines

The Council circulated proposed revisions in its guidelines for comment in January 1971 and adopted them in April.[33] These Revised Guidelines included at least three significant modifications.

First, they gave new emphasis to "building environmental considerations into the decision-making process." Where the Interim Guidelines had directed the agencies to assess environmental impacts "before undertaking" major actions, the revised version ordered them to do so "as early as possible, and in all cases prior to agency decision."[34]

Second, the revised guidelines were more detailed in their specification of the range of issues that agency guidelines must cover. Among other things, for instance, they must specify the points in the agency's decision processes when consultation with other affected agencies would take place; they must specify the review processes for which the detailed statement would be made available; and they must implement new requirements for public information by July 1. In addition, the agencies were required to consult with the Council in the course of establishing these or any other procedures related to NEPA.[35] The effect of these revisions was to leave the content of implementation guidelines still to the agencies' prerogatives, but to make each agency accountable for some explicit policy concerning each of the specified issues.

Third, and most significantly, the revised guidelines required that:

To the fullest extent possible, no administrative action subject to Section 102 (2) (C) is to be taken sooner than ninety (90) days after a draft environmental statement has been circulated for comment, furnished to the Council and made available to the public . . . or sooner than thirty (30) days after the final text of a statement (together with comments) has been made available to the Council and the public.[36]

This directive, which resulted directly from the insistence of the Dingell subcommittee (as noted above), had two noteworthy implications. It established a minimum time period for public review and comment prior to the actual administrative action, an important innovation in itself; but it also required public access to the *draft* environmental statement, rather than merely to the final one, before the action was taken. These two requirements had mutually reinforcing effects: the availability of the draft statements made the time period for review more likely to produce comments, and the establishment of the time period made the draft statement far more central in importance than it might otherwise have been.

Other substantive revisions in the 1971 guidelines included requirements that environmental statements be circulated for state and local review, rather then merely announced in the *Federal Register*; that the statements include descriptions, maps, and data concerning proposed actions as well as the information called for under the five points of Section 102 (2) (C); and that the comments of the Environmental Protection Agency rather than the "mere certification" of a state agency be obtained concerning impacts on water quality.[37]

The principal policy thrusts of the 1971 guidelines, then, were to make the detailed statements public before action was taken, to re-emphasize the Executive order's intent that the statements be linked to the decision process, and to remedy omissions that had become apparent in the Interim Guidelines. In general, however, the 1971 Revised Guidelines continued the Council's policy of deference to the other agencies concerning the *content* of their policies and guidelines.

CEQ Memoranda

The 1971 Revised Guidelines were not superseded by another revision *per se* until August 1973, but they were supplemented during this period by a series of "memoranda" from the Council, at least three of which amounted to further statements of Council policy concerning the implementation of NEPA.[38]

The first of these (dated May 24, 1971) directed that any benefit-cost analysis that was normally prepared for an action requiring an impact statement should be attached to the environmental impact statement and circulated for review with it.[39] The second (dated November 2, 1971) listed five "sample issues" that should be addressed in agency procedures and the Council's suggested treatment of some of them.[40] Finally, a memorandum of May 16, 1972, explicitly titled "Supplemental Guidance," contained ten CEQ "recommendations for improving agency NEPA procedures."[41] Each of these "recommendations" was carefully defended by quotations from the law's legislative history and judicial decisions; together, they amounted to a second revision of the Council's guidelines, by any other name.[42] Among the most important of these recommendations were suggestions that the agencies prepare "program" impact statements for complex actions, as well as individual detailed statements for major actions within these components; that they discuss all reasonable alternatives to proposed actions, even alternatives lying outside their jurisdictions, at a level of detail adequate to permit independent evaluation by a reviewer; and that they indicate, in each impact statement, the considerations that justified (or "balanced") the "unavoidable adverse effects" listed in the statement.[p]

Unlike the 1970 and 1971 guidelines, which were primarily procedural, the memoranda included some guidance concerning the appropriate *content* of agencies' procedures and detailed statements. This guidance was offered cautiously, couched in terms of "recommendations" rather than directives or formal guidelines. Significantly, each was justified by carefully argued appeals to judicial decisions and legislative history, rather than by reference to the Council's authority to issue guidelines and other instructions to the agencies. By appealing to outside authority rather than its own formal powers, the Council clearly was attempting to maintain a posture of accommodation with the agencies, of suggestion and negotiation rather than confrontation, and also to avoid any direct challenge over the legal force of those powers themselves. At the same time, however, the memoranda adopted more explicit bargaining positions than had their predecessor guidelines concerning the appropriate content of the agencies' procedures and thus hinted at a more active involvement by the Council in its oversight role.[q]

---

[p]Other recommendations in the May 1972 memo were that the agencies prepare lists in advance of all likely impacts of typical agency actions; that they consider and respond, in each final impact statement, to opposing views raised in comments on the draft statement; that they give early warning of their decisions to prepare impact statements for particular actions, including possibly the issuance of public "notices of intent" to prepare them; that each impact statement include references to underlying documents, and indications of how those documents could be obtained or examined; that the availability of each draft statement be adequately publicized; that joint statements be prepared for actions involving more than one federal agency; and that no actions be considered exempt from NEPA as "environmental regulatory activities" except the Water Quality permit program and other activities of the EPA specifically identified as such by the EPA and CEQ. See *102 Monitor* II (June 1972), pp. 1–21.

Note also that of the three principal recommendations identified in the text, the latter two were results of judicial decisions (*Calvert Cliffs Coordinating Committee v. Atomic Energy Commission*, 2 ERC 1779 [D.C. Circuit, July 23, 1971] and *Natural Resources Defense Council v. Morton*, 337 F. Supp. 165, 167, 458 F.2d 827, 337 F. Supp. 170). The question of whether the "balancing" of "beneficial" and "adverse" effects should be discussed in the impact statement itself has been a particularly controversial issue and will be discussed further below.

[q]An interesting question here is *why* the Council chose to attempt a stronger oversight involvement. Obvious reasons include the fact that it was beginning to develop clearer policies from its two years of experience with NEPA and that a series of tough pro-environmentalist judicial decisions had provided it with a new source of authority for more forceful interpretations of the law. Another possible explanation, however, is that the Council's strategy of "team-playing" was beginning to show its weaknesses and that the Council was therefore resorting more strongly to explicit guidance—which could later be used against uncooperative agencies by litigants in court, if they did not adopt it—out of frustration with the resistance of the agencies to its advice. Two of the memos were stern reminders that agencies had not yet revised their procedures as directed by the Council. Significantly, the period during which these memoranda were issued (1971–72) was also the period during which the White House began to back off from its environmental leadership to a position of compro-

1973 Revised Guidelines

In August 1973, the Council issued a second full revision of its guidelines, including a requirement that all agency procedures be brought into conformance with them by January 1974.[43] Among the most obvious features of these guidelines were the enormous increase in detail of the guidance offered, and the fact that most of the "recommendations" made in earlier memoranda were now established as guidelines. Even more significant, however, were a number of policy positions that had been absent in earlier guidelines and now received stronger emphasis.

First, the 1973 guidelines stressed NEPA's substantive policy, rather than merely its requirement of "detailed statements." Section 1(a) of the guidelines noted the agencies' responsibility not simply to prepare detailed statements and to "meet national environmental goals," in general, but to strive actively for the achievement of NEPA's specific policy objectives, which it restated. Section 4(a) added an interpretation of NEPA's provision (Section 105) that its requirements were "supplementary" to those of existing legislation: the guidelines interpreted this as "a mandate to view traditional policies and missions in the light of the Act's national environmental objectives," rather than treating the environment as merely one more disparate consideration to be traded off.

Second, augmenting this substantive emphasis, the 1973 guidelines paid new attention to NEPA's "other" requirements, especially the requirement of Section 102 (2) (A) that the agencies utilize systematically the natural and social sciences and the environmental design arts in their planning and decisions. Section 6(c) pointedly noted that only the "detailed statement" is limited in its applicability to "major federal actions significantly affecting environmental quality;" the rest of NEPA's requirements apply to *all* federal actions. Section 8(c) of the guidelines included expanded discussion of NEPA's Section 102 (2) (A); and Section 2(b) required that initial assessments of environmental impact be undertaken concurrently with initial technical and economic studies. All these provisions served to make more explicit the intended integration of impact assessment with traditional processes of planning and decision.

Third, the 1973 revisions added mild but explicit references to the various authorities of the Council and to the legal duties of the agencies to cooperate with it. Section 1(b) reminded the agencies of the Council's broad statutory authority to "review and appraise" all federal programs in the light of NEPA's substantive policies, as well as its further mandate under the Executive order.

---

mise, the period during which rhetoric promoting an "environmental backlash" and amendments to NEPA was being preached by some key Congressmen and Cabinet officers, and the period during which the Office of Management and Budget inaugurated its "quality of life reviews" mentioned below.

Probably both sets of factors and perhaps others were operating here, but it is important to recognize the extent to which the Council may have been negotiating out of weakness as well as out of strength.

Section 11(f) noted that the Act and the Executive order required the agencies to be "responsive" to the Council's instructions and requests for information, including requests that impact statements be prepared "unless the agency determines that an impact statement is not required." If such a determination were made, Section 6(e) of the guidelines required that it be formally stated and published (and hence reviewable by the courts). In short, in these guidelines the Council set a somewhat broader context for the implementation of NEPA's procedures and sought to remind the agencies of its own statutory role as well as the broader substantive purposes of the law.

Fourth, and finally, the 1973 revisions required that competing considerations, which were thought to offset or "balance" the environmental impacts, be mentioned *within* the detailed statement rather than simply in the agency's overall decision process. Section 8(a)(8) created this requirement, in a provision directing that not only a summary benefit-cost analysis, but also "an indication of what other considerations of Federal policy are thought to offset the adverse effects of the proposed action," be made part of the detailed statement.

This policy became a focus of intense controversy between the Council and several other agencies. Critics argued that the detailed statement was intended to be strictly an objective, factual declaration, whose content was to be considered along with the content of other project documents and evaluations in the agency's decision process. The attempt to force discussion of the "balancing" of environmental impacts against nonenvironmental considerations *within* the detailed statement, they held, would make the statement necessarily a justification of a proposed action rather than an objective declaration of impacts. Such a justification might take the form of either a slick public-relations piece, or a massive and technical "decision document"; but in either case, the goal of a neutral and factual declaration of probable impacts would be lost.

In fact, however, the language of NEPA required *both* an objective declaration *and* evaluative judgments about the merits of what was declared: a detailed statement not only of the impacts and alternatives *per se*, but also of the "adverse effects" of a "proposed action." Moreover, Section 102 (2) (B) of NEPA required that environmental values be considered "along with economic and technical considerations"; and there was no logical reason why these "offsetting considerations" should not be mentioned in the detailed statement once value judgments had already been introduced by the definition of "adverse" effects and the recommendation of a "proposed" action. In some cases, especially, the impact statement might be the only document in which all these considerations *were* balanced explicitly. The important point was that these two categories of information—factual statements and evaluative judgments—be *distinguished* from each other; and this distinction was perfectly possible, under the separate subheadings of the statement's content prescribed by the law and the Council's guidelines.

The real issue in this controversy, therefore, appears to have been not the interpretation of the law for its own sake, but the practical implications of the Council's policy. Its direct effect was to bring more and more of each action's decision record within the scope of the detailed statement, *thus making it legally reviewable by other agencies and citizens and discoverable in lawsuits*, under the procedures mandated by NEPA. As a consequence, it strengthened the authority of the courts (and hence of the Council's public constituency) to challenge the substantive merits of the agencies' decisions—that is, the balance that was struck between adverse impacts and offsetting considerations—rather than merely the descriptive completeness of the statement. The Council probably decided that since such balancing judgments and decisions would occur whether or not they were discussed in the detailed statement, the purposes of NEPA would be best served by requiring that they be on record in a document that was subject to external and judicial review.

The 1973 Revised Guidelines, then, expressed a more detailed and definitely more substantive policy of NEPA oversight on the part of the Council; and while they added further to the content and legal significance of the "detailed statement," they also gave new and strong emphasis to its broader purposes and to its role as one of a series of interrelated means created by NEPA for the fulfillment of these purposes.

Practical Problems

While the Council's official statements of environmental policy were expressed through its guidelines and public statements, the informal manifestations of environmental policy in its structure, staffing, and behavior were no less important in their implications.[r] By these measures the Council's environmental policy making encountered severe limitations, especially because of the small size and composition of its staff. The Council was never a large organization during this period: its total number of professionals was twenty-three in April 1971 and grew to a ceiling of fifty by 1973.[44] Such a size was probably adequate for the fulfillment of its advisory role, but grossly inadequate for oversight and "coordination" of the environmental activities of the federal agencies. OMB, the only agency comparable in its oversight responsibilities, was limited in its capabilities even with a staff of approximately 400. In effect, the Council had only one or two staff members to oversee the activities of each entire sector of government activities.[s]

---

[r]Official statements of policy have at least symbolic value and may have additional force if they take the form of regulations. In practice, however, their true significance depends upon how effectively they are implemented and enforced, especially by the issuing agency.

[s]The Council's staff was organized internally into four principal components: the General Counsel, the Secretary to the Council, the Program Development Staff, and the Federal Impact Evaluation Staff. Within the Impact Evaluation group, each staff member had

In addition, many early members of the Council's staff were administrators with little experience either in the federal government or in the sciences of the human environment. For its first full year, the Council operated with personnel borrowed from other agencies, since its budget was not appropriated until December 1970; by April 1971 it had recruited its own initial staff, but of these twenty-three, only four had master's degrees or doctorates in the sciences, and two in economics; the remainder were drawn primarily from policy professions such as law and public administration.[45] Only a handful of these staff members had had working experience in the programs or agencies whose activities they were to oversee.

The Council was also constrained by the organizations charged with oversight of *its* activities and resources. Its dependence upon Presidential favor was discussed above, but in addition it was subject to scrutiny and control both by the Office of Management and Budget and by the congressional subcommittees responsible for its allocations of budget and personnel. One manifestation of the Council's problems was OMB's treatment of its budget: OMB impounded $320,000 in Fiscal Year 1973 (14.3 percent of the total, or the equivalent of eight professional positions), cut fifteen positions as well as substantial funds from its budget request in Fiscal Year 1974, and held its staff and budget to virtually the same level in the budget for Fiscal Year 1975.[46] Another manifestation was the vesting of congressional control over the Council's budget in the House Subcommittee on Agriculture Appropriations (promptly renamed the "Subcommittee on Agriculture-Environmental and Consumer Protection Appropriations"), which was chaired by one of the handful of congressmen who had voted against the Council's creation in the first place.[t] While this committee was cordial to the Council during this period, it clearly was a constituency that the Council could not afford to antagonize, and this constraint undoubtedly limited the Council's policy leadership on such matters as the environmental impacts of agricultural activities.[47]

Because of these realities, the Council's exercise of its oversight authority was necessarily constrained, and governed by political criteria as much as by scientific or ethical principles of environmental policy. The Council could not conceivably conduct a careful review of more than a fraction of the detailed

---

responsibility for a particular set of federal programs, such as water resources, energy, transportation, and housing. This structure was patterned generally on the assignments of responsibility in the Office of Management and Budget, from which the Council's Staff Director had come. It differed somewhat from OMB in the background of its staff, however: OMB's examiners tended to be persons who had either strong analytic training (for instance, in economics) or substantial experience in the agencies whose programs they examined, while many of the Council's staff members had only more general qualifications.

[t]Representative Jamie L. Whitten (D–Mississippi), chairman of this subcommittee since 1949, was also the author of a book, *That We May Live* (Princeton, N.J.: Van Nostrand, 1966), which defended the importance of chemical pesticides in response to Rachel Carson's attacks on them in her book *Silent Spring* (New York: Houghton Mifflin, 1962).

statements submitted to it by the agencies, let alone monitor the full range of federal actions to identify those for which statements should have been prepared but were not. Moreover, there was no generally accepted empirical standard against which the quality of the statements could be evaluated, and the Council's staff had neither the time nor the qualifications to develop such a standard based upon objective premises. Its criteria for review, therefore, were primarily political. Was there local opposition to a proposed action with which the Council could ally itself? Especially, was there opposition from local or state government? Was there opposition from other federal agencies? Was a lawsuit likely? Was the action inconsistent with any expressed Presidential environmental policy? Was there an educational issue involved, a point that could be and needed to be impressed upon the sponsoring agency? And was the issue *winnable*, in the sense that Council intervention might sway the balance and increase its reputation for effectiveness?[48] Lacking direct power and authority itself, the Council depended for its effectiveness upon choosing issues where it could ally itself with active coalitions and constituencies that did have some levers of power and thereby lend its symbolic support to their efforts and gain their support and an enhanced reputation in return.[49]

During late 1973 and early 1974, the Council experienced a near-total staff change, the first major turnover of the staff members it had itself recruited. Council Chairman Train was named administrator of the Environmental Protection Agency and took with him Staff Director Alvin Alm; Council members Robert Cahn and Gordon MacDonald were succeeded by John Busterud and Beatrice Willard, General Counsel Timothy Atkeson accepted a position of the same title with the new Congressional Office of Technology Assessment; and by the middle of 1974 almost the entire senior staff of the Council, plus many of their less senior colleagues (including the entire professional staff of the General Counsel's Office) had resigned to take other positions.

With these losses, it is fair to say that the first major era of the Council's existence had ended and that the almost total turnover of top-level policy leadership and experienced staff members would bring a reassessment of priorities and strategy, rebuilding of staff, and different directions. Former Governor Russell W. Peterson of Delaware was named to replace Train as chairman of the Council; and the central thrust of Council policy and its effectiveness, under its second chairman and new staff, remain to be seen.

Summary

In spite of its constraints, the Council during its first four years made some limited progress toward fulfilling the purpose prescribed for it by NEPA: providing an institutional focal point for environmental policymaking in the Executive Office of the President. The discussion above has centered on the evolution of its oversight role and NEPA implementation guidelines, since this is the area of its policy that bears most directly upon the discussion of agency responses to NEPA that follows. In addition, however, the Council in its advisory capacity contributed to a wide range of executive policy actions favoring environmental protection and made numerous policy recommendations to the White House (whether or not they were heeded).[u]

The logic of the Council's environmental policy during this period was fundamentally the logic of its own efforts to establish itself, and to achieve sufficient political leverage in the administrative process to fulfill its two competing roles effectively. Its initial strategy of Administration "team-playing" and accommodation with the agencies was well suited to its status as a new and inexperienced agency trying to guide the implementation of a new and ambiguous law, especially in a period when environmental policy goals were matters of strong political consensus and Presidential initiatives. The effectiveness of this strategy diminished, however, as Presidential leadership retreated to a posture of compromise and thence to other priorities, and the continued attempts by the Council to retain its credibility within the Administration resulted in a diminution of its credibility with the public as a voice for responsible environmental policy. It needed, therefore, some new source of policy leverage to replace direct Presidential backing, without the risks of overtly seeking public support independent of the White House. It found such a source in the judiciary, whose unprecedented activism in the interpretation of NEPA provided both an authoritative basis for tougher interpretation of the law's mandate and a rallying point for the Council's public constituency. As the courts' interpretations of the law grew stronger, the Council's guidelines followed; and as the courts gradually moved beyond matters of definition and procedure toward issues of substantive policy, the Council's 1973 guideline revisions incorporated language designed to pave the way further.

With the support of the courts, therefore, and through them of an active public constituency, the Council was able to establish—at least for a time—both an initial place for itself and a modicum of effectiveness, despite a gradual decline in Presidential policy leadership and severe constraints on its staff, budget, formal authority, and political power.

---

[u]Among the environmental policy actions for which it could claim partial if not full credit were at least half a dozen Executive orders; reversal of a ruling by the Internal Revenue Service that would have denied tax exempt status to environmental law groups; recommendation that construction be terminated on the Cross-Florida Barge Canal, among other projects; formulation of the President's annual environmental legislative programs and guidance of these programs in the legislative process; special studies leading to legislative initiatives by the President (for instance, on control of ocean dumping and of toxic substances and on integrated methods of pest management); and regular staff work for the President on numerous issues as diverse as eagle killings, oil spills, channelization of streams, nuclear testing, international treaties, land use conflicts, and the 1972 United Nations Conference on the Environment. See, for instance, U.S. Congress, *Administration of the National Environmental Policy Act,* House Report 92–316, Washington, D.C., pp. 40–43.

The Office of Management and Budget

The question from other agencies' points of view, however, was how much credence should be given to the President's environmental rhetoric and the Council's constrained authority. Until the law had been tested repeatedly in the courts, the Council's authority was clearly dependent upon Presidential support; and while the President had demonstrated a symbolic commitment to environmental quality, this commitment did not in practice override his greater competing commitments to certain major and environmentally hazardous actions of public works and "high technology." These commitments included, for instance, the supersonic transport or SST (1970), the Tennessee-Tombigbee Waterway (1971), the Liquid Metal Fast Breeder Reactor or LMFBR (1971), offshore oil leasing (1972), the Trans-Alaska Pipeline System or TAPS (1972, 1973), drastic increases in timber cutting on the National Forests (1973), and numerous energy exploitation proposals in 1973 and 1974. All of these latter commitments might reasonably lead agency officials to decide that their missions too were of higher priority than the environmental "fad," in spite of that issue's rhetorical prominence at the time. The President did not apply the substance of NEPA's policy goals to the evaluation of such major symbolic actions as these, and this failure may well have encouraged discounting of his rhetoric by the agencies that had to decide how strongly to react to new "environmental policy goals."

Most significantly, especially on a day-to-day level, the environmental commitment espoused in the President's rhetoric and the Council's policies received little consistent reinforcement in the normal planning process of the Executive Office itself: the annual cycle of budget preparation, review, and allocation.[50] The authors of NEPA intended that the Office of Management and Budget (then the Budget Bureau) play a central role in NEPA's oversight and implementation that was consistent with its key role in oversight and implementation of all federal activities. Instead, however, OMB willingly left the onus of NEPA oversight to the CEQ and took pains to avoid engaging itself either in the oversight of its implementation by other agencies, or even in the implementation of it in its own activities.

The Office of Management and Budget issued only three instructions to the agencies during this period concerning fulfillment of the requirements of NEPA, and all of these were limited to procedural considerations in the routing and processing of information.[51] One of these, Circular A-19, simply referred the agencies back to the guidelines of the Council on Environmental Quality. The other two did direct that relevant information about the environmental impacts of budgetary actions be provided to OMB personnel with the agencies' annual budget requests, but did not require that environmental impact statements *per se* be prepared for such actions. Only for water resource projects were environmental impact statements required prior to OMB review, a circumstance that probably says more about the OMB's traditional battle for control of the water resource "pork barrel" than about its concern for the environment.[52] Significantly, the second bulletin *eliminated* a requirement of the first bulletin that an impact statement accompany each legislative proposal, thereby leaving only the requirement of Circular A-19 that "information copies of required 102 statements should be submitted to OMB *if available at the time clearance is requested*" (emphasis added).[53] Such a position clearly indicated that the agencies need not take trouble to comply with NEPA in order to survive the OMB clearance process, since OMB was not interested in using the statements itself unless they happened to be available at the appropriate time.

A particularly significant procedural change occurred in 1971, when OMB quietly inaugurated its so-called "quality of life reviews." OMB traditionally reviewed agencies' legislative proposals and congressional testimony confidentially prior to publication of them, to insure their consistency with the Administration's policy positions. In contrast, proposed rules and regulations of the agencies were normally reviewed openly, by publication in the *Federal Register* with a period for responses and comments. Beginning with the guidelines for implementation of the Clean Air Act amendments of 1970, however, which were published by the Environmental Protection Agency in 1971, the OMB confidentially directed that all proposed federal regulations that dealt with the "quality of life"—specifically including environmental quality, health, and consumer protection—must be submitted to OMB for confidential review *prior* to their publication. OMB would then circulate them for review and comment by other affected agencies of government, such as the Department of Commerce, which might exert pressures to modify them prior to their publication. In the case of the Clean Air Act guidelines, EPA published a notice of proposed rule making in the *Federal Register* in April 1971: the guidelines were called in by OMB for "routine" review in June, shortly before they were due to be published, and in August they were finally published, in a form somewhat stronger than the April proposals but considerably weaker than the June draft.[54]

The implication of such reviews was far from routine; they amounted to a privileged channel through which the subjects of environmental and other "quality of life" regulations could exert private political pressures and special pleading for modifications before a proposed regulation was made public, rather than responding openly with comments on the proposed regulations as published in the *Federal Register*.[55]

OMB also successfully resisted an attempt by the Council on Environmental Quality to include stricter reporting requirements in its 1973 Revised Guidelines. CEQ sought to require that to the maximum extent practicable, no legislation to which the impact statement requirement applied would be sent to OMB until a draft statement, with agency comments appended, had been filed with the Council and that "reports, reconnaissance studies and feasibility studies . . . required by law to be submitted to Congress" would also be accompanied by impact statements.[56] OMB objected, however, and these proposed changes were stricken before the guidelines were issued.

So far as is known, OMB provided no further instructions to its own professional staff during this period as to how information obtained from environmental impact statements should be utilized in budgetary decision making. Some OMB staff members developed working relationships with their CEQ counterparts, but these appear to have been individual rather than official or systematic forms of policy coordination. CEQ staff members began sitting in on some of the annual budget hearings in the fall of 1971, and Chairman Train wrote a memorandum of understanding to OMB Director Caspar Weinberger in September 1972 expressing agreement on closer staff cooperation;[57] but while these actions indicated some improvement in coordination, reports from staff members of the two agencies indicated that OMB had not pursued or encouraged such coordination to any significant extent in its internal guidance to its staff. It appears that OMB's staff were encouraged to take an interest in the environmental implications of federal actions only when they provided a convenient reason for preventing actions that OMB opposed for budgetary or other reasons.

Finally, it is particularly significant that during the same period when OMB was deliberately avoiding any central role in the review of environmental impact statements, it was creating the requirement that all new "quality of life" regulations pass through its review prior to publication. Why the one and not the other, especially in light of NEPA's intent that the impact statement be considered along with the proposed action at each level of review? If OMB had been genuinely interested in implementing environmental policy, it should have been interested in the environmental consequences of nonenvironmental proposals as well as the nonenvironmental consequences of environmental regulations. It was not, however, except in the case of water resource projects. One may infer that OMB's priorities were governed not so much by the broad, policy-shaping role that it in fact occupied (by virtue of its powers of budget allocation and legislative clearance), but by narrower, more fiscal and business-oriented values held by its political appointees and senior staff members. Environmental protection was not a priority to OMB; it was at best a transitory political issue to be contained, more likely a headache that would result in more paperwork, and at worst a threat to the budget—that is, a new area of federal activity that would bring new pressures to spend more federal money.[v] It is such values that proba-

---

[v]It is only fair to note that in at least one major respect, environmental quality clearly *was* a major threat to the federal budget during these years. NEPA itself was not, despite certail increases in costs necessary to perform adequate environmental analyses prior to taking major federal actions. However, especially between 1970 and 1972 President Nixon and Senator Muskie were engaged in intense competition for symbolic leadership of the environmental issue, and a result of this competition was Muskie's "bidding up" the budget for pollution control into one of the costliest single public works programs in history. The Clean Water Act Amendments of 1972, for instance, Public Law 92–500, authorized the expenditure of more than $6 *billion* per year for the first three years in grants for construction of local wastewater treatment plants. Such expenditures were unquestionably matters for serious OMB concern, though the extension of that concern to implementation of other environmental policy matters (especially those the President had adopted in his public policy statements, such as NEPA) appears unwarranted and unfortunate.

bly best explain OMB's simultaneous insistence on reviewing environmental protection regulations and disinterest in reviewing environmental impact statements. It was interested in the *fiscal* and *political* consequences of federal actions, not in the full range of environmental, social, and economic consequences whose consideration and balancing NEPA was intended to insure.

Conclusion

Within the context of these three sets of signals from the Executive Office, the operating agencies of the federal government were left with the responsibility of *implementing* environmental policy. It is clear that these signals did not always carry the same message and that each was based to a significant extent upon its author's perception of politics rather than of principle. President Nixon's rhetorical commitment to environmental policy was evident in many of his statements and actions, especially during 1970 and 1971, but this commitment was not supported by change in other priorities because of their environmental impacts. The preferences of the Council were clear, but so were the limitations on its ability to enforce them. The Office of Management and Budget continued to conduct business as usual—that is, setting up a new branch to oversee the budgets of the environmental agencies (EPA and CEQ) as a new sector of federal activity, but making no attempt to treat environmental policy goals as major considerations in the activities of all federal agencies as NEPA intended.

 The net effect of these signals was to leave the operating agencies with substantial discretion in interpreting and implementing environmental policy. Agencies that wanted to change their policies in the direction of NEPA's goals appeared to have *permission* to do so; but agencies that preferred not to change were not given an unambiguous mandate by the Executive Office. It is interesting to examine, therefore, the ways in which the agencies exercised this discretion. Which ones changed, and in what ways, and which did not? Did agencies with similar missions react in the same way? If not, why not? It is not only interesting to ask these questions, but important as well, for the answers may reveal important realities about the workings of the federal government and about the effectiveness of various strategies for trying to change its priorities and activities.

4 NEPA and the Army Corps of Engineers

Background

The Corps of Engineers is both one of the largest and by far the oldest of the federal agencies responsible for water resource development.[a] Established by act of Congress in 1802, it was given general responsibility for civil works in 1824, for rivers and harbors work in 1852, and for related flood control work in 1917.[1] The Flood Control Act of 1936 authorized it to undertake flood control work in the nation generally; the Flood Control Act of 1944 expanded the definition of "flood control" to include major drainage works for economic gain; and amendments to the Fish and Wildlife Coordination Act in 1958 added responsibilities to mitigate or prevent damage to fish and wildlife resources.[2] Its budget during fiscal year 1971 was approximately $1.3 billion, of which roughly sixty percent was for construction; and its budget for fiscal year 1972 provided funds for 323 general investigations (surveys and planning), preconstruction planning of 81 projects, and construction of 234 projects.[3]

Structure and Planning Process

The Corps' civil works program is divided administratively into eleven divisions corresponding to eleven major watersheds of the United States; and these divisions are composed of thirty-six engineer districts, the basic organizational units. Each engineer district is administered by a District Engineer, who is a military officer and reports (with respect to civil functions) through the Division Engineer to the Office of the Director of Civil Works, a component of the Office of the Chief of Engineers; the Chief of Engineers in turn reports directly to the Secretary of the Army. As of 1966, the policy-making chain of authority in the Corps consisted of approximately 235 military officers, of whom approximately 114 were assigned to Civil Works; the remainder of the Corps' 30,000 personnel are civilians.[4] The engineer officers, however, normally are rotated every two to three years, while civilian staff members often are promoted within their district organizations over long periods of time. Of its professional staff members, the

---

[a]It also has major military responsibilities for combat, combat support, and military construction. This study will be confined to its civil works activities in water resource development, which are administratively independent of its military activities.

47

majority are engineers, but a range of other disciplines are also represented, such as biologists, landscape architects, planners, and economists, to name a few.

With the exception of some small projects constructed under continuing authority, all Corps water resource projects require specific authorizations and appropriations by the Congress and must undergo a lengthy process of planning and review before they are ready for construction.[5] The normal Corps planning process begins with a local request, typically made through the appropriate Congressman, for a study by the Corps. Such requests frequently originate in communities that experience periodic flooding or that have political leaders or interest groups eager to promote economic development of water resources.[6] If no survey has been carried out by the Corps on the area in question, a survey must be authorized by inclusion in the biennial "omnibus rivers and harbors authorization bill" (or by a separate bill). In many, if not most cases, however, the Corps has already carried out some study in the past either on the same area or one close by within the same river basin; and in these cases, a restudy of the earlier recommendations may be directed merely by a resolution of the Public Works Committee of either House of the Congress.[7]

Following authorization for a survey or restudy, funds must be appropriated for it, which requires an average of four and a half years' wait;[8] after these funds are received, a survey is undertaken. The survey itself requires an average of four and a half years to complete[9] and is intended to identify a recommended proposal among alternative possibilities—based primarily upon economic and engineering standards, but including also local preferences and other statutory considerations—for the development of the water resource.[10]

In the course of the survey, three public meetings are held, all of which are "informational" rather than adversary or formal in character, and each is preceded by public notice in local newspapers and to a cumulative mailing list of persons and groups known to be interested in the project. At the first such meeting, the District Engineer explains—and requests public views on—the water resource problem that is to be investigated, and discussion centers on this problem. At the second, some time later, he presents alternative solutions that he considers feasible to deal with this problem, and at the third, he presents the solution that he has decided to recommend.[11]

The survey report is then reviewed by the Division Engineer and by the Board of Engineers for Rivers and Harbors (BERH), an advisory board of senior engineer officers in the Office of the Chief of Engineers.[12] Concurrently, it is sent for review to other affected federal agencies at the Washington level and to the states involved. It then goes to the Chief of Engineers for final recommendation, to the Secretary of the Army, and to the Office of Management and Budget for review and clearance. This review process requires just over two years, eleven months of which is taken up by review and coordination within the Corps itself.[13] Unfavorable reports may be appealed to the Board of Engineers for Rivers and Harbors by any interested party. According to estimates of Corps officials, approximately half of all survey reports submitted are unfavorable, though no information is available on how many of these are later reconsidered by committee resolution.

Once the survey report is completed and submitted to the Congress, the projects that it recommends must be authorized for construction, funds must be appropriated for them, and the Corps must plan each project in full engineering detail—the "advanced engineering and design" phase. The Congress rarely refuses to authorize a project upon which the Corps has submitted a favorable survey report,[14] but as at the survey stage, there is a waiting period of over two years for appropriations for engineering and construction. As of 1969, the Corps had over 450 active, authorized projects, costing by conservative estimate $9.7 billion, that had not yet been funded for construction.[15]

During advanced engineering and design, which takes approximately two years, many of the planning studies must be redone in detail and others updated; design memoranda and other detailed studies are completed; a "definite project report" is prepared by the district on the basis of these memoranda and studies, and approved by the Division Engineer and the Office of the Chief of Engineers; and construction contracts are developed and let. Construction of the project then commences and is continued at whatever pace funds are appropriated by the Congress and apportioned by the Office of Management and Budget.[16] The average time required for construction is two years and eight months.[17] The average time required for planning a project in full, then—from the time a study is authorized by the Congress until the initiation of construction—is approximately fifteen years and three months; construction requires an average of thirty months beyond this.[18]

Planning Objectives and Criteria

The history of the Corps reveals a cumulative broadening of the range of purposes that it was directed to consider in planning the development and management of water resources. During its first century of civil works, activity was limited almost entirely to navigation projects, but over the course of the past fifty to sixty years other major goals and categories of activities were assigned to it by the Congress, including flood control, hydroelectric power production, agricultural drainage and irrigation, water quality management, and the prevention of beach erosion.[19] Within the past two decades, further changes in public and congressional preferences and the emergence of other issues on the national agenda have led to the inclusion of even more objectives, such as the protection of fish and wildlife resources, development of recreational opportunities, and now the production and enhancement of "environmental quality" in general.

Many of these additional purposes were far removed from the traditional activities and professional goals of civil engineers. Moreover, the more that were added, the more frequently conflicts would arise concerning the mixture of them that should be achieved in a particular project. All, however, were significantly affected by the management of water resources if not dependent upon it, and in recognition of this relationship, the Congress gradually added them to the Corps' responsibilities.[20] In short, long before the enactment of the National Environmental Policy Act, the Corps had been charged by the Congress with the mission of *multiple-purpose* management of water resources.

While the purposes of the Corps' activities were established by congressional authorization, however, the *criteria* for the achievement of those purposes, and for the evaluation of specific projects, have traditionally been set by the executive (through the Office of Management and Budget, its predecessor Bureau of the Budget, and the Water Resources Council established in 1965).[21] At least four sets of these criteria have been promulgated: the so-called "Green Book" of 1950,[22] Budget Circular A–47 of 1952,[23] a set published as Senate Document 97 in 1962,[24] and most recently, the "Principles and Standards" of the Water Resources Council, which were officially promulgated in 1973.[25] Underlying all of these criteria was the principle established by the Flood Control Act of 1936, that the federal government should undertake such projects only if "the benefits, to whomsoever they may accrue, exceed the costs."[26]

In principle, these various sets of evaluation criteria gradually broadened the range of benefits and costs that might be included in the calculation. Senate Document 97, for instance, explicitly provided for consideration of "all pertinent benefits and costs, both tangible and intangible," and for "study of all [area] resources, an assessment of their functional relationships, their development protentials, [and] possible adverse effects . . . ."[27] In practice, however, the Budget Bureau insisted that all projects first meet a strict test of *economic* efficiency—that is, that they have discounted economic benefits greater than economic costs—before other merits or impacts of a project might be considered; and it tended to give preference to projects that exhibited high *ratios* of economic benefits to economic costs. The result was an incentive for the water engineering agencies to create economic surrogates for intangible values wherever possible (such as fifty cents per recreational "user-day") and to ignore or underestimate intangible costs and other values that could not be so quantified. According to Corps testimony in 1971:

In practice . . . only demonstrable economic benefits and costs based on market values were considered . . . It wasn't until the passage of the National Environmental Policy Act that we really had in our hands the authority to spend money, time, and effort in this field over and above what were the precedent-setting studies in which economic development and the benefit-cost ratio were the be-all-and-end-all.[28]

The Budget Bureau's insistence upon strictly economic criteria undoubtedly stemmed from both economic and political considerations. As guardian of the federal budget, it argued that such projects were not sound investments of federal funds unless they were expected to yield benefits greater than their costs. This argument might sound reasonable except that water resource projects are the only form of federal investment that must be so justified and that many others are undertaken precisely to achieve public benefits that are not economically quantifiable (for instance, national defense).[29] Politically, however, water resource projects have served historically as a form of congressional political currency, primarily to benefit the congressional districts of powerful majority party Congressmen, Public Works committee members, and enough other Congressmen to ensure passage of legislation authorizing and funding them.[30] In order to set limits upon this phenomenon, therefore, and to prevent federal support of economically wasteful projects for political reasons (and sometimes to prevent the support of projects that would benefit administration opponents in the Congress), the Budget Bureau adopted narrowly defined economic criteria of benefit and cost as its instrument.

The enactment of NEPA and the promulgation of the new "Principles and Standards" have probably resulted in some broadening of these criteria in practice but not in any change in the ultimate test of a project's acceptability. They have undoubtedly introduced greater flexibility into the balancing of noneconomic considerations once a project has been shown to have economic benefits at least marginally greater than economic costs, and they may thus have reduced the previous emphasis upon a high *ratio* of economic benefits to costs for its own sake. There is no reason to suppose, however, that OMB will abandon the economic criterion as a necessary threshold test unless water projects cease to have value as a political currency, and unless Congress ceases to approve them by "log-rolling."[b]

Interagency Coordination

In addition to considering the broadening range of objectives and criteria that define their own missions, the water engineering agencies are also obliged to "coordinate" their activities with those of other agencies whose missions might be affected by their actions. Long before the requirements of NEPA that "de-

---

[b]"Porkbarreling" refers to the practice of seeking expenditures of federal funds to benefit one's own region or congressional district at the expense of the country as a whole; it includes water resource projects as well as defense installations and contracts, construction grants for sewage treatment plants, and many other forms of federal subsidy. "Logrolling" refers to the form of congressional cooperation by which expenditures of such region-specific benefit are approved, whereby a Congressman will support such expenditures in other regions as *quid pro quo* for other Congressmen's support of his. In the absence of some objective criteria, such a process may easily ignore the relative merits of the proposals even for achieving their intended purposes, let alone for achieving an efficient and equitable allocation of public resources.

tailed statements" be circulated to other agencies for review and comment, for instance, proposals for water resource projects were already subject to such reviews.[31] There were, however, at least three important differences: the number of reviewing agencies was smaller, their comments were not subject to public disclosure, and the review process did not extend to water resource *related* actions such as nuclear power plants, highway bridges, sewage treatment plants, and other water-using facilities.

The requirements for coordination of water resource development proposals are of several types, but all share a common effect: to insure that the diverse interests of many federal agencies in the use of water resources are represented in the processes of planning and decision making concerning those resources.[c] The *purpose* of this representation, however, has been perceived differently by the Executive Office and the Congress, and by various agencies and interest groups. From the standpoint of the Executive Office, such coordination would hopefully reduce wasteful competition and duplication among the agencies and make the functioning of government more efficient; it would also provide a substitute for centralized comprehensive planning by the executive branch, which the Congress was unwilling to permit.[d] To the agencies whose missions involved nondevelopmental uses of water resources (such as the Bureau of Sport Fisheries and the National Park Service), however, and to the supporters of these agencies in the Congress, such coordination provided a new and two-fold degree of political power. It provided access for them to the water resource project decision process and thus opportunities to lobby for greater consideration of their purposes by the water engineering agencies (which otherwise tended to show greater interst in traditional purposes such as economic development and structural engineering); and through this access, it provided them also with a partial counterpoise to the narrowly economic evaluation criteria established for water projects by the Budget Bureau.[32]

---

[c]These mechanisms of coordination were of several types. Some required direct review of proposed actions by affected agencies (for instance, the Fish and Wildlife Coordination Act); others required coordination by agencies of the Executive Office of the President (for instance, Executive Order No. 9384); still others required project review or even "framework" planning by an interagency committee (for instance, the Water Resource Planning Act of 1965). Maass comments that "the planning process has come to be rated by the quantity of coordination that is practiced, that is, by the extent to which all conceivable interests have been given a voice in planning." See Arthur Maass, "Public Investment Planning in the United States: Analysis and Critique," *Public Policy XVIII* (Winter 1970), p. 216.

[d]During the period in which many of the requirements for coordination (and multiple-purpose water resource planning itself) first arose, President Roosevelt tried repeatedly to establish a "National Resources Board" to provide such a capacity. The Congress repeatedly refused to act upon this request, however, during the period 1936-1943; and in 1943, it eliminated the "National Resources Planning Board" (successor of the "Natural Resources Committee") that Roosevelt had established by fiat, by striking its appropriation from the budget. See Arthur M. Schlesinger, *The Coming of the New Deal* (Boston: Houghton Mifflin, 1958), p. 352; also Frank E. Smith, *The Politics of Conservation* (New York: Harper and Row, 1966), pp. 267–69.

These perceptions of the purpose of coordination are obviously in conflict and illustrate precisely the problem that gave rise to the National Environmental Policy Act: the "jurisdictional externalities" among the missions of the various federal agencies concerning the use of a common resource and the absence of any common "environmental policy" for the resolution of these conflicts. Increasingly comprehensive "coordination" was the nearest existing approximation to such a resolution; but such coordination was only partially developed even for water resource projects and absent for most other federal actions. Without a substantive basis in an "environmental policy," moreover, it was more a political bargaining process among the agencies than a rational allocation of public resources. In practice, the agencies frequently worked out accommodations that obscured or submerged the major points of difference among them rather than continuing to force confrontations that the reviewing agencies lacked the power to win.[33]

In this context, NEPA itself had the potential to become at least the culmination of one trend and perhaps the catalyst for change in some new direction. Its procedural requirements for review and comment on "detailed statements" extended the principle of comprehensive coordination to include not only all affected agencies, but also all categories of major federal actions that might have significant environmental impacts (rather than just water projects), thus stretching that principle almost to its logical limit. The very magnitude of these requirements might force the principle to collapse of its own weight, or to yield to some further innovation.[34] At the same time, NEPA's substantive policy and other requirements (such as integrated multi-disciplinary planning) provided at least a glimpse of what one such innovation might be; namely, broadening the responsibility of the *initiating* agency to consider the impacts of its activities upon the social values and purposes that relied upon the same resources. If the agencies were to accept this responsibility, both formally and by developing broader disciplinary expertise and goal sets, presumably the need for comprehensive coordination among limited-mission agencies would be greatly diminished.

Initial Response to NEPA, 1970–71

The response of the Corps to NEPA took several forms, and it must therefore be examined from several perspectives. The obvious starting point is its headquarters policy directives as expressed in its guidelines, regulations, and public statements. Such official positions, however, are only as meaningful as the extent to which related decisions are visibly consistent with them. We must therefore look also at other actions during the same period to understand the extent to which environmental policy objectives affected the normal activities of the agency. At the most immediate level, the treatment of the required "detailed statements" provides an indication of how seriously committed the agency was to implementation of the law. A more significant though less tangible indicator is the extent to which agency officials attributed modifications, delays, and cancellations of projects in progress during this period to the requirements of NEPA. Finally, a possible indicator of long-term response is the extent to which new environmental policy directions were reflected in organizational structure and personnel decisions, since these elements provide the preconditions for the "integrated use of the natural and social sciences and the environmental design arts" that NEPA directed.

Policy Statements and Guidelines

Within four months after the enactment of NEPA, the Office of the Chief of Engineers had issued three circulars to its districts and divisions concerning the implementation of NEPA.[35] The message of these circulars was clear. The spirit and intent of NEPA were to be effectuated by the Corps in all of its activities; its requirements were applicable to the water resource development activities of each district; and its procedures were to be complied with immediately. The first of these was issued two days before even the President's Executive Order and almost two months before the CEQ's Interim Guidelines; it stated a general policy position on environmental quality, defined the law's applicability as covering all pre-and postauthorization activities (including all survey reports and requests for construction funds), and directed that detailed statements be prepared for each survey report "not essentially complete" as of that date.[36] The second circular underscored these points by adding a more detailed list of the categories of action that would require detailed statements and stressing priority attention to detailed statements for upcoming budget materials and "projects whose starting time is imminent."[37] Finally, the third circular provided detailed instructions for implementation of the law; this circular was published the same day that the Council on Environmental Quality issued its Interim Guidelines.

The detailed instructions of this third circular consolidated the contents of the two earlier directives and went beyond them in three respects. First, they declared a Corps policy that impact assessment and preparation of detailed statements were to be made an integral part of the pre-authorization planning process, as directed by the Executive order.[38] Second, they consolidated and clarified the list of categories of Corps actions for which detailed statements were to be prepared and applied the law broadly and explicitly to include nearly all the agency's major categories of action.[39] Finally, they directed that the public be kept fully informed concerning the environmental impacts of proposed actions, not only after the detailed statement was released but also during the development of it.[40] These policies provided the Corps' official guidance to its staff for the first nine months of NEPA's implementation.[e]

---

[e]One further statement of general policy on environmental quality was issued by the Chief of Engineers, in the form of a "multiple letter" to all districts and divisions; 26 engineer cir-

In September 1970, the Chief's Office issued another circular concerning the preparation of detailed statements that provided additional guidance and clarification based upon the CEQ Interim Guidelines and upon its own review of seventeen statements prepared by the districts prior to that time.[41] This circular had two thrusts: it specified in greater detail the proper tone and content of the detailed statements, and it directed more fully the steps that were to be taken to integrate the preparation of detailed statements with the Corps' normal planning process. It gave examples of problems that had been identified in environmental statements so far and stated the lessons that were to be drawn from these problems.[42] It also included an illustrative "checklist" of possible environmental impacts that were to be considered,[f] and it directed that alternatives favoring environmental quality enhancement be developed and discussed, including the alternative of no action, and that environmental impacts be discussed in an objective manner.[43] To integrate this activity into the planning process, it required that possible impacts be identified at the first "checkpoint conference," be discussed beginning with the second of the three public meetings during the survey, and be specifically and thoroughly aired at the third public meeting.[44] It required the District Engineer to circulate a "preliminary draft" statement for initial field review by other agencies and the public;[g] and it required consideration of "feasible" alternatives favoring environmental quality even for projects that had already been recommended, authorized, or partially constructed.[45]

---

culars (EC), engineer regulations (ER), and other existing policy instructions were revised to bring them into compliance with NEPA: and 45 more standard operating policies were identified as subjects of immediate or planned revision for the same reason. By August 10, 3 final and 14 draft environmental statements had been submitted to the Council on Environmental Quality (though only one of the three final statements was on a proposed project); and on August 25, the Corps submitted its report—required by Section 103 of NEPA—on actions taken to bring its policies and regulations into compliance with NEPA. A complete list of these actions is printed in U.S. Congress, House Committee on Merchant Marine and Fisheries, *Administration of the National Environmental Policy Act*, Hearings, Serial 91-41, Washington, D.C., 1971, Part 2, pp. 804-14.

fAmong other "working papers," a check list of pertinent environmental elements of the project and their importance was to be kept by the Corps' planners, and a list of categories and sample elements was included—including, for instance, geological, hydrological, botanical, zoological, historical/cultural, and miscellaneous (national parks, scientific areas, wildlife refuges, contemporary human features) elements. The "working papers" designation is explicit and legally significant, however: for unlike the detailed statement itself, "working papers" are exempt from public disclosure under the provisions of the Freedom of Information Act (5 U.S.C. 552 *et seq.*).

gThe reporting officer (District Engineer) was directed to prepare a "preliminary draft statement" for initial review by other agencies and the public; the Division Engineer was then to prepare a "draft statement" to submit with his recommendations on the survey report; and the Chief of Engineers would then circulate the draft statement for formal review at the department level.

Note that all project review up to and including review by the Board of Engineers for Rivers and Harbors was thus based upon the draft or even the unofficial "preliminary draft" environmental statement, which lacked the official comments of the reviewing agencies. This fact was noted critically by the General Accounting Office in its review of agency response to NEPA. General Accounting Office, *Improvements Needed in Federal Efforts to Implement the National Environmental Policy Act of 1969*, Washington, D.C., 1972, pp. 16-17.

Further policy guidance was provided by four additional instructions during the fall of 1970. The first of these established procedures for preparation of detailed statements concerning operation and maintenance actions, and the second created an "Environmental Advisory Board" in the Office of the Chief of Engineers.[46] The third, issued in November, reiterated and emphasized the message of the September circular:

Purpose. This circular reiterates and emphasizes the need to resolve policy problems and assure the adequacy of environmental considerations in the execution of Civil Works planning studies.... Adequate consideration must be given to the potential impact of plan proposals on the environment. Such consideration must be integrated into the planning process from the beginning. Full and objective appraisal must be made of environmental effects, both good and bad, and of reasonable alternatives. This matter must be a major discussion topic at public meetings and in conferences where decisions are made to proceed with successive phases of study.... Following each checkpoint conference, Division Engineers will advise the Chief of Engineers in writing on the status of policy and environmental aspects for each study involved.[47]

Finally, the fourth instruction provided "environmental guidelines" for the consideration of environmental factors in the planning, design, construction, and operation of civil works projects.[48] This document lacked the specificity of the September circular and contained many of the generalizations and ambiguities that were present in NEPA itself (for instance, "select and recommend the optimum solutions considering all pertinent factors"). However, it also was identified as a set of guidelines for the *normal conduct of civil works activities*, rather than merely for the preparation and coordination of the new required statements; and it thus served to reiterate the policy that environmental considerations were henceforth to be considered an issue in project planning rather than merely a new form of paperwork.

In May 1971, the Corps issued two new instructions on NEPA-related matters to all its districts and divisions, and these two instructions completed the basic substance of its policy guidance on this subject until early 1972.

The first of these instructions revised the September 1970 circular on the preparation and coordination of environmental statements, and redesignated it an "engineer regulation."[49] Among other things it incorporated the revisions that had been made in the guidelines of the Council on Environmental Quality. It directed a three-year review of all projects with impacts that "might be considered significant for any reason," with priority going to those projects having the greatest impact and those in which scheduled actions would preclude the adoption of alternative plans,[50] and it directed that "unresolved conflicts must be clearly set forth with a full and complete discussion of both sides of the issue."[51] It also put increased emphasis on the incorporation of public participation at all stages of the planning process,[52] and it expanded the list of "environmental elements" that were to be considered, as stated in the appendix to the September circular, to include "economic conditions, social relationships, and human well-being."[53]

This regulation did not, however, include other substantive changes that might have been beneficial. It provided no further clarification, for instance, of the extent to which the law was to be applied to existing projects, and it provided no criteria for weighing impacts on the physical environment against impacts on the newly added "economic conditions, social relationships, and human well-being." It also gave no indication as to whether any change should be made in project proposals themselves as a result either of the information developed in the statement or of the comments of other agencies on it. The latter point is a particularly important one, for the Corps is constantly considering projects that were originally approved for planning or even authorized for construction years before but were not funded until the present.

The second May instruction did not refer directly to NEPA, but it appeared to have sprung from it. This circular, entitled "Public Participation in Water Resources Planning," emphasized the importance of earlier and more broadly based participation in the Corps' planning and directed that each survey include an explicit "public participation plan."[54] These plans, it directed, were to be an integral part of each Plan of Survey; they were to be developed for all ongoing preauthorization survey studies; and they should be considered for postauthorization planning studies whenever there were substantial changes made, new interests affected, or changes in conditions that might warrant it.[55] In addition to the three public meetings previously required, the circular stressed the importance of conscious *two-way* communication at every stage of the survey process, from the preliminary evaluation until the survey report was prepared, and on through the review process.[56]

With the issuance of the May 1971 regulation and circular, the official policy response of the Corps to NEPA appeared to have stabilized for a time, thereby leaving further implementation to the project-by-project process of planning, review and—in some cases—legal action. Later revisions of these instructions will be mentioned below, but these directives more or less complete the substance of the Corps' initial policy response to NEPA during 1970 and 1971.

These policy statements and guidelines exhibit important strengths and were identified both then and since as examples of outstanding policy responses among the federal agencies.[57] First, they began with an *immediate* response without waiting even for the Executive order or the Interim Guidelines of the CEQ.[58] They applied NEPA not only to new actions but to projects already underway if significant actions remained to be taken, and they gave examples of the sorts of actions included.[h] They exhibited a rapid evolution by providing

---

[h]That is, they identified the categories of action and the stages of completion at which the *procedure* of preparing an environmental statement was to apply. They did *not* specify how much, if any, *re-evaluation* of ongoing projects was to be done as a basis for preparation of the statement, nor did they indicate whether application of this procedure should ever bring about review or change in the plan or design of the project itself.

increasingly detailed guidance and feedback to their field personnel concerning both the emerging interpretation of the law and the inadequacies and problems of impact statements that were first submitted from the field.

Second, the Corps' policy statements interpreted NEPA as a *substantive mandate*, not merely a procedural law, which directed it to recognize environmental quality as a new and legitimate purpose of its planning and actions. The balance that was to be struck between this and other purposes was not clearly specified, but the acceptance of a new purpose was clearly and repeatedly stated.

Third, the Corps took policy positions *stronger* than those of the Council on Environmental Quality on at least two major points: integration of the detailed statement into normal planning processes and provision of environmental impact information to the public. Integration of the detailed statements into planning was directed by the Executive Order and adopted by the Corps in April 1970, though it was not stressed in the Council's guidelines until their 1971 revision. Early public discussion was likewise a policy of the Corps right from the start, while the Council explicitly refused to require it until 1971 after direct congressional threats. In the words of the Corps' Director of Civil Works, *"We want [potential controversies] out just as soon as we can get them out"*[59] [emphasis added]. It appears clear, in short, that at least the Corps' official stance was one of commitment to the purposes of NEPA and to immediate implementation of its requirements.

At the same time, however, these directives did not establish *how much* change in previous priorities was to take place in order to accommodate environmental values, nor did they establish operational definitions of many of the terms left ambiguous by the Act, by the Executive Order, and by the Council's guidelines. They thus left considerable responsibility and discretion to the divisions and districts to interpret what specifically was required of them. Like the concurrent policy documents of both the Congress and the Executive Office, and perhaps for the same reasons, they served primarily to put procedural mechanisms into motion and to leave substantive choices for case-by-case resolution.

The lack of clear criteria for change in decisions suggests two important cautions against reading too much significance into policy directives issued by the Corps' headquarters. First, the Corps functions organizationally as a decentralized federation, in which lateral relationships at the field level between district officials and regional political forces may be at least as significant as policy statements issued in Washington. Second, even at the Washington level NEPA policy statements and guidelines were prepared by a relatively small group of advocates in the Office of the Chief of Engineers, the Office of the Secretary of the Army, and the Institute for Water Resources. The fact that this group succeeded in having its position issued as headquarters policy, therefore, has only potential significance as a force shaping the agency's substantive output at the operational level.

Table 4–1

Environmental Statements Submitted by Corps, as of December 31, 1971

	Jan	Feb	Mar	Apr	May	Jun	Jul	Aug	Sep	Oct	Nov	Dec
						Month						
1970				1	1		1	1	1	3	90	18
1971	13	25	30	42	32	44	30	21	34	12	12	21

Total Received (as of December 31, 1971):   435

    Final   265
    Draft, no final   170

Sources: Council on Environmental Quality, "Environmental Impact Statements Received by the Council on Environmental Quality to February 1, 1971," in U.S. Congress, House Committee on Merchant Marine and Fisheries, *Administration of the National Environmental Policy Act*, Hearings, December 1970, Serial 91–41, Washington, D.C., Part 2, pp. 20, 28–30. *Final Statements only* (draft statements were not officially listed by the Council as publicly available prior to 1971). Also, Council on Environmental Quality, *102 Monitor* I (February 1971–January 1972). Includes final statements, plus draft statements for which no final statements had yet been received by the Council.

Detailed Statements

By the end of 1971, the Corps had submitted 435 "detailed statements" to the Council on Environmental Quality, a number which far exceeded the total submitted by any other agency except the Department of Transportation.[60] Of these, three final and fourteen draft statements, which had been prepared by the districts by the end of August 1970, formed the basis for the Corps' September 1970 guideline revisions.[61] Eighty-five final statements, covering the projects included in the omnibus authorization bill,[62] were released as a group in November 1970, and the remainder were released at a rate of approximately 25 per month over the remaining thirteen months.[63] Table 4-1 shows the total number of statements received from the Corps by the Council during this period, and their distribution by months.

A principal reason for the large number of these statements was the Corps' policy that the law was to be applied immediately to all of its actions in progress. The Corps had 234 projects under construction in Fiscal Year 1972, and 404 more were budgeted either for survey or for engineering and design.[64] It also had approximately 700 more projects authorized but not yet funded, and 1,300 non-project actions (such as permits) that might require the preparation of detailed statements.[65] The Corps' commitment to apply the law to this backlog as well as to its "new" actions, therefore, necessarily resulted in a substantial workload, and by the end of 1973, it was still submitting statements at a rate of approximately twenty per month.[66] By contrast, other agencies whose activities also involved substantial volumes of environmentally impacting actions prepared far less statements during this period: by the end of 1971 the Department of Commerce had submitted only 8 statements, the Environmental Protection Agency 16, the Department of Housing and Urban Development 26, the rest of the Department of Defense (excluding the Corps) 32, and the entire Department of Health, Education and Welfare only 1.[i] By this standard, at least, the Corps took NEPA far more seriously than did most other agencies (see Figure 4-1).

The detailed statements submitted by the Corps during this period exhibited some gradual improvement, but continuing deficiencies were evident in several important respects. Statements submitted during 1970 were almost without exception paperwork documentation exercises prepared under a "crash program" to meet the deadline for November hearings on the omnibus authorization bill. Their tone was superficial; they were not based upon any new studies or reassessments; and a substantial number of them probably were simply written up by the Washington staff rather than by the districts.[67] Four general criticisms may be made of virtually all of these statements: they provided no detail concerning the magnitude or significance of adverse effects, they ignored areas of uncertainty as well as secondary impacts (chains of consequences) of the actions, they contained little or no detail in the discussion of alternatives, and despite the requirements of both Corps and CEQ guidelines, they frequently presented only the judgments of the District Engineer, unsupported by documentation or by sufficient evidence to permit independent review of their justification.[j]

---

[i]At the end of 1973, the same relative standings were still evident: the Department of Commerce had submitted 35 statements, the EPA 56, HUD 74, non-Corps Department of Defense 75, and HEW 15, compared to the Corps' 889 and the Department of Transportation's 2460. See *102 Monitor* III (January 1974), p. 98. Some of the environmentally significant activities of these agencies include economic development grants of the Department of Commerce, waste treatment plant grants by EPA and HUD, HUD's housing and "new communities" programs, numerous facilities and munitions disposal actions as well as land use changes and military exercises by the Department of Defense, and a wide range of actions by HEW (grants for construction of regional hospitals and schools and other facilities, environmental health research activities, and Food and Drug regulatory actions).

Obviously, the Corps simply plans more actions that may "significantly affect the quality of the human environment" than many agencies, such as the Tennessee Valley Authority or the Treasury Department, whose programs either are small or have only indirect impacts upon the environment. This argument, however, does not explain the great gap between the number of statements submitted by the Corps and DOT and the number submitted by all other agencies.

[j]Three assertions, for instance, appeared with such regularity, and without supporting detail from the specific project involved, as to appear to have been written by formula: first, that since the proposed plan did not make any significant change in the existing environment, it was the preferred plan from an environmental point of view (an assertion that does not necessarily follow from its premise in the abstract, let alone in the specific projects involved); second, that alternatives, and particularly the alternative of no action, did not offer any significant environmental advantages over the proposed plan and would involve the loss of the alleged environmental advantages of the proposed plan; and third, that not constructing the project would be at best only a temporary solution (based upon unsupported assumptions that projected "needs" were immutable requirements to be met, and that if the Corps project were not built, unplanned development would result in the same adverse en-

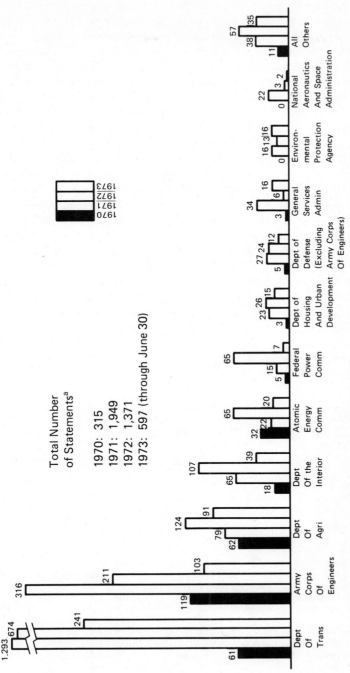

[a]Includes, through 1973, all final statements and draft statements on actions for which a final has not yet been filed.

Source: U.S. Council on Environmental Quality, *Environmental Quality–1973*, Fourth Annual Report (Washington, D.C.: U.S. Government Printing Office, 1973), p. 244.

Figure 4-1. Environmental Impact Statements Filed with the Council on Environmental Quality by Agency, for 1970, 1971, 1972, and 1973

Statements submitted after February 1971 contained more detailed descriptions, as well as maps, of the proposed projects. The sections on "coordination with other agencies" also were more informative and contained summaries of comments submitted and their disposition rather than merely lists of the agencies contacted.[k] Most of these statements still did not devote more than a single summary paragraph to the possible adverse effects of the action, however, or to the description and evaluation of alternatives. The alternative of no action was usually mentioned, but others were discussed only briefly if at all, and virtually never was any careful or quantitative comparison of alternative actions included. Even in cases of projects that involved obviously major modifications of the physical environment, such as extensive stream channel excavation and new impoundments, the reader usually was provided only the general judgments of the District Engineer, rather than information upon which he could base his own understanding and opinions. Table 4-2 lists eighteen projects that would clearly involve major modifications of these types and includes the number of pages in the "detailed statement" submitted for each during 1971. Despite the magnitude of these actions, their "detailed statements" averaged nine pages of narrative each— hardly a "detailed" statement of impacts and alternatives.[l]

A study was commissioned by the Corps in 1971 to evaluate the quality of the more than 200 final detailed statements prepared through August 1971; and this study identified a wide range of deficiencies in the majority of them.[68] Among the most significant of these were frequent failures to include:

Water-quality changes due to stream impoundment;
Effects of spoil disposal from dredging projects;

---

vironmental effects in any case). Any of these three assertions may have been justified in the cases in which they were made. The point here is that in the majority of cases, they were not supported by sufficient evidence to permit independent review of their justification, as required by Corps policy and by the guidelines of the Council on Environmental Quality.

[k]One apparent reason for these changes was the publication of proposed revisions in the Interim Guidelines by the Council on Environmental Quality, which occurred in January 1971. The inclusion of specific responses to comments submitted on the draft, however, was almost unique to the Corps and rarely if ever present in the detailed statements prepared by other agencies during this period.

[l]These eighteen projects are not a complete list of the Corps' major or significantly impacting actions, nor are they a random selection. They include only projects whose significance could be inferred from their stated magnitude and exclude a few projects for which more detailed "revised" statements were later submitted as a result of public controversy or litigation (See Table 4-3). They do, however, provide a legitimate basis for questioning the level of detail in "detailed statements" concerning large-scale actions during this period.
Final statements submitted during 1971 were somewhat longer, but not much so: of 30 final statements submitted on major impoundments and channelizations (excluding four statements revised after public controversy or litigation), the average number of pages including the comments of other agencies was thirty-five. Since comments required at least five pages on virtually all projects and far more on some, we may estimate that the average length of most final environmental statements on major Corp projects during this period was between 20 and 30 pages, and probably closer to 20. See *102 Monitor* I (1971).

Table 4-2

Draft Statements on Selected Major Corps Projects (Pages), June–October 1971

Statement Date	Name of Project	Size	Pages in Statement
June 16	West Tennessee Tributaries	31 miles channelized	9
July 1	Applegate Lake, Oregon	988 acres inundated	20
July 1	Clayton Lake, Oklahoma	44 miles long[a]	13
July 6	Mill Creek Lake, Ohio	1,064 acres inundated	10
July 6	Longview, Little Blue R. Lake Missouri	930 acres inundated	7
July 6	Yatesville Lake, Kentucky	20,800 acres inundated	13
July 8	Big Creek, Arkansas	68 miles channelized	9
July 23	Spewrell Bluff Lake, Georgia	13,300 acres inundated	19
July 23	Peacock Creek, Georgia	24 miles channelized	9
July 29	Long Branch Lake, Little Chariton River, Mo.	2,430 acres inundated	7
July 29	Fort Scott Lake, Kansas	5,000 acres inundated	8
Aug 26	Papillon Creek, Nebraska	system of 21 dams[b]	10
Sept 3	Laneport, North and South Fork Lakes, Texas	8,700 acres inundated	9
Sept 9	Los Esterios Lake, N.M.	7,360 acres inundated	11
Sept 13	Blue Springs Lake, Missouri	560 acres inundated	7
Sept 22	Taylorsville Lake, Kentucky	7,850 acres inundated	4
Oct 7	Licking River Lake, Kentucky	12,300 acres inundated	4
	Mean number of pages:	9.6	
	Median number of pages:	9.0	

[a]Number of acres inundated was not specified.

[b]Number of acres inundated was not specified.

Source: Council on Environmental Quality, *102 Monitor* I (July–November 1971), passim.

Specific changes in ecological systems;

Quantified estimates of environmental change (other than acreages to be inundated;

Qualification of speculative or controversial impacts;

Documentation or resolution of controversies;

Identification of uncertainties;

Identification of recipients of impacts;

Distinctions between statements of fact and value judgments;

Discussion of environmental impacts of alternatives;[69]

Responses to comments of other agencies concerning possible nonstructural alternatives.[70]

The authors of this study noted that there were legitimate reasons for many of these deficiencies, including severe constraints on time, personnel, and project budgets, as well as the newness and ambiguity of the legal requirements themselves. They concluded, however, that for whatever combination of reasons the 234 statements that they examined were not especially useful:

On the basis of casual observation, we found the later statements to be longer, slightly more complete, and somewhat more carefully written . . . . However, with relatively few exceptions, the only statements that appeared to be *substantially* more thorough and sophisticated, were those associated with projects involved with litigation alleging violations of the NEPA.

To summarize, the general impression we received upon reviewing 234 environmental statements, is that these statements, as presently prepared, are of extremely limited usefulness.[71]

These criticisms are not intended to imply that the Corps' "detailed statements" were unusually deficient compared to those of other agencies. On the contrary, casual comparison suggests that most were no worse and some were far better than those submitted by other agencies during this period. A learning process was required, and several distinct improvements *were* evident during this period, particularly in the sections of the statements dealing with project descriptions and coordination with other agencies.

Four important deficiencies, however, continued. First, many statements *failed to mention potentially important impacts*. However meager the information may have been concerning the precise effects of an impoundment upon water quality, for instance, change in it would clearly take place, and the likelihood of uncertain impacts upon this resource and others should therefore have been noted despite the absence of sophisticated analyses.

Second, most statements *failed to identify gaps and uncertainties* in their environmental analyses. Such gaps could have been identified as legitimate deficiencies in projects planned prior to NEPA's enactment and targeted for improvement in later projects, but frequently the statements resorted to false specificity and unsupported judgments instead.

Third, most statements *failed to describe alternatives* in sufficient detail to permit independent review of them. The availability of alternatives undoubtedly varied with the degrees of the projects' completion, but many of the statements made little effort to describe even alternatives that had been considered and rejected by the Corps, let alone environmentally oriented alternatives to actions not yet taken.

Finally, many of the statements *indiscriminately mingled factual statements and value judgments*, suggesting a desire simply to justify preconceived projects through the detailed statement rather than to detail their impacts and alternatives objectively. During this initial period, the Corps could legitimately have justified projects whose impacts were admittedly adverse or uncertain, on the grounds that they were planned prior to enactment of an environmental mandate. Instead, however, it frequently tried to convey the impression that adverse or uncertain effects simply did not exist—a position which opened it to considerable criticism and litigation.[m]

These deficiencies in the detailed statements are interesting in their own right, and numerous attempts have been made elsewhere to evaluate and improve them.[72] The key issue here, however, is not the content of the statements *per se* but the development and use of that content by the Corps. In this regard, it is particularly significant that despite their deficiencies, these statements were approved and released by the Office of the Chief of Engineers rather than returned to the districts for improvement. The statements were deficient not only by academic criteria, but even by comparison with the Corps' own official guidelines. The September 1970 circular included explicit discussion of deficiencies in earlier statements, and the four problems listed in the preceeding paragraphs were all issues that were treated in the Corps' circulars and regulations; yet detailed statements exhibiting these problems were routinely approved and released by the agency in spite of them.

In short, there was some disparity between the Corps' official policy and its practice concerning the implementation of NEPA, even at the level of the Chief's Office. Its policy statements directed immediate implementation of both the letter and the spirit of NEPA, both its procedures and its substantive purposes; but its practice, at least initially, permitted preparation of the new "detailed statement" as simply a mechanical documentation process with only indirect quality control. This practice suggests that the Corps had adopted an incremental approach to the implementation of NEPA that permitted gradual learning and improvement rather than demanding any immediate change in priorities to reflect NEPA's substantive purposes. It undoubtedly signalled to the districts that implementation of NEPA should not necessitate reassessment or disruption in the schedules for completion of previously authorized projects.[n]

Effort

In contrast to the deficiencies of most of the Corps' "detailed statements" during this period, Table 4-3 lists a few projects whose statements, whatever their deficiencies, were at least far more detailed than those previously discussed. These

---

[m]Other deficiencies included relatively superficial treatment of elements of the human environment other than physical and biological entities (showing a tendency to identify the "environment" narrowly with fish and wildlife conservationists and antipollution interests, rather than with the broader mandate of NEPA's policy statement) and other problems that have been identified in later guidelines and judicial decisions. For the best available summary of early judicial decisions under NEPA, see Frederick R. Anderson, *NEPA in the Courts* (Baltimore: Johns Hopkins, 1973).

[n]Note that the House Committee on Public Works, which had demanded that the Corps prepare detailed statements for the 85 projects included in the 1970 omnibus authorization bill, exhibited the same policy. It accepted these statements as adequate, but only—significantly—"in view of the short period of time that has elapsed since the promulgation of the guidelines [of the Council on Environmental Quality]." See U.S. Congress, *Omnibus River and Harbor and Flood Control Act of 1970*, House Report 91-1665, December 3, 1970, Washington, D.C., 1970, p. 3.

Table 4–3
Unusually Detailed Statements Submitted by Corps, as of
December 31, 1971

Project	Pages
Cache River Basin, Fish & Wildlife Mitigation Plan, Revised Statement	152
Central & South Florida Flood Control	127
Gillham Lake (Ark.) Revised Statement	400+
LaFarge Lake (Wis.)	200
Lower Granite Lock & Dam, Snake River, (Wash. and Idaho)	163
New Hope Lake (N.C.) Revised Statement	600+
Oswego Steam Unit 5, Niagara Mohawk Power Co.	192
Perry Co. Drainage & Levee Districts 1, 2, & 3 (Missouri and Illinois)	201
Tocks Island Lake (Pa., N.J., and N.Y.)	214

Source: Council on Environmental Quality, *102 Monitor* I (1971).

statements do not display a "trend" of increasing detail in the Corps' statements, for they were distributed relatively evenly over the latter half of 1971; moreover, there was a sharp discontinuity between the length of these statements (over 100 pages each) and the length of all other Corps statements during the same period, none of which were over 60 to 70 pages.[73] They also originated in at least eight different districts, not in one or two that were more "progressive" than others. Why the difference?

The only apparent feature that these projects had in common was that nearly all of them were *controversial*. Not all controversial Corps projects had detailed statements this long (at least not by the end of 1971); but with only one or two possible exceptions, all statements that were over 100 pages long concerned projects that were at least controversial if not under litigation.[o] This supports the conclusion of Ortolano and Hill, quoted above, that "the only statements that appeared to be *substantially* more thorough and sophisticated, were those associated with projects involved with litigation alleging violations of NEPA.[74]

Additional evidence for this conclusion is provided by the districts' own estimates, in late 1971, of the amounts of effort they devoted to the preparation of detailed statements for controversial and noncontroversial projects.[75] Table 4-4 shows that more than double the effort was devoted to the preparation of detailed statements on controversial projects over the amount that was devoted to the same task for noncontroversial actions, and that significantly greater effort than the average was devoted to statements for both controversial *and*

[o]The Oswego Steam Unit statement was probably prepared with data and assistance from the applicant power company; the status or controversiality of the Perry County drainage project is not known to the author. All others were definitely controversial.

Table 4–4

Estimated Effort Required for Preparation of Corps Environmental Statements, per Project, as of October 1971

	Man-hours, All Districts Responding[a]	Man-hours, Districts in Which Litigation Occurred[b]	Percent Increase, Litigated Districts
Noncontroversial Projects			
Mean	443	495	11%
Median	275	300	9%
Controversial Projects			
Mean	1798	2382	32%
Median	620	880	42%
Percent Increase, Controversial Projects			
Mean	306%	381%	
Median	125%	193%	

[a]N = 22, or 60% of all Corps districts (including its two operating divisions).

[b]N = 9, or 90% of all responding districts that reported that litigation had occurred.

Source: Survey of U.S. Army Corps of Engineers, District and Division Engineers, October 1971.

noncontroversial projects by those districts that had been defendants in lawsuits under NEPA.[76]

It is possible, of course, that districts that had been sued would have had a greater propensity to overestimate their efforts; but presumably they would also have had a greater propensity to exaggerate the difference in effort required between controversial and noncontroversial projects, an hypothesis which the data do not confirm. It seems, therefore, that litigation induced those districts to take more pains in the preparation of detailed statements for noncontroversial as well as controversial projects and that this factor, more than the policy statements or practices of the Chief's Office, was the principal motive force for improvement in the content of the Corps' detailed statements.

Project Modifications

To the extent that it can be measured, the ultimate indicator of an agency's responsiveness to NEPA is whether or not its *actions* changed as a result of it. Policies and procedures, laws and documents, organizational structures, and personnel changes are not ends in themselves, but instruments, and changes in these instruments are of little use if they do not lead to changes in those actions of the agency that directly affect the quality of the human environment.

Table 4–5

Number of Corps Projects Reported Modified in Response to NEPA, as of October 1971

	% Cancelled (n = 7)	% Postponed (n = 48)	% Significantly Changed (n = 23)
Stage of Completion			
Not yet designed	–	40%	57%
Designed, under construction, or in operation	100%	54%	39%
Not reported	–	6%	4%
Total	100%	100%	100%

Note: Number of districts reporting = 32, or 87% of the total, plus the Office of the Chief of Engineers.
Source: October 1971 Survey.

Table 4–5 shows the number of Corps projects that were reported to have been cancelled, postponed, or "significantly changed" as a result of the mandate of the National Environmental Policy Act, as of October 1971.[P] Seven projects were reported cancelled, which speaks for itself as an indicator of the paucity of projects that NEPA stopped outright, but also indicates that a precedent had been set whereby "reasonable consideration" of new environmental factors *could* lead to termination of previously planned actions.[q] Forty-eight projects were reported postponed, of which more than half had already advanced to the

---

[P]All District Engineers, plus officials of the Board of Engineers for Rivers and Harbors and the Office of the Chief of Engineers, were asked to identify all projects that had been cancelled, postponed, or "significantly revised" as a result of the requirements of NEPA. They were also asked to indicate the stage of completion at which the change occurred (investigated; recommended; authorized; budgeted; designed; under construction; in operation), and to identify which of a number of possible proximate causes were responsible for the decision to change the project: internal re-evaluation, adverse comments from other federal agencies, adverse comments from state and local governments, public controversy, impoundment of funds, court decisions, and "other." The categories appear to have been well chosen in the sense that only two project modifications were attributed to "other" causes (the Cross-Florida Barge Canal cancellation, which was attributed to a Presidential order, and one other).

[q]But note that the Corps' environmental chief stated in January 1972 that only three projects had been terminated as a result of NEPA. These projects were the Buffalo Bayou (Texas), Carrabelle to St. Mark's River (Florida), and Jack and Simmerly Sloughs (California). Only one of these was reported in the survey responses, and it was reported as "significantly changed" rather than as cancelled. See statement of Donald Lawyer, in Robert B. Ditton and Thomas I. Goodale, *Environmental Impact Analysis* (Madison, Wisc.: Wisconsin Sea Grant Program, 1972), pp. 56–57.

design stage or beyond, and 23 projects were reported "significantly changed" as a result of NEPA, in the views of the District Engineers.[r]

These 78 projects probably were not a significant proportion of the total number of Corps actions taken during this period; the omnibus bill of 1970, for instance, authorized a greater number of projects than this just for one two-year period, and 78 projects represented less than 6 percent of the estimated 1,338 Corps projects already authorized or budgeted that would require preparation of detailed statements under NEPA.[77]

On the other hand, they did represent nearly 20 percent of the 435 projects for which detailed statements were prepared during this period, and there were some indications that even greater numbers might be affected as the "learning process" created by NEPA progressed.[s] Significantly, too, more than half of the projects reported to have been "significantly changed" in response to NEPA were projects that had not yet been designed, while more than half of those postponed and all of those cancelled had already entered the design stage. These data as well as common sense suggest a greater willingness to make significant modifications in projects that had not yet been planned and designed in detail.

Irrespective of the number of projects reported to have been affected by NEPA, the *reasons* given for these modifications provide striking insights into the "action-forcing mechanisms" by which NEPA had its effect on the Corps. Table 4-6 lists the reported causes of the project modifications that were displayed in Table 4-5, and Table 4-7 shows the percentage of the 78 projects for which each individual causative factor was mentioned. One clear conclusion emerges from these tables, especially from Table 4-6: *external pressures* on the Corps, from nonfederal agencies as well as public controversies and lawsuits, played an overwhelming role in decisions by the Corps to modify projects in any

---

[r]But note that the Corps' environmental chief stated in January 1972 that only seven projects had been modified in response to NEPA. These seven were the Big Walnut Reservoir (Indiana), Oakley Dam (Illinois), Morrison Creek (California), LaFarge Lake (Minnesota), Red River (Kentucky), Tennessee Colony Dam (Texas) and the Columbus Lock and Dam (Mississippi). Three of these were listed as "significantly changed" in the survey responses below; two were listed only as postponed; and two were not reported in the survey responses. See ibid.

[s]For instance, a later study conducted by the Corps itself, in June 1973, concluded that NEPA had had some substantive effect on at least 265 Corps projects, which represented fully 36 percent of the 736 projects for which detailed statements had been prepared as of that time. Of these, 24 had been cancelled, or negatively reported by the District Engineers; 44 had been postponed, or ordered deferred or restudied by the Board of Engineers for Rivers and Harbors; and 197 had been "modified." While these modifications may not have been "significant" changes (in one case, for instance, it included merely the addition of facilities for jetty fishing), the attribution of them to the requirements of NEPA displayed an attitude of responsiveness to this law on the part of some Corps officials. See U.S. Army Corps of Engineers, "Effect of NEPA on Corps Studies and Projects," Staff study, June 1, 1973.

Table 4-6
Causes of Corps Project Modifications Reported in Response to NEPA,
as of October 1971

	% Cancelled (n = 7)	% Postponed (n = 48)	% Significantly Changed (n = 23)
Cause of Modification			
Internal re-evaluation only	14%	10%	9%
Internal re-evaluation plus			
External pressures[a]	43%⎱ 86%	35%⎱ 73%	56%⎱ 73%
External pressures only	43%⎰	38%⎰	17%⎰
Comments of other federal agencies only	–	–	9%
Other cause (unspecified)	–	2%	–
Cause not reported	–	15%	9%
Total	100%	100%	100%

Note: Number of districts reporting = 32, or 87% of the total, plus OCE.
[a]"External pressures" refer to pressures from outside the federal administrative structure and include three subcategories in the survey: comments of state and local government agencies, public controversies, and judicial decisions.
Source: October 1971 Survey.

way in response to NEPA. Table 4-6 shows the combined effect of these pressures, both as a group and in combination with internal re-evaluation of projects by the Corps; Table 4-7 shows the frequency with which each individual factor was mentioned.

Of the projects that were reported cancelled, internal re-evaluation by the agency was the reason most frequently cited, followed by public controversy; but in only one instance was internal re-evaluation the cause of cancellation in the absence of one of the three forms of external pressure—adverse state and local comments, public controversy, or a judicial decision. Adverse comments from other federal agencies were not identified as a reason for any of these cancellations.

A similar pattern is evident among projects reported postponed in response to NEPA: of these postponements, fully half involved public controversy, and 73 percent resulted in part from at least one of the external causes. Internal re-evaluation was the reason given second most frequently, but as in the case of cancellations, it appeared as the sole cause of only 10 percent of the modifications; and the adverse comments of other federal agencies again played only a minor role.

Finally, external pressures figured in 73 percent of all "significant changes" attributed to NEPA, while internal re-evaluation alone was the cause of only 9 percent of such changes. A somewhat different pattern of individual factors ap-

Table 4-7

Frequency of Mention, Causes of Reported Modifications of Corps Projects in Response to NEPA, as of October 1971

Cause of Modification	% Cancelled (n = 7)	% Postponed (n = 48)	% Significantly Changed (n = 23)
Internal re-evaluation	57%	44%	65%
Federal agency comments	–	13%	30%
State and local agency comments	29%	33%	61%
Public controversies	43%	50%	43%
Judicial decisions	29%	25%	4%
Other cause (unspecified)	14%	2%	–

Note: Number of districts reporting = 32, or 87% of the total, plus OCE. Since several causes were sometimes mentioned, columns do not sum to 100%.

Source: October 1971 Survey.

pears here—primarily a stronger combination of internal re-evaluation with the comments of state and local agencies as well as other federal agencies—concerning projects that were less fully developed (compare Tables 4-5 and 4-7); judicial decisions also were virtually ineffective here, while they had figured in more than one-fourth of all cancellations and postponements. The strong role of factors external to the federal administrative structure, however, is still clear here.

The role of such "external pressures" during this period was not only a perception of the District Engineers, but a perception that had a strong basis in reality. The reality was that during the initial period of NEPA's implementation, the Corps *was* subjected to more intense external pressures to implement environmental policy than nearly any other federal agency.[t] In addition to increased levels of general pressure from individual citizens and environmental interest groups, at least six legal complaints alleged NEPA violations in Corps projects before the law was even eight months old.[78] Two judicial decisions were issued: one of these stopped a Corps project that was already under construction until NEPA requirements had been met, and the other upheld the Corps in its denial of a permit for environmental reasons.[79] Many more complaints were filed during 1971, and at least eight more judicial decisions involving the Corps were issued: one case was dismissed, a second supported the Corps in another permit denial

[t]A possible exception was the Federal Highway Administration. By late 1971 the Atomic Energy Commission could be added to this category, and the Environmental Protection Agency was the target of numerous lawsuits by 1972; but the Corps was clearly one of the two agencies that experienced the heaviest initial pressure in the courts.

for environmental reasons, and the other six all supported environmentalist plaintiffs in their challenges to proposed Corps actions.[80]

Many of these early decisions served only to define the law's applicability to actions initiated prior to its enactment, rather than adding much to the interpretation of its content, and many provided only temporary injunctive relief to litigants rather than changes or permanent abandonment of Corps projects.[u] As a group, however, they clearly demonstrated that the Corps had a new environmental mandate that must be applied to all its actions; and they proved that opponents of its projects now had dramatically increased chances of obtaining judicial review and of securing injunctions unless at least the procedural requirements of that mandate were taken seriously.

The Corps was also subjected to pressures from several sources other than the courts during this period, some of which were shared by other agencies but not to the same degree. The House Committee on Public Works, for instance, required that environmental statements be prepared for all 85 projects included in the 1970 omnibus authorization bill, and it delayed action on the bill until they were received.[81] While a subcommittee of this Committee also staged hearings in 1971 to mobilize pressure against the "red tape" of environmental statements, the Committee itself did continue to require the submission of environmental statements for all projects sent to it for its consideration.[82] Other congressional committees also put pressure on the Corps and other agencies: Congressman Dingell's NEPA oversight hearings in December 1970 have already been mentioned, and Congressman Henry Reuss' Subcommittee on Conservation and Natural Resources also held extensive hearings on the environmental impacts of stream channelization in 1971, the main targets of which were the Corps, the Soil Conservation Service, and the Tennessee Valley Authority.[83]

The President, too, chose the Corps' Cross-Florida Barge Canal project as an action to halt in order to dramatize his commitment to NEPA implementation,[84] and the evolving guidelines of the Council on Environmental Quality as well as the decisions of the courts sustained an ongoing climate of such pressure around the activities of all the agencies.[85] In the case of the Corps, however, it seems clear that the reinforcement of these general pressures by *specific* pressures on its districts from nonfederal sources, particularly through the courts, both were and were perceived as NEPA's principal "action-forcing mechanism."

In summary, then, the data presented here suggest five conclusions about

---

[u]The Gillham Dam and Tennessee-Tombigbee injunctions, for instance, were dissolved after the Corps prepared more detailed environmental statements; and a February 1974 decision in the combined Cross-Florida Barge Canal cases overturned the President's termination of that project by directing the Corps to proceed with preparation of an adequate environmental statement and thence to the likelihood of a resumption of work on the project. See *Canal Authority of Florida v. Callaway*, 6 ERC 1808 (M.D. Florida, 1974). By June 1973, however, a Corps staff report cited one project postponed, one modified, and seven stopped or abandoned as a result of judicial decisions, and sixteen still pending in the courts. See U.S. Army Corps of Engineers, "Effect of NEPA on Corps Studies and Projects."

the initial effects of NEPA on the Corps' procedures and program, and about some of the proximate causes of those effects. First, rarely during this period did any cancellations, postponements, or significant changes of existing projects result from internal re-evaluation by the Corps in the absence of some form of pressure from outside the federal government. Insofar as actual project modifications were concerned, the Corps clearly was responding to project-specific threats, political pressures, and controversies associated with NEPA, rather than more systematically to the law itself. This pattern has potentially crucial implications for prediction of the law's long-term effectiveness, and during the short-term period studied, it confirms the importance of NEPA's public disclosure provisions, which were added to the bill at the last minute before it was sent to conference.

Second, the comments of other federal agencies proved to be one of the least significant factors in decisions to cancel, postpone, or significantly change projects. This conclusion may tend to bear out Gilbert White's assertion that agencies establish patterns of accommodation that submerge their conflicts; it probably reflects also the absence of resources or incentives that would encourage most agencies to take their commenting role seriously, in the absence of direct conflict with their plans or jurisdictions.[86]

This finding must be interpreted with some care, for two reasons: coordination with other agencies might already have taken place with respect to existing projects, while similar commenting procedures in the cases of new projects might elicit more significant and effective comments. In addition, the adverse comments that *were* submitted by other federal agencies may have had *indirect* effects out of proportion to their direct impacts—for instance, judicial decisions and public controversies have sometimes relied upon adverse comments and other materials submitted by (or subpoenaed from) other federal agencies. If interagency coordination *was* an important factor in the Corps' NEPA—related decisions to alter projects, however, it was so only through the medium of public pressure and not in its own right: most effects were attributed to pressure from sources wholly external to the federal administrative structure, not to coordination or negotiation among the various federal agencies.

Third, despite the number of lawsuits brought against the Corps under NEPA few "significant changes" in projects were attributed to judicial decisions. The Corps evidently preferred to change the environmental statement to conform to the procedural letter of the law, rather than change the projects themselves either to conform more closely to the law's substantive spirit or to meet the objections of litigants.[v] Two reasons for this phenomenon may be surmised: first, actions reviewed by the courts are more difficult to change than others, since the courts traditionally decline to review agency actions until they are in

---

[v]This conclusion is borne out by the facts of several of the most controversial projects: for instance, Tocks Island Lake (Pennsylvania), New Hope Lake (North Carolina), Gillham Lake (Arkansas), and the Tennessee-Tombigbee Waterway.

Table 4–8
Relationship of Reported Corps Project Modification to Litigation, as of October 1971

	% Districts in Which Litigation Reported (n = 10)	% Districts in Which No Litigation Reported (n = 22)
Percentage of All Districts Reporting	27%	73%
% of Projects reported cancelled (n = 7)	100%	0
% of Projects reported postponed (n = 48)	58%	42%
% of Projects reported significantly changed (n = 23)	35%	57%[a]
% of *All* Projects reported affected by NEPA (cancelled, postponed, or significantly changed) (n = 78)	55%	42%[a]

[a]The districts having jurisdiction over two projects reported as significantly changed by the Office of the Chief of Engineers were not identified.
Source: October 1971 Survey.

some final form and administrative remedies have been exhausted;[87] and second, agency personnel and their lawyers undoubtedly tend to react with defensiveness and self-justification when their actions are challenged, even though they may at the same time modify other actions to avoid similar challenges.

If court decisions involving NEPA had little direct effect on projects, however, the evidence suggests that their indirect effects were more substantial. Table 4–8 shows the percentages of projects cancelled, postponed or significantly changed within the jurisdictions of the ten districts that were subjected to lawsuits during this period (whether the lawsuits were directed at the projects in question or not), as opposed to projects similarly affected in the jurisdictions of other districts. It is clear that disproportionally high numbers of all projects affected in *any* way by NEPA fell within the jurisdictions that were sued at least once, a finding that underscores the importance of litigation as an instrument of administrative change. Not only did litigation apparently lead to the investment of increased effort in the preparation of environmental statements, it also resulted in more cancellations, postponements, and significant changes in projects that were not sued, even though it resulted in few changes in the projects that were actually the subjects of suit. In short, while litigation had little substantive effect in the particular cases litigated during this period, it appears to have had a "multiplier effect" on changes in other agency actions.[w]

---

[w]The possible presence of other factors must be noted here, though these factors probably would not seriously affect the conclusions. Some districts, for instance, may be more tech-

Fourth, adverse comments by state and local agencies were significantly more important as causes of significant *change* in projects than of cancellation or postponement of them; they figured in 61 percent of the former though only 29 and 33 percent of the latter, respectively. The reason for this is probably that the Corps simply was more accustomed to coordinating its planning with such agencies than it was to interacting with the general public.[88] Changes would be more apt to result than postponement if a coordinated working relationship existed to resolve conflicts among such agencies.

The fifth and final conclusion to be drawn is a cautionary one; namely, that far more projects were merely *postponed* during this period than were cancelled or significantly changed. These projects might well become the subjects of significant change before they are constructed, though they had not yet been so changed at the time of the survey.[x] On the other hand, they might also be reintroduced at a later time without change, if pressure for change in them were not evident and effective or if only limited time were available for their re-evaluation. In short, the presence of this large number of projects that were merely postponed is a significant uncertainty in evaluating the Corps' response to NEPA.

Budget, Staff, and Structure

The analyses above were based primarily upon three bodies of information about the Corps: its official policies and procedures, the "detailed statements" that it prepared and submitted during 1970 and 1971, and the modifications in previously planned actions during that period that were attributed to NEPA by Corps officials. All of these data, however, provide relatively short-term indicators of administrative change. The first two sources are merely changes in documents, which may or may not indicate changes in the tangible impacts of Corps actions. The third source is limited predominantly to projects that were substantially developed prior to NEPA's enactment, since most such projects require ten to fifteen years of planning while the scope of this study covers a much shorter time period.

---

nically proficient than others, especially large districts whose budgets permit the hiring of a more diversified staff. Similarly, some districts may be headed by officials more sensitive to environmental issues than others; and some districts may simply have more controversial projects than others. Notwithstanding these qualifications, however, the magnitudes of the disproportions shown in the table are striking; and none of the other possible factors explain them convincingly. Size of district did not show any clear relationship to these figures, nor did the distribution of "controversial" projects. The attitudinal data gathered in the survey do not appear to be reliable evidence either for or against the possibility that attitudes were a significant factor, but no correlation was evident. Response to litigation remains the most convincing explanation of the disproportion.

[x]According to the survey responses, only three projects had been *both* postponed and significantly changed during this period.

In order to predict the long-term response of the Corps to NEPA, therefore, other indicators must be sought, and several such indicators are changes made by the agency in its budget requests, professional staff, and organizational structure. These are all tangible indicators, and as a group they tend to define, far more than any official document, the capability and commitment of the agency to the "integrated use of the natural and social sciences and the environmental design arts" called for by NEPA. These indicators, therefore, may provide some portent of the treatment of less-developed and "new" projects by the Corps in the future and also of the fate of the projects that were merely "postponed" during 1970 and 1971.

The Corps did not request increases in the funding of many projects that had already been authorized in order to meet the requirements of NEPA (or if it did, it did not attribute these requests to the requirements of NEPA). This fact appears consistent with the conclusion, suggested above, that the agency sought to push on with most previously initiated projects after completing token environmental statements. The Corps did, however, request budget increases for fiscal year 1972 in 140 of its 142 general investigations, and increases averaging 10 percent per survey were specifically attributed to new studies necessitated by NEPA.[89] Such studies would not ensure that the outcomes would reflect a different mix of objectives than earlier projects. However, they did justify an expectation that new projects would at least reflect more sophisticated information about probable environmental impacts than earlier ones.

With regard to professional manpower, several important changes were clearly evident in recruitment as well as in the allocation of effort by existing personnel, though these changes were generally limited to junior and staff employees rather than supervisory or "line" positions. As of August 1971, an average of five to six persons per district were devoting at least one-fourth of their time specifically to the preparation and coordination of NEPA's detailed statements; of those persons, three-fourths were either civil engineers, biologists, landscape architects, or recreation planners.[90] Of the twenty supervisory personnel included in this group, however, at least 65 percent were civil engineers. It is likely, therefore, that while more environmental information might be gathered as a result of these efforts, the weighting of that information in Corps decisions would continue for some time to reflect the traditional priorities and values of the civil engineering profession.[91]

The Corps did hire new personnel also, to assist in meeting its new environmental responsibilities under NEPA, and this fact—like the increased budget requests—provides modest grounds for the expectation of change in the evaluation of new projects. Responses of the District Engineers indicated that an average of four to five new positions per district had been requested, and three positions per district had been filled as of October 15, 1971. "Biologists" were the most frequently cited classification of these positions, with the other three professions mentioned in the preceding paragraph plus unclassified "environmental resources section" positions next most frequent.[92]

The fact that new personnel were hired to assist in responding to NEPA suggests the likelihood of some increased consideration of environmental values in the Corps' planning.[y] On the other hand, one member of the staff of the Office of the Chief Engineers estimated unofficially that perhaps twenty new personnel per district (rather than the four to five requested or the three hired) would be necessary to carry out the agency's environmental responsibilities effectively; and if this estimate is accurate, the agency's performance during 1970 and 1971 appears considerably less adequate to the task at hand.[z]

Finally, considerable variation was evident among the Corps' districts in the extent to which they recognized environmental analysis as an identifiable unit of their organizational structure. Table 4-9 shows the numbers of environmental resources branches and sections that had been established by the Corps' districts and operating divisions as of June 1971.[aa] Over half the districts had established environmental sections, and 11 percent had gone so far as to establish environmental branches; but fully 30 percent apparently had not yet created any identifiable organizational unit for environmental analysis.[93] No significant differences were evident between districts that had and had not been sued.

This information must be interpreted with some caution for several reasons. First, the absence of identifiable units in one-third of the districts may reflect simply a lag in short-term response rather than an unlikelihood of long-term change (though such a lag is significant in itself when compared against the speed of other districts' responses). Second, and more important, the creation of an identifiable unit *per se* does not insure that unit's effectiveness in achieving its stated purposes. Depending upon the power structure within the district organi-

---

[y]Although there was always a danger that in any personal cutback or "Reduction in Force," these "last-hired" persons would also be the first fired.

[z]The numbers of new positions that were filled was not entirely under the districts' control. Other federal agencies and private employers were competing for environmental scientists as well; and federal agencies including the Corps were handicapped by the Administration's concurrent efforts to reduce the average pay grade in the federal government (the campaign against "grade creep"), which limited their ability to recruit at the GS-12 level that most scientists could command.

On the other hand, none of the districts even requested anywhere near twenty new positions during this period, and substantial differences in initiative were evident among the districts in the extent to they sought to utilize other manpower pools such as the reserve officer corps (which included some individuals trained in the environmental sciences) and private contractors.

[aa]Each Corps district is normally subdivided into major "divisions" (for instance, the engineering division, the operations division, and in some districts the planning division); each division in turn is divided into "branches" (for instance, a district not having a separate planning division might have a planning branch within the engineering division); and each branch is composed of "sections."

Table 4-9
Environmental Units in Corps Districts, June 1971

	Number of Districts Having
Branch	4 (11%)
Section	22 (57%)
No identifiable unit	11 (30%)
Total	37 (100%)

Source: List of Participants, Corps of Engineers Civil Works Environmental Planning Conference, Washington, D.C., June 28–July 1, 1971.

zation, for instance, an environmental resource section might function either as a minor adjunct or "window dressing" to an engineering division, or as a relatively autonomous unit of a separate and more environmentally oriented planning division.[bb] It might provide the "critical mass" necessary to give environmental policy goals a real voice in district decisions, or it might merely *segregate* such goals in a relatively powerless unit divorced from the planning and decision process.[94] Third, and finally, implicit in the uncertainty regarding the unit's role in the district power structure is the importance of district officials' attitudes toward the environmental unit, particularly the attitudes of the division chiefs and the District Engineer. Where these individuals were not committed to implementation of environmental policy purposes, designation as a branch probably would not add much to the unit's effectiveness.

The formal status accorded to environmental information gathering is significant, however, both for the power that it might give to the chief of the unit to influence planning and decision making and especially for what that status may reveal symbolically about the degree of importance attached to environmental analysis by command officials in each district. As of June 1971, a substantial number of these officials had not yet attached any such symbolic importance to it. In those districts where such units had been established, however, they did in fact serve as symbols of the changing orientation of the Corps towards its mission.

Discussion

The foregoing analysis suggests four major conclusions about the response of the Corps of Engineers to NEPA during 1970 and 1971. First, the Corps' head-

---

[bb]In the Baltimore district, for instance, the environmental unit was officially a branch of the planning division, but its division chief and District Engineer allowed it substantial autonomy to work directly with any of the district's divisions whose activities might involve environmental considerations. This was not the case in many other districts.

quarters policy statements clearly interpreted NEPA's purposes and procedures as a new range of criteria by which its actions were to be evaluated, and they established both an inclusive definition and a detailed list of the "significant environmental impacts" that were to be considered more thoroughly. The Corps repeatedly stated a policy that change was called for; it issued instructions that identified both environmental elements that were to be considered in planning and deficiencies that were to be corrected; and it requested increases in its staff and budget in order to discharge the new responsibilities imposed upon it by NEPA. It also directed that environmental statements be prepared on *all* Corps projects, including not only projects not yet under construction but all projects on which any significant actions remained to be taken. In short, it specified in considerable detail the new mandate to consider environmental impacts, the "significant environmental impacts" that were to be considered in the formulation of projects, and the categories of actions that were likely to have such impacts and should therefore be accompanied by environmental statements.

Second, Corps policies encouraged public involvement not only in comment on the environmental statement itself, but from the earliest point in planning, in order to meet and resolve objections as soon as possible. The Corps stated its intention to plan "in a fishbowl," in order to "get objections out as soon as possible"; and it required at least three public meetings during planning of each project, including discussion of the environmental impacts of alternative actions and presentation of the draft environmental statement before a recommendation was forwarded to Washington. Later instructions, while not mandatory, urged public involvement at *every* stage of the planning process. In addition, the Corps' treatment of comments on its draft statements was somewhat more responsive than that accorded them by most other agencies: these comments were appended to the final statement, including the comments of nongovernmental groups and individuals, and in many cases they were also summarized with point-by-point response to their major themes. While these responses were not always as complete or as factually detailed as one might ask, the practice itself was a significant improvement over the practices of many other agencies.[cc]

Third, however, the official policies stopped short of specifying how much change was to be made in project *decisions* as a result of environmental considerations; and in practice, the Corps was less than wholehearted in the application of these new criteria to projects already in progress. Environmental statements were approved and released, despite the nonconformity of many of them with the guidelines both of the Council on Environmental Quality and

---

[cc]Most agencies during this period simply appended the comments to the final statement without detailed responses. A few did not even do this much: the policy of the Tennessee Valley Authority, for instance, was not to even attach the comments except in cases "where in TVA's judgment they raise significant environmental issues not raised in the official review process"—thus concealing the magnitude of any public objections to its projects. See *Federal Register* XXXVI (November 2, 1971), pp. 21010–14.

of the Corps itself. Less than 20 percent of all projects for which environmental statements were prepared were modified in any substantive respect, and of these, more than twice as many were merely postponed as were significantly changed (in addition, official estimates of these modifications ran considerably lower). Requests for new professional positions were considerably less than the Corps' estimated needs, and in a significant minority of the Corps' districts, environmental staff members appeared to have no recognizable status as a unit within the agency's structure. These indications suggest that at least in the short term, the Corps was willing to settle for the letter of the law in practice even while it preached its spirit in official statements.

Finally, the survey results indicated that factors external to the federal administrative structure were among the causes of three-quarters of all substantive changes in projects resulting from NEPA. Adverse state and local comments, public controversies and judicial decisions were thus collectively the most significant reason for all substantive effects attributed to NEPA on pending projects, while factors internal to the federal administrative structure—interagency coordination and re-evaluation of projects by the Corps in the absence of external forces—played minor roles by comparison. Judicial decisions did not appear to have brought about many significant changes in projects that were sued during this period, though they were a factor in one-fourth of all reported postponements (which might or might not later lead to revision); but they did appear both to have increased the propensity of the districts sued to alter other projects within their jurisdictions and to have increased the effort put into the preparation of environmental statements by those districts on both controversial and noncontroversial projects.

While these conclusions do not tell the full story of the Corps' response to NEPA, they do illuminate key elements of it. By doing so, they illustrate one model of initial agency response to NEPA—a response shaped to a considerable extent by the external forces acting on the agency to reinforce the law's message. Other agencies exhibited significantly different responses, and the reasons for these differences may lie not only in differences between the agencies themselves, but also in differences among the constellations of external pressures to which each was subjected.

1972-1974

During the two years following the initial period discussed above, there was continued evidence of pressures on the Corps, not only from sources external to the federal government but also from all three branches of that government. These pressures were not always consistent in their direction, but on balance they tended to encourage further implementation by the Corps of its environmental policy mandate. There is at least some evidence, though most of it is in the form of policy statements and experimental innovations rather than everyday action, that the Corps continued to evolve somewhat as a result.

External Forces

The courts, which were perhaps the most significant single source of pressure on the Corps during the initial period, seemed by 1973 a less potent force for further innovation and change. Initially, both the agencies and the Council on Environmental Quality focussed on implementation of the law's *procedures*, especially the "detailed statement" requirement. The courts were vigorously active in this process and exhibited their traditional talents in the interpretation of matters of law and procedure. Anderson, in his definitive review of the early judicial interpretation of NEPA, concludes that this strict enforcement of NEPA's procedures laid an important foundation for possible substantive changes in the future.[95] During 1972 and 1973 the courts continued to develop some further concepts and interpretations, such as the requirement of "programmatic" environmental statements for research programs;[96] but the number of such major new interpretations was considerably less than during the initial period, and in general the courts appeared to have settled into a pattern of procedural review that stopped short of enforcing the law's substantive purposes.[97] Significantly, many projects that had been enjoined pending preparation of "adequate" environmental statements were later released, as the courts accepted the revised versions as adequate.[98]

One potential exception to this pattern, however, was a 1973 decision against the Corps' Trinity River project, in which the judge took pains to show the intimate interrelationship of environmental impact information with economic benefit-cost analysis, with the consideration of unquantifiable values also required by NEPA and with NEPA's substantive policies.[99] Like the others, this decision was concerned with the procedure by which a decision was reached rather than with the merits of the decision itself; but its explicit integration of the various forms of project planning information brought it to the brink of reviewing compliance with NEPA's substantive purposes as well as its procedural requirements.[100]

Despite a diminution in the rate of their new interpretation of the Act, however, the courts continued to exert an important form of sustained pressure, thereby insuring that challenged projects would be brought up at least to the standards of their established precedents. One cannot assume that the agencies would automatically implement judicial precedents in all their actions, any more than they automatically implemented the legislative mandate of NEPA. The continuing availability of the courts as a recourse for project opponents thus forced more widespread response to the Act than would otherwise have occurred.[101] Corps projects continued to be held up by the courts periodically during 1973 and 1974, and these decisions undoubtedly served to keep pressure at least for procedural compliance on the less innovative districts, as well as to remind the agency's staff generally that NEPA must continue to be taken seriously.[102]

The Corps was also confronted with a mixture of pressures from the executive branch, including not only the Executive Office policies discussed in the previous chapter but also the report of the National Water Commission and the new "Principles and Standards" of the Water Resources Council.

The Water Commission's report was not binding on the Corps, but it did provide a wide-ranging overview of federal water policy and of important priorities for future action. Among other themes, it stressed the use of a *range* of alternative future situations as a basis for planning, rather than simple acceptance of trend projections; it predicted a change in future priorities from traditional water development to water quality management; it urged the development of water conservation policies and of closer links between water resource and land use planning; and it advocated an expanded policy of user charges to recapture the windfall benefits of water projects to identifiable individuals and groups.[103]

The "Principles and Standards" of the Water Resource Council were binding on the Corps, but the strength of their mandate was questionable because of the unacceptability of some of their provisions to the Office of Management and Budget and the Congress.[104] The OMB, on the one hand, supported the guidelines' higher discount rate but opposed the dilution of the economic benefit-cost criterion that was implied by the addition of other separate objectives (such as "environmental quality"), and it continued to insist that projects meet the economic criterion before their noneconomic merits would be discussed. The Congress, conversely, supported the multi-objective framework but flatly rejected an elevation of the discount rate that would lead to rejection of many previously authorized projects, and in the Water Resource Development Act of 1973, it established its own lower interest rate and "grandfather clause" for previous projects by statute.[105] The principal effect of the WRC guidelines, therefore, was simply to legitimize some of the directions in which the Corps was moving, particularly the adoption of environmental quality as one of the two formal objectives of Corps activities and the accounting of benefits and costs of projects in terms of multiple objectives rather than merely economics.

Pressures on the Corps from the Congress through 1974 seemed to carry three messages: insistence on procedural compliance with NEPA's detailed statement requirement, permissive support for new initiatives and innovations by the Corps, but opposition to delays or abandonment of previously authorized projects. As far back as 1970, Section 122 of the Rivers and Harbors Act had been added to require balanced assessment of social and economic, as well as "environmental," effects of proposed actions, apparently to avoid any precipitous policy change that would stress the physical environment to the exclusion of economic and social values. The Congress also provided substantial increases in funding for the accomplishment of new environmental studies necessitated by

NEPA, and it fostered dramatic growth in support of Corps involvement in comprehensive urban water use/water quality studies during Fiscal Years 1972 through 1974.[106] Many Congressmen had personal commitments to previously authorized projects, but they were willing to support new roles and missions for the Corps as well—perhaps simply in the expectation of a new form of "environmental pork," but perhaps also in a broader philosophical belief that capable agencies whose missions were becoming outdated should be redirected rather than eliminated or weakened.

The most significant Corps-related action of the Congress in 1973 was enactment of the Water Resource Development Act, the new name for the omnibus biennial River and Harbor and Flood Control Authorization Act.[107] As reported by the House Committee on Public Works, this Act included a complex mixture of provisions, some of which were foresighted recognitions of the stronger role that environmental policy should play in the Corps in the future, while others were less consistent with such policy, and some were even clearly inconsistent with it. On the environmental side, the Committee directed that nonstructural alternatives be considered for all flood protection projects, authorized federal payment of 80 percent of the costs of such measures, and also authorized three flood protection projects in which nonstructural rather than structural solutions had been recommended.[108] It also increased the federal share of fish and wildlife enhancement costs from 50 to 75 percent; it authorized a new mission for the Corps in the study and control of streambank erosion; and it authorized an expanded program of technical assistance by the Corps to the states for the planning of water resources and related land uses.[109] In recognition that most detailed planning of Corps projects normally occurs after project authorization, it established a new point of congressional review and approval after preparation of the "Phase 1 Design Memorandum" and before "Advanced Engineering and Design," at which point the environmental statement and "Statement of Findings" could be reviewed before land acquisition and construction commenced.[110] Finally, like the WRC "Principles and Standards" it permitted de-authorization of projects more than eight years old unless Congress specifically directed their continuation.[111]

On the other hand, the same report also laid heavy stress upon the *development* of water resources to meet an upcoming "crisis" of water supply, while unlike the 1970 report, it did not single out environmental protection for such special emphasis. It fixed the discount rate for project evaluation at 5 5/8 percent, rather than the 6 7/8 percent established by the "Principles and Standards," and it expressed general displeasure with other aspects of that document; it also added a "grandfather clause" freezing the discount rate for pre-1969 projects at an archaic 3 1/4 percent.[112] The effect of these provisions was to roll back the WRC "Standards" by statute to the rates fixed in Senate Document 97 eleven years before. Finally, this Act approved federal payment of 100 percent of the costs of operating and maintaining "general navigation features of small boat harbors," thereby repudiating Administration attempts in recent years to recoup such costs from local beneficiaries and spurring further federal subsidies to recreational development interests.[113]

These few examples can do no more than highlight the evolving climate of events in which the Corps found itself during the early 1970s, but they do serve to illuminate the broader context within which the Corps' implementation of NEPA took place. Not all these events were consistent with NEPA's purposes, and some clearly served to perpetuate traditional activities with little consideration of their relationship to those purposes. On balance, however, they tended to reinforce NEPA in two ways. First, despite the inconsistencies and despite periodic threats of an "environmental backlash" during this period, none of the events directly *repudiated* the purposes of NEPA, a fact that contrasts sharply with the congressional rejection of key elements of the WRC "Principles and Standards" and with the judicial rejection of numerous "inadequate" environmental statements during the same period. Second, while many traditional activities were perpetuated, new missions were also created for the Corps in several areas of environmental protection, thus permitting it to respond further in positive ways to NEPA's mandate rather than merely pressuring it to curtail its activities altogether. In both these respects, the flow of events following NEPA served generally to encourage the Corps toward further implementation of NEPA's environmental policy mandate.

Corps Response

C. Grant Ash, Chief of the environmental resources branch in the Office of the Chief of Engineers, has characterized the Corps' response to NEPA as a three-stage evolution—that is, a period of interpretation involving a great deal of talk and not much action; a period of procedural compliance with the letter of the law; and finally what he calls an "integrated planning" or "spirit of the law" phase. He asserts that the first of these periods was relatively short and was succeeded by the second primarily in response to pressures from the judiciary, but that the Corps "is now [fall 1973] well along into the third and, hopefully, last phase in the scheme for preparing EIS." The impetus for entry into the third phase, he states, was the Corps' own recognition of the inadequacies of letter-of-the-law compliance, particularly duplication and inconsistencies between environmental and planning documents, overemphasis on raw data that was difficult to relate to impacts and alternatives, and after-the-fact preparation of environmental statements.[114]

The evidence for Ash's optimism is not conclusive, and other Corps staff members estimate that full implementation of new environmental policies and experimental innovations might not occur for five to ten years, if ever. The Corps' policies did continue to evolve, however, and its actions included new initiatives that were consistent with the directions of change mandated by NEPA, even if only partially attributable to it. While these represented the frontier rather than the day-to-day norm of Corps activity, they were indicative of directions in which the agency might move, and in which at least its innovators were moving.

Guidelines

Between 1972 and 1974, the Corps issued two further revisions of its guidelines for preparation and coordination of NEPA environmental statements, and it also issued numerous other related guidelines and policy statements, at least three of which should be mentioned here.[115]

Revisions of the Corps' NEPA regulations were issued in February 1973 and April 1974, and these guidelines continued to be exemplary among those of other federal agencies in their interpretation of the Act.[116] The 1973 revision was considerably more detailed in its guidance than the 1971 version, and included major emphasis on integration of impact assessment—including social and economic as well as "environmental" impacts—into the Corps' planning and design processes. Among other things, it required coordination with other agencies and with interested citizen groups early and throughout the process; it required the development of alternatives specifically weighted toward environmental protection and enhancement and a balanced assessment of these alternatives; and it directed that environmental investigations be carried to the same scope and level of detail as engineering, economic, and other studies. It also created a new document to accompany the detailed environmental statement required by NEPA, a "Statement of Findings," in which the responsible official must lay out his judgments on the *rationale* for his choices among the impacts and alternatives discussed in the impact statement.[117] This "Statement of Findings" provided an innovative approach to the "balancing process" required by NEPA, while at the same time distinguishing it clearly from the objective disclosure of alternatives and impacts. The 1974 revision continued these directions by adding language to incorporate the broader thrust of the CEQ's 1973 Revised Guidelines; it also included even more detailed instructions concerning the required purposes and content of detailed statements.

A related regulation was issued in December 1972, entitled "Guidelines for Assessment of Economic, Social, and Environmental Effects of Civil Works Projects."[118] This directive, known as the "122 guidelines," was intended to supplement and extend the requirements of NEPA; its basis was Section 122 of the 1970 River and Harbor Act, which required the unified assessment of all of these categories of effects.[119] While the apparent intent of this provision's congressional sponsors was to dilute the effect of NEPA, by incorporating economic "benefits" into the detailed statement, in some instances it was used by the

Corps to *strengthen* the integration between environmental statement preparation and project planning, as NEPA intended.

Like the CEQ's early guidance, the Corps' NEPA guidelines had focussed
primarily upon the "preparation and coordination of environmental statements,"
as *documents*, and they had defined "the environment" primarily in terms of
physical, biological, and aesthetic impacts that were the concerns of environmental lobby groups rather than more inclusively to include the full range of significant effects upon the human environment. The "122 guidelines," in contrast,
emphasized the process of information gathering and assessment that must underlie the statement.[120] They directed the balanced assessment of social and economic effects as well as these "environmental" ones, and by so doing, they
fostered the development of a new model of planning directed toward the objective prediction of multiple dimensions of project impact rather than merely
justification of preconceived choices. Beginning with the 1973 revision of the
Corps' NEPA guidelines, the policies and procedures of the 122 guidelines were
linked directly to the requirements for preparation of detailed statements; together they required, at least on paper, an integrated approach to planning analysis and assessment of impacts.

In December 1972, the same month in which the 122 guideline regulation
was promulgated, the Corps issued a new summary of all its basic policies and
authorities that superseded a version that had been in effect since 1966.[121]
Among other things, this digest gave strong recognition to the broadening scope
of the Corps' objectives, to the mandates of NEPA and Section 122 as well as
other authorities for multiple-objective planning, and to the philosophy that
thorough assessment of alternatives and their consequences should be used as
the basis for all water management proposals. It also reiterated the requirements
that nonstructural as well as structural alternatives be considered, that the consequences with and without each alternative be determined, that options fore-
closed by proposed actions be carefully analyzed and avoided where possible,
and that cumulative effects of proposed actions and related activities be carefully
identified. The digest did not spell out new policies, but it served to pull together
the many policies and directives that had been promulgated in recent years,
many of them intimately related to environmental policy goals, and to integrate
these with the agency's more traditional policies and authorities.

Citizen Participation

While the NEPA and 122 guidelines were concerned primarily with the information *content* of water management plans and decisions, a concurrent evolution
was occurring in the *process* by which planning information was collected from
and disseminated to the public. Earlier studies of the Corps have noted its traditional alliance with the construction industry and other economic beneficiaries

of water resource development,[122] but both the Freedom of Information Act and NEPA as well as a series of judicial decisions favoring environmental interest groups drastically increased the power of these latter groups to challenge Corps projects that served economic beneficiaries at their expense. The Corps responded to these pressures, therefore, with new policy emphasis on the early involvement of *all* affected interests in the planning of its actions.

This new emphasis was by no means the norm in the Corps' districts, since it was not only more costly but more threatening for planners and District Engineers to actively solicit the views of hostile interest groups.[123] Despite these disincentives, several districts did try new approaches to public involvement at least on an experimental basis between 1971 and 1974. While it was too soon to tell whether these experiments would be implemented on a regular basis, they clearly increased the Corps' responsiveness to constituencies voicing environmental concerns in instances where they were employed, and several of them appeared to have significant merit. Among these were such changes as having public meetings conducted by technical staff rather than merely by administrators, holding public workshops rather than merely informational meetings, and distributing sequences of "brochures" describing the various alternatives under consideration and their expected impacts, along with decisions made to date and the reasons for them. One district in particular received extensive publicity for its efforts to plan "in a fishbowl"—that is, by using open workshops and brochures as well as other devices in order to involve as wide a range as possible of the affected publics in discussion of alternative actions and their consequences.[124]

Environmental Reconnaissance Inventories

Another experimental activity undertaken by the Corps was the preparation of four pilot "environmental reconnaissance inventories" that attempted to compile environmental information from a wide range of available sources on a statewide or Corps districtwide basis. This idea originated with a recommendation of the Chief's Environmental Advisory Board, and while serious questions were raised about the quality of the data and the "statewide significance" threshold upon which the pilot inventories were based, they did represent an experimental attempt by the agency to inventory not only hydrologic and physiographic, but also biotic and cultural resources that might be affected by its actions.[125]

Urban Studies

A related activity of the Corps during this period, and an important initiative in itself, was a new program of comprehensive urban water quality and water use studies, which was inaugurated by congressional authorization in 1971. This program was first conceived as a "Pilot Wastewater Management Program," to explore experimentally a role for the Corps in planning for water quality management in five urban areas.[126] As these studies progressed, it became obvious that wastewater management was intimately bound up with broader questions of water availability and use, and that it was equally intimately related to other considerations such as solid waste disposal, facilities siting, and land use planning in general. The Corps therefore received congressional approval for more comprehensive studies of urban water use, and it also received congressional mandates to increase the number of studies, to include up to twenty-six urban areas in Fiscal Year 1973 and more yet in Fiscal Year 1974.[127]

Unlike most of its traditional activities, the Corps had no authority to implement the recommendations of its urban studies. It undertook them in the role of the "consultant-planner," in which it could only develop its studies and recommendations, present them to the governments and agencies that had jurisdiction over their implementation, and hope that they would be acted upon.[128] The Corps did put considerable money into these studies, however—approximately one-third of its total study funds during Fiscal Year 1974, or $6.8 million—which represented a significant commitment to the new activity and a direct reallocation of priorities away from the planning of more traditional types of projects.[129] It thus began to lay the foundations for a major new agency mission of managing the quality of water in urban areas in close and logical conjunction with its more traditional mission of insuring the availability of sufficient quantities of this resource. If its recommendations appeared sound but were not implemented by the other agencies and governments, it would hardly be surprising if the Congress were to broaden the Corps' implementation authority once again in the future, as it has repeatedly in the past, in order to include these activities.

Flood Management Innovations

A final area of new Corps initiatives was its recommendation of *nonstructural* solutions to flooding problems in at least three 1973 proposals. Such solutions, including flood-plain land acquisition to prevent development as well as relocation of existing development in flood-prone areas, have long been advocated by environmental interest groups, but they have also been considered outside the Corps' jurisdiction as well as being opposed by economic interest groups. In 1973, for the first time, the Corps recommended these measures as its preferred solutions in three projects, and all three were authorized by the Congress in the 1973 Water Resource Development Act.[130] Like the other new initiatives noted above, these recommendations were experiments that involved only a small number of projects: just over one-tenth of the Corps' 1973 authorization requests, one author notes.[131] They also were opposed not only by some of the Corps' traditional constituency but by the Office of Management and Budget, which was concerned about the precedent of major land acquisitions by the Corps for planning purposes rather than merely as a necessity of water impoundment. Even as experiments, however, they provided an important precedent for Corps activities in the future as well as a demonstration of the viability of nonstructural solutions.

Conclusion

It is tempting to conclude analyses of the Corps with categorical generalizations that support either a glowing endorsement or a damning indictment of it. The reality that emerges from this study is mixed, however, and none of its indicators are entirely definitive. Should one judge the agency by the foresightedness of its paper policies, or by its reluctance to redesign previously initiated projects? By the experiments of its innovators, or by the more marginal changes in the everyday actions and values of its staff? By its explicit response to NEPA, or by the environmental policies implicit in the broad pattern of its behavior during the period of following NEPA's enactment? Many of these indicators suggest different results, but all of them provide pieces of the response of the Corps to its new environmental policy mandate.

Perhaps the most important conclusion to be drawn is that the Corps *was changing*, partly in response to NEPA but also in response to the broader set of pressures and opportunities in which it found itself during the early 1970s. Some of these changes were merely symbolic, and others were experimental rather than pervasive; many must realistically be viewed as more corrective than innovative, at least in terms of the conflict between NEPA's mandate and the Corps' traditions. All, however, indicated at least an openness to new directions and missions that is frequently absent among long-established agencies.[132]

NEPA was a threat to many of the Corps' traditional priorities and constituencies and could easily have triggered a protective recalcitrance or defensiveness by the agency in the face of attack. This defensiveness was the initial response of many of the Corps' districts and of many other federal agencies as well. The response of some of its headquarters staff, however, which gradually made itself evident at least in the better districts, was to *accept* environmental policy as a new mandate and to *broaden the planning mission* of the Corps to encompass it. Rather than simply defending traditional forms of activity, the Corps sought out new activities through which it could bring its capabilities to bear on the new priorities.

This was basically a healthy and encouraging form of response, despite the fact that after four years it was still only the vanguard rather than the mainstream of Corps activities. Even as Washington issued better and better guidelines and some districts experimented, others continued to turn out the same old projects, perhaps with wildlife refuges added as "mitigation" measures.[dd] While some units geared up for urban wastewater studies, others plunged into recreational harbor and marina projects.[133] The openness of the Corps to all these new missions was an important characteristic, however, that suggested a flexibility that would permit adaptation over time rather than parochial protectiveness of its traditional domain against change or incursion.

These signs are important and tentatively encouraging indicators of the Corps' long-term responsiveness to the environmental policy mandate established by NEPA. Perhaps the most important remaining uncertainty, however, was still the fate of the Corps' backlogged and "postponed" projects. The Corps' new projects would almost certainly reflect greater awareness of environmental impacts and alternatives, assuming that the general public climate of concern over such consequences is not dramatically repudiated, and the Corps' newly authorized activities were clearly weighted toward environmentally oriented missions and solutions.

But the Corps does not undertake many new projects and with an average planning period of fifteen years, its response time to new mandates would be intolerably slow if response were limited to new actions. Many of its key decisions concern not new actions, but the order of priority in which previously studied and partially planned projects will be pursued further—and how much restudy and replanning will be devoted to each. The extent to which NEPA's purposes will shape these priorities, and will be invoked in developing new recommended solutions in such cases, is a crucial question whose answer is not yet clear.

The most reasonable conclusion, therefore, seems to be a cautious optimism that the Corps *will* continue to change its priorities with the times, but that the change process will continue to be burdened with the baggage of past commitments, with the preferences of more parochial Congressmen and district units and with the sluggishness of any large or old organization in altering its accepted ways of doing business. The appropriate question is no longer whether NEPA's procedural requirements would bring about change in the Corps, for the agency's policies and behavior after four years exhibited clear evidence of some such changes. Rather, one must turn to questions that go beyond NEPA's procedures. How much change in *substantive* priorities will result now that NEPA's procedures have been implaced? How widely will experimental changes come to pervade the daily priorities of the district? And how vigorously will the environ-

---

[dd]This is a curious but widespread misuse of the concept of "mitigation," frequently implying that the purchase of a new area by the government provides a substitute (and hence "mitigation") for the irreversible destruction of an existing wildlife habitat. In some cases it may provide such a substitute, but in many others either the substitute is not equivalent in its ecological composition or value, or it may simply transfer to public ownership lands that would have been preserved anyway thus leaving the same net impact of the project.

mental quality objective hold up in practice against new "crises," new political realities and concerns, and other future occurrences? The answers to these questions must be sought in the unfolding flow of events, but NEPA's "action forcing" procedures clearly did catalyze action-forcing *political pressure* on the Corps during the initial period of its implementation.

5 NEPA and the SCS Small Watersheds Program

Background

The Soil Conservation Service is of more recent origin than the Corps, and while its original mission was very different, it does carry out sufficiently similar activities in the area of water resource development to merit comparison. Originally created as the Soil Erosion Service of the Department of the Interior in 1933, it was transferred to the Department of Agriculture in 1935 and given its present name.[1] At the field level, its staff is organized along state rather than district lines, and directed in each state by an SCS State Conservationist. Its central mission was not public works, nor even water resource development for its own sake: it was the conservation of soil, particularly agricultural soils that were severely depleted by poor agricultural practices and droughts in the 1930s. This mission is still identified by SCS officials as the agency's principal charge.

The conservation of soil, however, is inseparably linked with the management of water, since it is water that washes away soil, it is the lack of water that permits soil to be blown away by windstorms, and it is soil properties that govern water uptake by the land and runoff from it. The Flood Control Act of 1936, therefore, authorized the SCS to "study watersheds above existing and future flood control projects to determine the effect of watershed treatment methods in reducing erosion and providing runoff and waterflow retardation." The Flood Control Act of 1944 expanded this mandate into an authorization to "plan and carry out a complete watershed protection and flood prevention program in eleven designated river basins."[2] In 1953, a new Pilot Watershed Program was initiated, to test the concept of federal *assistance* for watershed planning (as opposed to the previous practice of direct federal planning and installation), and in 1954, this concept was institutionalized in the Watershed Protection and Flood Prevention Act, commonly known as Public Law 566, which is the basic authority for the program that is the subject of this chapter.[3]

Public Law 566 authorized water resource development activities by the Department of Agriculture towards two general purposes: preventing damages due to erosion, floodwaters and sediment, and furthering the conservation, utilization, and disposal of water.[4] Under P.L. 566, water resource development was to be carried out through *technical assistance* to "local sponsoring organizations," rather than by direct planning and implementation. These organizations might be either "soil and water conservation districts," many of which had been established under state enabling legislation developed with SCS assistance since 1935,

93

or they might be units of state or local general purpose government (such as counties), or they might be "watershed improvement districts" established specifically for the purpose of seeking P.L. 566 assistance.[5] In any event, they must be legally and financially responsible entities and in return for SCS technical and financial assistance, they must secure agreements, from the owners of at least 50 percent of the lands in the watershed above any water control structure, to develop farm plans and implement conservation farming practices.[6]

Like the Corps, the SCS is responsible for numerous programs and activities in addition to water resource management, but there is an important difference between the two agencies in the relationship which these other responsibilities bear to each agency's water-related activities. In the case of the Corps, the agency's principal mission is public works engineering, and water resource development is one of the primary arenas for the application of its considerable capabilities in this area. The Corps' other major activities also contribute to this mission: military construction, post office construction, combat support, and so forth. In the case of the SCS, however, the principal mission is the conservation of soil, and most if not all of the agency's activities are directed toward this end: for instance, soil and snow surveys, testing of plant species for conservation characteristics, a national land inventory and monitoring program, and technical and financial assistance in the conservation of cropland, pastures, woodlands, wildlife, and other soil-related resources.[7]

In short, most of the activities of the SCS do in fact serve a mission of environmental protection; only in its watershed projects, and perhaps a few other activities, have serious questions been raised as to whether economic and engineering considerations have taken precedence over environmental and conservation goals. Since these projects and their apparent impacts are at least superficially quite similar to those of the Corps, it seems useful to compare the effects of NEPA on the two programs, while bearing in mind the differences that exist between the agencies as a whole.[a]

---

[a]Critics charged, for instance, that with the initiation of the Public Law 566 program in 1954 the SCS, which had previously been dominated by professionals in fields of physical conservation of resources (agronomists, biologists, land use planners), took on a civil engineering–economic development mission more similar to that of the Corps than to its own traditional conservation mission. They asserted that:

The channelization emphasis in the Public Law 566 program has to be changed because it leads to the same basic blunders and environmental damages that have resulted from similar projects carried out by the Corps of Engineers and the Bureau of Reclamation. These damages are in the lowering of water tables, the elimination of flood plains as natural reservoirs and recharge basins or aquifers, the elimination of wildlife cover and of stabilizing vegetation along the streambanks, an increase in water temperature and turbidity, elimination of desirable sport fisheries, and decimation of a whole host of stream-related wildlife.

See the testimony of Charles H. Callison, Executive Vice President of the National Audubon Society, in U.S. Congress, House Committee on Government Operations, Subcommittee on Conservation and Natural Resources, *Stream Channelization*, Hearings, June 1971, Wash-

In its Small Watershed Program, the SCS like the Corps had a considerable backlog of projects that were in one sense or another pending at the time NEPA was enacted. In all, some 1,270 projects had been authorized for planning under Public Law 566, which had not yet been completed and which thus might be affected by the requirements of NEPA.[b] Since the agency completes only about 50 such projects per year, at least 800 and possibly as many as 1,200 of these projects might conceivably have sufficient work remaining to make them subject to NEPA's impact statement requirement, if significant increments of federal action remained to be taken.[c] The federal costs of completing the 1,001 projects that had been authorized for operation but not yet completed was estimated at $727 million, and its budget for P.L. 566 projects in fiscal year 1971 was approximately $82.4 million, of which $76.4 million was for construction.[8]

SCS watershed projects have one other important similarity to these of the Corps, and that is their primary economic purpose. The SCS regularly invokes its "conservation" label to suggest a presumption that its activities are beneficial. In fact, however, its projects are multiple-purpose water development actions just as those of the Corps are, and historically they have been evaluated and justified by precisely the same predominantly economic criteria as those of the Corps of Engineers.[9] In addition, unlike the Corps, the SCS must also plan its water resource projects to fit the preferences of "local sponsoring organizations," which are sometimes general purpose governments but more often associations of presumably profit-motivated landowners. For both these reasons, the small watersheds program of the SCS must be clearly distinguished from most of that agency's other activities, in that like the Corps' civil works program, this program has historically been a means to the achievement of primarily *economic* objectives, rather than to the conservation of soil as a physical resource.

Three other important differences stand out between the water resource programs of the Corps and the Soil Conservation Service. First, the projects of

---

ington, D.C., 1971, Part 1, pp. 9-10; also Peter Harnik, "Channelization: Streamlining Our Nation's Rivers," *Environmental Action* III (March 4, 1972).

[b]As of June 30, 1970, the SCS had 1,324 unprocessed applications on hand, of which it estimated that 824 would be found suitable for assistance, as well as 1,561 applications which it had approved for planning. Of the approved applications, planning was in process on over 300. One thousand and one projects had been authorized for "operation" as of this date (that is, for design and construction), either administratively or by the Congress, as appropriate; of these, 223 were receiving preconstruction land treatment and engineering, 429 were under construction, and construction had been completed on 291. See U.S. Congress, House Committee on Appropriations, *Agriculture-Environmental and Consumer Protection Appropriations for 1972*, Hearings, Washington, D.C., Part 3, pp. 498, 500, 511-12.

[c]Normally the last major federal action on an SCS watershed project is the signing of a construction contract or of a "project agreement" signed after preconstruction engineering and before the beginning of construction. If a project is divided into several portions under separate project agreements or contracts, however, there might be "major federal actions" to which NEPA must be applied during construction. The backlog of projects to which NEPA might be applicable was thus at least 800 and probably less than 1200.

the SCS are limited by statutory ceilings on physical capacities and maximum costs, while those of the Corps are not. Projects under P.L. 566 were limited to watersheds or subwatersheds not larger than 250,000 acres, and no single structure could exceed a storage capacity of 12,500 acre feet for floodwaters or 25,000 acre feet total. Projects storing more than 2,500 acre feet or costing the federal government more than $250,000 must be authorized by congressional committee resolution and reviewed by the Secretaries of the Army and the Interior, and projects storing more than 4,000 acre feet of water must be approved by the Public Works rather than the Agriculture Committees.[10] As a result, the SCS has a narrower range of project alternatives open to it, and probably a more limiting constraint on the amount of resources it could reallocate to the fulfillment of any new mandate, than did the Corps. Needless to say, however, neither size nor cost provides a definitive indicator of the magnitudes of environmental impacts that might result from such a project.

Second, the SCS Small Watersheds Program is by law a program of federal *assistance,* both technical and financial, to local sponsoring organizations, while the Corps' civil works program is primarily a program of direct federal decision making and construction.[d] P.L. 566 provided *financial assistance* to these "local sponsoring organizations" in amounts up to 100 percent of the costs of flood prevention and up to 50 percent of the costs of land and basic facilities for such public purposes as public recreation and fish and wildlife development. It also authorized federal loans and advances to these organizations for land acquisition and for the construction of storage capacity to meet future water supply needs, subject to assurances of local repayment, and it allowed the federal government to arrange contracting for construction when requested to do so by the local organization.[11] Despite the similarity of their actions, therefore, important differences may arise from the fact that the SCS is more closely bound to clients who apply for its assistance than the Corps is to the wide range of interests that may benefit from its discretionary actions.

Third, despite the historical broadening of its statutory purposes, the SCS was still more limited than the Corps in the range of purposes open to it and in the percentages of costs of their achievement that could be charged to the federal government. No cost-sharing was permitted for water quality management in P.L. 566 projects, for instance, and local sponsors were required to pay 50 percent of *all* costs allocated to fish and wildlife protection, while in Corps projects such sponsors must pay only 50 percent of the *additional* costs of such measures over and above joint costs with other purposes.[12] The SCS has no authority in such areas as navigation and hydroelectric power production.

Irrespective of the mandate of NEPA, therefore, a more difficult balancing

---

[d]Local cooperation is required in some matters concerning Corps projects, such as repayment of benefits attributed to water supply, and provision of lands, easements, and rights-of way for local protection projects, but otherwise the difference is clear.

process is involved in the SCS than in the Corps, between the agency's responsibilities to federal objectives on the one hand, and its mission to provide both technical and financial assistance to a narrower constituency of *local* organizations for the pursuit of *local* objectives, within the means and ends of such organizations' constituencies.[13] Since it must work through local sponsors, its capacity for centralized planning and objective setting is constrained by its lack of authority for direct implementation, and its balancing of federal and non-federal objectives takes place in a context of multilateral negotiation with the state soil conservation committees and the conservation districts, rather than of a strict administrative chain of command.[14] In practice, the balance struck by the SCS on this issue appears to be a permissive one that defers to the wishes and objectives of the local sponsors whenever possible as long as the project is, in the SCS' opinion, "sound."[15]

Formally, the SCS' response to NEPA is comparable to that of the Corps, since both accepted the principle that NEPA was applicable to their water resource projects and the projects of both must meet the same federal criteria. In practice, however, the achievement of administrative change in the SCS is complicated by its dependence upon independent organizations for the realization of its purposes and by its greater ability to shelter its own decisions and priorities behind those of its clients.

Initial Response to NEPA, 1970–71

Three key points stand out in the initial policy response of the Soil Conservation Service to NEPA, and these points differ in important respects from the official response of the Corps of Engineers. First, the SCS took an official position that NEPA was *consistent* with its previous mission and objectives and thus established no new mandate and required no change in policy for the agency. The testimony of SCS officials in 1971 shows this position clearly:

... we took the National Environmental Policy Act which said in substance that you will do the maximum *under the law that you now operate on* in this direction. And we did ask our field offices to take a fresh look at going projects, ones in the formulation stage, to be sure that everything had been done to carry out the will of Congress in the direction of *maximum development for the total environment* [emphasis added].[16]

In essence, this position implied the SCS' adoption of the position of Congressman Aspinall, whose interpretation of NEPA as requiring no change in the existing authority of agencies to consider environmental purposes had been rejected by the other members of the conference committee.[17] It also differed from the interpretation of the Corps, whose policy from the outset was that

NEPA did establish a new mission for the agency's water resource activities, and that it both authorized and required the consideration of environmental factors that had been ignored by previous practices under Senate Document 97.

Second, SCS policies showed little appreciation of the significance of the environmental impacts that might be caused by its actions, and they seemed to treat these impacts as primarily a *political* matter of environmental "acceptability" and justification, rather than as consequences to be objectively documented as a basis for decisions. The SCS guidelines did not include operational definitions of the environmental impacts that should be categorized as "some" and "serious," and unlike those of the Corps, they did not even provide illustrative examples of such impacts to guide field officials. On the contrary, the SCS discounted and downplayed the possible adverse effects of its channelization projects, while emphasizing their economic benefits,[18] and its guidelines also failed even to mention important categories of environmental impacts, such as impacts other than sedimentation and fish and wildlife damage.[19] It created a limited outline for "effects assessment" rather than adopting the more detailed materials that were already in use by the Corps,[20] and it required impact statements for projects in progress only on a "case-by-case basis," in contrast to the Corps policy of preparing them for all water projects and despite strong scientific evidence of the serious environmental impacts of this practice.[21]

The SCS did accept the applicability of NEPA's procedural requirements to its watershed projects, and under questioning, its officials acknowledged the agency's authority to require minimization of significant environmental damages—"just like we would require a certain design and construction"—as a condition of federal assistance.[22] Its instructions concerning the identification and evaluation of such damages were not specific, however. They were less complete than those of the Corps with respect to some major categories of potential impacts, and they were predicated upon the projects' environmental "acceptability" to sponsoring organizations and fish and wildlife agencies, rather than upon comprehensive and objective balancing of the projects' consequences.

Third, SCS policies concerning implementation of NEPA reflected that agency's traditionally client-centered, negotiative patterns of decision making, and consistent with this, they gave far less encouragement than did Corps policies to public involvement in project decisions, even though they did insist that public information programs be undertaken and documented by project sponsors. SCS officials insisted that project objectives were the responsibility of the sponsors rather than the SCS, though under questioning they acknowledged the agency's authority to withhold assistance if in its judgment "significant biological losses" would result and "feasible" alternatives were available.[23] The SCS did not hold hearings itself concerning proposed projects, although it did have the authority to do so,[24] and the environmental statement itself was withheld until tentative agreement was reached on a final work plan. Prior to this point the public was to be given "adequate information," but not opportunities to review and comment upon the environmental statement itself.[25] Even the other agencies were not to be given advance copies of the environmental statement along with their advance copies of work plans: the environmental statement was to be a final, formal piece of paper documentation in the work plan approval process, rather than an active element of that process as it developed.[26]

In short, SCS policies and public statements during 1970 and 1971 suggested an official willingness to listen to the comments of other agencies and individuals, but no inclination to change priorities or projects as a result unless both its own staff and the local sponsors wished to do so.[27]

Policy Statements and Guidelines

The initial response of the SCS to NEPA was a claim that NEPA required no change in its previous policies and activities. Like the Corps, the SCS responded to NEPA's enactment with a flurry of official documents during the first half of 1970. Several of these were simply informational transmittals, enclosing copies first of the Act and then of the Executive Order and the CEQ Interim Guidelines; others were later attributed to NEPA, but made no specific reference to it and may well have been under development by the agency prior to NEPA's enactment.[28] In any case, they contributed to the attention on "environmental policy" during this period; but all were explicitly introduced as *re-emphases* of previous policies rather than acknowledgments of any *new* environmental mission or emphasis.[29]

The SCS' first guidance on the implementation of NEPA *per se* was issued in a memorandum of May 1, 1970, just before the agency received the CEQ's Interim Guidelines.[30] This memorandum stated three principal policies. First, it asserted that NEPA did not change the traditional relationship between the SCS and the local organizations to which it gave assistance, but that it was the SCS' responsibility to "bring (environmental effects) to the attention of" these local groups and to "encourage" them to consider national environmental objectives along with their own objectives. Second, it affirmed the applicability of NEPA to watershed projects and itemized the major requirements established by the Executive Order. Finally, it directed the preparation of an environmental statement for each new watershed work plan, especially for those projects requiring congressional approval.

The SCS transmitted departmental policy statements regarding environmental policies and implementation of NEPA to its field offices in September 1970, and two supplements to these policies just prior to the Dingell oversight hearings in December.[31] These policies restated the language of the CEQ Interim Guidelines and added a directive that environmental statements itemize "favorable" as well as "adverse" environmental effects. They also directed that public information efforts were to be expanded and preferably improved. The SCS did not issue further NEPA guidance of its own during 1970, although by December 11 it had submitted 49 environmental statements on watershed plans to the Council on Environmental Quality.[32]

In February 1971, the SCS issued one of its most important policy directives. "Watersheds Memorandum 108," as it was identified, called for an interdisciplinary review of all pending projects that included stream channel modification measures ("channelization"). It directed that all channelization projects be classified in three groups according to the extent of modifications that might be necessary to make them environmentally "acceptable," and it ordered that the economic justifications for each be reviewed also in the light of these modifications.[33] The memorandum also drew together and restated the agency's various policies concerning the circumstances in which stream channel modification was to be employed.[34]

An important point in this memorandum was its implication that NEPA did require the review and possibly the modification of projects initiated before its enactment. Unlike the Corps, the SCS did not direct the completion of environmental impact statements for all its pending projects, but it did direct a review of all those projects that involved channel modification, which amounted to over 67 percent of its authorized projects and which were generally thought by environmental and conservation groups to have the most serious environmental consequences of any of the SCS' actions.[35] The memorandum stated that NEPA was a primary basis for this review, and that project modifications were to result from it where indicated.[36]

While the memorandum did direct substantive review of channelization projects, however, it also had three important defects. First, it did not mention the requirement of NEPA that a detailed statement be prepared on every project having a significant impact on the environment, nor how the review and classification process directed by the memorandum was to be coordinated with that requirement. This was an important omission, since on the one hand, assignment of the project to Group 1 would appear to imply that an environmental statement was not required, while on the other hand, operational criteria for assigning projects to these three groups (and definitions of adverse environmental effects) were nowhere spelled out.[37]

Second, the memorandum failed to provide any new *criteria* to guide the review of channelization projects, beyond the reviewers' judgments of "some" or "serious" environmental impacts and of "environmental acceptability." Significantly, it did not indicate that NEPA required any change in the agency's traditional purposes and objectives for the use of channelization. It did suggest that "serious consideration be given" to nonstructural measures—such as floodproofing and flood plain zoning—but the mission was still to permit the "profitable" use of flood plains, rather than the full range of ecological functions of these lands.[38] Channelization might not be used where the "primary" purpose was to develop new land, but it could be used where this purpose was secondary, or where "retardation is obviously impractical"—such as in the southeastern coastal plain, the location both of important estuarine wetlands and of many SCS channelization projects.[39] The extent to which SCS-sponsored channelization might encourage private drainage of wetlands after project installation was also ignored.

Third, the memorandum required SCS reviewers to consult only with sponsoring organizations and fish and wildlife agencies, not with the general public or even with agencies having "jurisdiction or special expertise" regarding other impacts of channelization (for instance, water quality agencies); yet on the basis of this review, determinations would be made concerning whether each channelization project had "significant environmental impacts" or not. The memorandum did require Group 2 or 3 classification for all projects to which fish and wildlife agencies objected, but it did not prevent the possibility of compromises between SCS and those agencies that might ignore other potentially significant impacts. By the end of 1971, the SCS was negotiating modifications in Group 2 and 3 projects to permit their reclassification into Group 1,[40] while proceeding ahead with Group 1 projects—since by its own definition these did not have "significant environmental impacts." This reclassification process thus permitted an unfortunate sort of evasion of the EIS process established by NEPA, since it was based simply on SCS and fish and wildlife agencies' agreements concerning "environmental acceptability" rather than upon the responses of other agencies and individuals to an EIS.[41]

In short, Watersheds Memorandum 108 directed a review of all work plan agreements and proposals involving channelization, but it did not provide strong authority or operational criteria for change in them, and without such authority, few State Conservationists would be likely to bargain single-handedly for significant changes in previously approved projects.

In March 1971, the SCS finally issued its *Environment Memorandum 1*, "Interim Environmental Policies and Procedures."[42] Like earlier memoranda, this directive asserted that NEPA only reinforced the agency's previous mission rather than conferring a new mandate,[43] and while it applied NEPA's requirements to all new project agreements, it directed (in contrast to the Corps) that older projects be reviewed only on a "case-by-case basis."[44]

The position that NEPA reinforced the mission of the SCS was true as a general statement: even many vocal critics of some of the agency's practices conceded that the environmental impact of many of its activities was beneficial rather than adverse.[45] *Environment Memorandum 1*, however, showed no recognition that *some* of the agency's activities—specifically, its water resource engineering activities, which were guided primarily by the economic criteria of Senate Document 97 and of local sponsors—might require redirection in order to give more balanced consideration to environmental as well as economic and technical factors. In the absence of any language distinguishing these economic development–related activities from the agency's broader mission to conserve the quality of agricultural lands, the memorandum failed to address the need for new priorities in water resource development, and the inconsistency of traditional water project evaluation criteria with the new environmental mandate.

In April 1971, the SCS incorporated its previous instructions (and some new material) into its handbook of standard operating procedures.[46] Three points stand out in the notice effecting these changes. First, it directed SCS personnel to demonstrate "forceful leadership" in the selection of alternatives, in order to insure that all environmental values were carefully considered. This seems a distinctly stronger exhortation than the generally passive, facilitative role that SCS had previously advocated.

Second, the notice emphasized the importance of an interdisciplinary approach to watershed planning,[47] but it remained highly ambiguous regarding public involvement in that planning. It stressed the importance of a public *information* program, to be carried out by the sponsoring organization, beginning at the time of the preliminary investigation, but it stated that outside comments need not be solicited by SCS field offices on "preliminary draft statements" unless there was a need for consultation or special expertise on a particular environmental problem.[48] It also directed that the EIS itself be prepared in Washington, and not be released until the final work plan was completed and circulated for review.[49] Copies of the final work plan could be circulated in advance of formal approval, "to facilitate review" by concerned federal and state agencies, but the draft environmental statement was *not* to be circulated with these advance copies, despite NEPA's requirement that the environmental statement "accompany the proposal through the existing agency review processes," since this statement "may be modified by the Washington office before it is sent with the final work plan for interagency review."[50]

In short, while the SCS encouraged the dissemination of general information about its projects from their early stages on, it was far more reticent about publicizing, and soliciting comments on, the "detailed environmental statements" themselves. This position may be contrasted with that of the Corps of Engineers, which assigned responsibility for the preparation of environmental statements to the District Engineers, directed them to involve the public actively at every stage of planning, and required them to release and defend environmental statements in the field before submitting them with their recommendations to Washington. The Corps appears to have sought an active, two-way public *involvement* program, in order to surface and resolve value conflicts as early as possible; the SCS preferred a more passive, one-way public *information* program, to avoid an image of secrecy between the sponsors and the SCS but not to legitimize broader involvement in the sponsors' decisions.

Third, *Notice 1-17* included an annotated outline of the information that was to be included in each environmental statement, but this outline was not only six months later, but less detailed and distinctly different from that of the Corps.[51] No detailed listing of the environmental elements to be considered was provided, in contrast to the September 1970 circular of the Corps, which had attached such an illustrative list as an appendix.[52] Detailed measures of the project's beneficial impacts were specified (e.g., reduction of erosion rates, reduction of floodwater damages, reduction of sediment damages, amounts of water made available for beneficial purposes, number and kind of project beneficiaries), but only crude measures for the project's potentially damaging impacts: for instance, miles of stream fishery destroyed, acres of wildlife habitat destroyed, and "secondary impacts, such as greater vehicular traffic, etc."[53] The notice did require discussion of alternatives meeting different mixes of objectives, and alternatives outside the authority of the agency, but its tone did not convey the concept of a genuinely balanced approach. Few examples of the expected content were included other than the ones quoted above.

In September 1971, the SCS directed that economic as well as environmental impacts be discussed in all detailed statements.[54] This order resulted from a request by the congressional conference committee on agricultural appropriations for fiscal year 1972, which was similar in authorship and intent to Section 122 of the Corps' River and Harbor and Flood Control Act of 1970.[55] In contrast to the Corps, however, the SCS chose to approach such impacts in the traditional, justificatory manner. The Corps used this direction as a mandate for "effects assessment," to provide a full and balanced view of the consequences of alternative projects, and it created a whole new concept of the process for carrying out such an assessment, rather than merely extending traditional justification practices.[56] The SCS, however, directed that "with project" effects be calculated by using traditional justification procedures "except that more emphasis should be given to employment factors," and instead of a "without project" scenario, it directed only that the statement show "economic benefits foregone if the chosen project were to be delayed or terminated." The benefits foregone measure provides only one indicator of economic impacts, and a politically loaded one at that; the SCS' reliance on it suggests a desire to justify projects despite environmental impacts, rather than to identify objectively the impacts that might occur in the presence or absence of a project.

In October 1971, the SCS issued another notice updating the SCS *Watershed Protection Handbook*, and this directive included several policy changes.[57] In regard to public involvement, *Notice 1-18* directed for the first time that the State Conservationists rather than the Washington staff prepare the environmental statements, and it directed also that the "preliminary drafts" of these statements be circulated at field level to state and local agencies as well as the regional offices of federal agencies. A direct effect of these changes was to make information about the environmental impacts of such projects more accessible to the public earlier in the process, as the Corps had directed for some time previously. A longer-term consequence was to encourage greater environmental awareness among *all* of the agency's staff, as NEPA intended, rather than just among a specialized group of environmental statement writers in Washington.

In regard to mitigation, the notice directed that special measures be employed for alleviating the adverse impacts of stream channelization projects, and it defined mitigation as a *construction* cost "unless the primary effect is clearly enhancement" (rather than merely mitigation) of environmental effects.[58] The significance of the latter point is that it permitted federal payment of the costs of most of these measures, thus allowing more substantive change in such projects than would be possible if they must be paid for by the local sponsors.

In November 1971, the SCS issued a revision of *Environment Memorandum 1* that incorporated some new language from the revised guidelines of the Council on Environmental Quality but otherwise added little new substance.[59] Despite statements in *Notice 1-17* that environmental quality be considered an objective of watershed projects, this revision also reiterated the policy that NEPA merely reinforced the previous mission and practices of the agency.[60]

The SCS issued one additional document in August 1971 that is of interest here, though it was not an official directive to its staff at the time.[61] This was a series of "questions and answers" concerning the agency's stream channelization policies and practices, prepared in response to congressional inquiries. This document made several revealing admissions in its attempt to defend the agency's existing policies and practices.

First, it admitted that in many areas of knowledge, the SCS had no basis in research to support its standard claims and practices, because "the Soil Conservation Service is not authorized to conduct research."[62] These areas included the erosive and sediment transport characteristics of streams; the environmental impacts of channelization, the claim that P.L. 566 projects "preserve and enhance fish and wildlife resources"; the effects of channelization on the water table, on downstream flood peaks, on downstream erosion, and on fish, wildlife, wetland vegetation, and sediment production; the effectiveness of creating new "substitute" wetlands as a "mitigation measure"; and the impact of marsh drainage on floods, sediment production, and land productivity. In some of these areas, SCS answers indicated that other authors had performed such studies and that SCS relied upon these studies in formulating its actions. In others, it relied simply upon "established principles" or on its own "records of accomplishment." In still others, particularly the effects of channelization upon various resources and its environmental impact generally, it claimed that overall evaluation would be "valueless" and that "the only documentation we consider valid is that which is specific to a particular ditch or channel reach modification and the particular environmental resources or values present to be affected."[63] It made no such disclaimer, however, concerning its "established principles" of engineering or its reliance upon other authors' studies when these studies supported its traditional practices.

Second, SCS answers revealed the absence of follow-up studies of the effects of its own projects. Specifically, SCS had no information, and "did not see a need for information" concerning the condition of riparian lands before and after SCS project installation,[64] the extent to which stream riffles and pools were eliminated permanently by channelization, the extent to which lands benefitted by SCS projects were allowing farmers to receive additional benefits from the government for nonproduction, or the cost-benefit projections for completed projects (according to the SCS, "we had no reason or occasion to study the economic aspects of completed channel modification").[65] In fairness, most federal agencies fail to perform such studies, but in their absence, there is no valid performance measure for the value of the program except the political measure implied by continued congressional funding.

Third, the "questions and answers" admitted that the SCS had made no attempt to comply with Section 102(2)(B) of NEPA, which required development of methods to insure proper consideration of unquantified environmental amenities and values, except through the "detailed statements" required by Section 102(2)(C). The SCS erroneously claimed that the environmental impact statement was the vehicle intended by NEPA for such consideration, and it excused itself further by claiming that the Council on Environmental Quality was not yet ready to pursue this objective, a claim which incorrectly suggests that this was the Council's responsibility.[66] In fact, NEPA assigned this responsibility clearly to "all agencies of the federal government," subject only to consultation with the Council.

As in the case of the Corps, the end of 1971 provides a reasonably stable stopping point for summarizing the SCS' initial policy response to NEPA. Further development between 1972 and 1974 will be discussed later in the chapter.

Detailed Statements

As of October 1971, the Corps and the Soil Conservation Service reported similar numbers of partially planned projects in progress: 1,046 by the Corps, and 1,270 by the SCS.[67] Unlike the Corps, however, the SCS decided to apply the requirements of NEPA to these projects only on a "case-by-case basis," and as a result, during this period the SCS submitted only one-fifth as many detailed statements as the Corps. Table 5-1 shows these results and reveals a similar pattern (initial bulge, followed by relatively stable monthly output) but a far lower level of production. Whatever the merits or usefulness of the detailed statements may have been, the SCS clearly got far less practice at preparing them during this period than did the Corps, and this in itself suggests that the educational process intended by NEPA was slower and less widespread in the SCS.

Like those of the Corps, most of the environmental statements submitted by the SCS during 1970 were prepared hastily in response to the request of a congressional committee. Eighty-five statements were submitted *en bloc* by the Corps in November 1970, to meet the request of the House Committee on Pub-

Table 5–1
Environmental Statements Submitted by Soil Conservation Service, as of December 31, 1971

	Jan	Feb	Mar	Apr	May	Jun	Jul	Aug	Sep	Oct	Nov	Dec
						Month						
1970:								34	5	9	0	2
1971:	1	1	6	2	3	2	2	6	5	4	3	2

	SCS	Corps *(for comparison)*
Total:	87	435
Finals (with or without draft)	51	265
Draft, no final	36	170

Source: Council on Environmental Quality, *102 Monitor* I (1971).

lic Works; similarly, 28 of the 34 statements submitted by the SCS in August 1970 were submitted in a single batch to meet the request of the Senate Committee on Public Works.[68] Fifteen of the projects for which these initial statements were written included, in all, over 845 miles of stream channelization—an average (mean) of 60 miles per project, or a median of 25 miles per project—yet none of these statements was longer than three pages, and all were grossly superficial in their content.[69]

The deficiencies of these early statements were conceded by SCS witnesses at the Dingell hearings in December 1970, in a statement in which they also claimed that their standards for the preparation of such statements had since improved.[70] Examination of environmental statements submitted on channelization projects from September through December 1970, however, does not show that such improvement was significant. Seven such statements were submitted, and four changes were evident in the information they contained. First, all but one included somewhat longer and more detailed descriptions of the natural and economic setting of the project, but like earlier statements they included no maps of the project areas, and they still averaged less than five pages long.[71] Second, while they did show some improvement in their handling of comments in that they at least represented these comments fairly, and in all but one the comments had at least been incorporated into the text of the statement, there was no evidence of further change in response to these comments.[72] Third, all but one of these statements mentioned the number of acres of land and miles of stream that would be affected by the project, but none described any adverse impacts other than the commitment of acres and stream miles. Finally, six of the seven mentioned the alternative of not undertaking the project, but each discarded this alternative without further analysis on the basis of net economic benefits that would allegedly be foregone if no action were taken.[73]

Despite some improvements, in short, the environmental statements submitted by the SCS through December 1970 remained seriously deficient, a conclusion that was also expressed in an evaluation of them by the Council on Environmental Quality. In a December 1970 letter, CEQ Counsel Timothy Atkeson criticized the SCS for merely "going through the motions" in preparing impact statements and having them written up in standard language by the Washington staff; he suggested that the SCS develop a form for the preparation of such statements and listed nineteen illustrative items that such a form might cover.[74] The SCS' spring 1971 guideline revision did include an outline for preparation of impact statements, but this outline was relatively general and did not list the nineteen items suggested by the Council.

Environmental statements prepared by the SCS during 1971 displayed modest improvements, but remained seriously deficient in important respects.[75] They were somewhat more detailed and averaged ten pages each rather than five or less (four were over thirty pages each, including other agencies' comments); they included at least passing mention of "secondary" impacts; and they identified alternatives more specifically than did earlier statements, in some cases including general reasons for their rejection. In accordance with new departmental policies, they also included summaries of "favorable effects" as well as "adverse effects" of the proposed action. Unfortunately, however, the substance of many of these changes continued to be superficial, and the rationales for rejection of the alternatives seemed still to have been written by formula rather than by examination of each individual case.[76] The summaries of "favorable" effects were frequently repetitive while those of "adverse" effects were overgeneralized,[77] and many potentially important impacts still were rarely discussed at all.[78]

In short, by the end of 1971 SCS impact statements still were generally brief, superficial, and slanted in favor of justifying a previously selected action. These deficiencies were not significantly worse than those of the Corps or other agencies on the average, but SCS statements clearly were no better than average and were distinctly poorer than the best Corps statements.

Project Modifications

Table 5-2 shows the numbers of SCS projects reported to have been affected by NEPA, by stage of completion. *No* projects were reported cancelled as a result of NEPA (in contrast to 7 reported cancelled by the Corps), the SCS Administrator explained this circumstance by reasoning that "we haven't turned them down, because when you make the 102 study and you find out that you have problems, we are then back in the process of attempting to modify or change or adjust to make a determination on those projects." He conceded that no project had ever been turned down as a result of such a determination.[79]

Forty-four SCS projects were reported postponed, and 22 significantly changed as a result of NEPA. These figures are surprisingly similar to those of

Table 5–2.
Number of SCS Watershed Projects Reported Modified in Response to
NEPA, as of October 1971

	% Cancelled (n = 0) (7)		% Postponed (n = 44) (48)		% Significantly Changed (n = 22) (23)	
Stage of Completion						
Not yet designed	–	(–)	34	(40)	48	(57)
Designed, under construction, or in operation	–	(100%)	63	(54)	52	(39)
Not reported	–	(–)	3	(6)	–	(4)
	100%		100%		100%	

Note: Number of State Conservationists reporting = 38, or 76% of the total. Comparable figures from the Corps are noted in parenthesis, from Table 4–5.
Source: Survey of Soil Conservation Service, State Conservationists' Offices, October 1971.

the Corps, despite the agencies' divergent policies toward the preparation of environmental impact statements. The only obvious difference between these reports was the stage of project completion at which the modification occurred: more than half the "significantly changed" SCS projects were already being designed at the time they were changed, while more than half of those changed by the Corps had not yet reached the design stage. This difference is probably attributable to the difference in policy response of the agencies to NEPA: the Corps had directed that environmental impact statements be prepared for all its backlogged projects, but not that the projects themselves be reviewed, while the SCS directed that environmental statements be prepared only on a "case-by-case basis," but that all channelization projects be substantially reviewed and potentially modified. As a result, the Corps prepared "paper statements" on older projects and concentrated its project modifications on newer ones, while SCS staff members were compelled to re-examine the substance of some projects that were already partially designed.

As in the case of the Corps, these 66 projects represented only a small fraction (5 percent) of the 1,270 projects that were under development by the SCS during this period. Unlike those of the Corps, however, they cannot meaningfully be compared to the number of actions for which EIS's were prepared during the same period (87), since the SCS used project modifications in conjunction with its 108 review as a substitute for, rather than a consequence of the preparation of impact statements.

The effects of NEPA upon SCS watershed projects must include the effects of *Watersheds Memorandum 108*, itself a byproduct of NEPA, which directed classification of all channelization projects by degree of environmental impact and potentially the modification of them to insure their "environmental accepta-

Table 5–3.
Classifications of P.L. 566 Watershed Projects under Watersheds
Memorandum 108, Summer 1971

	Number of Projects	Stream Miles Channelized
Group 1 (little or no adverse impacts)	155 + parts of 44	4921.7
Group 2 (some adverse impacts)	148 + parts of 45	5478.7
Group 3 (serious adverse impacts)	43 + parts of 23	1626.9

Source: U.S. Congress, Senate Committee on Public Works, *The Effect of Channelization on the Environment*, Hearings, July 1971, Serial 91–H24, Washington, D.C., 1971, pp. 101–07.

bility."[e] Table 5–3 shows the initial results of this classification process: 155 projects and parts of 44 more were rated as having "minor or no adverse impacts," 148 projects and portions of 45 were classified as having "some adverse effects," and 43 projects and portions of 23 were considered by the SCS review teams to have "serious adverse effects."[f]

In all, the SCS estimated that not more than 16 percent of all its watershed projects, or 14 percent of the stream miles to be channelized, would involve seriously adverse environmental effects.[80] However, a significantly different view was evident in comments on these classifications by the Bureau of Sport Fisheries and Wildlife (BSFW), the most active of the reviewing agencies. Table 5–4 shows the differences in percentages of projects assigned to each group by the Bureau and by the SCS, in each state in which the Bureau participated in the review.[g] Undoubtedly these differences stemmed in part from differences in the

[e]One problem of interpretation here is the large number of projects—165 and portions of up to 62 more—that were classified in either Group 2 or Group 3 under the *Watershed Memorandum 108* review, but not reported as postponed or revised in response to NEPA. They need not necessarily have been revised, of course, especially in view of the brief time that had elapsed since classification under *WS-108*, but postponement for review and possible revision was a mandatory consequence of classification of a project into either of these groups. There seems, therefore, to have been some difference of opinion as to whether postponement under *WS-108* should be considered a consequence of NEPA, since not only were a large number of postponed projects not reported as consequences of NEPA, but 34 projects classified in Groups 2 or 3 *were* so reported.

[f]Note, however, SCS testimony that it does not even consider all projects classified in Group 3 to have serious environmental effects: some, it states, were placed there for economic or other reasons (Letter from Kennneth E. Grant, Administrator, to Congressman Henry S. Reuss, August 20, 1971, printed in *Stream Channelization*, Hearings, Part 4, p. 2704.

[g]According to the SCS, reviewing agencies in thirty-eight states concurred in the classifications of all projects; agencies in four states concurred in some but not all classifications; and no concurrence was obtained in the remaining eight states. See U.S. Congress, Senate Committee on Public Works. *The Effect of Channelization on the Environment*, Hearings,

Table 5-4

**Comparison of Recommended Classifications of SCS Channeliza-
tion Projects, Summer 1971**

	BSFW[a]	SCS[b]
Group I	31.7%	41.2%
Group II	43.4%	44.3%
Group III	24.9%	14.5%
	100 %	100 %

[a]Bureau of Sports Fisheries and Wildlife, of the U.S. Fish and Wildlife Service in the Department of the Interior, N = 343 projects.

[b]N = 449 projects. SCS totals include only those for states in which the BSFW either participated in the review or supported the recommendations of the state fish and wildlife agency.

Source: U.S. Congress, House Committee on Government Operations, Subcommittee on Conservation and Natural Resources, *Stream Channelization*, Hearings, June 1971, Washington, D.C., 1971, Part 2, p. 486.

values of the two agencies' constituencies, farmers versus sportsmen, but since the Bureau was the agency best qualified by its jurisdiction and expertise to comment upon fishery and wildlife impacts, the lower estimates of the SCS suggest either inadequate understanding of the ecological functions of streams, or inadequate appreciation of the impacts of its activities upon other values of the resource.[h]

These data suggest that some project modifications, at least mitigation

July 1971, Serial 91-H24, Washington, D.C., 1971, p. 101. In contrast, the Bureau of Sport Fisheries and Wildlife claimed that agreement had been reached among the agencies in only ten states, that it had not even participated in thirteen states, and that in twenty-three other states "there was disagreement by the SCS in Bureau classification ranging from a few projects in some states to total disregard in others." See *Stream Channelization*, Hearings, Part 2, p. 486.

[h]Such underestimation was consistent, of course, with the limited definition of "significant environmental impacts" that was evident in the SCS' guidelines. See also end note 19.

The definition of "significant impacts" also appears to have differed from state to state even within the SCS organization. Thirteen State Conservationists, for instance, classified virtually all their projects in Group 1; six classified nearly all in Group 2; only one classified all in Group 3 (Virginia), and only five classified a total of more than three projects in Group 3 (Arkansas, Georgia, Illinois, Mississippi, and Virginia). At least two of the most controversial projects pending in the SCS—the Lost River Watershed in Indiana, and Chicod Creek in North Carolina—were both classified in Group 1, as was the Marshyhope Creek project (Delaware and Maryland) for which the BSFW had requested Group 3 classification. (See *The Effect of Channelization*, Hearings, pp. 101-07, and *Stream Channelization*, Hearings, Part 4, pp. 2209-41, 2719-24.) The Bureau also requested Group 3 classification for the Chicod Creek project, which later was to become the first SCS project enjoined by the courts for noncompliance with NEPA. (See *The Effect of Channelization*, Hearings, p. 111.) The attitude of the SCS exhibited here may help to explain the complaints of fish and wildlife officials that the SCS listened to their comments but rarely acted upon them. (See, for instance, *Stream Channelization*, Hearings, pp. 169, 183, 213, 412, 1287, 1373-75.)

Table 5-5
Causes of SCS Watershed Project Modifications Reported in Response to NEPA, as of October 1971

	% Cancelled (n = 0) (7)		% Postponed (n = 44) (48)		% Significantly Changed (n = 22) (23)	
Cause of Modification						
Internal re-evaluation only	—	(14)	18	(10)	39	(9)
Internal re-evaluation plus external pressures[a]	—	(43)	4	(35)	—	(56)
Internal re-evaluation plus federal agency comments	—		18		4	
Internal re-evaluation plus external pressures plus federal agency comments	—		2		17	
External pressures only	—	(43)	9	(38)	—	(17)
Federal agency comments only	—		3		—	(9)
External pressures plus federal agency comments	—		25		9	
Other	—		—	(2)	—	
No report	—		21	(15)	31	(9)
			100%		100%	

Note: Number of State Conservationists reporting = 38, or 76% of the total. Comparable figures from the Corps are noted in parenthesis, from Table 4–6.
[a] As in Table 4–6, "external pressures" refer to pressures from outside the federal administrative structure, including three subcategories: comments of state and local agencies, public controversies, and judicial decisions.
Source: October 1971 Survey.

measures, would be added to between 200 and 300 proposed projects as a result of the 108 review. This suggestion should be interpreted with caution, however, since according to the SCS some Group 3 classifications were for economic rather than environmental reasons.

Table 5-5 shows the reasons given for the project modifications, and Table 5-6 shows the frequencies with which these reasons were mentioned. Several interesting patterns are evident here. First, internal re-evaluation dominated nearly all other factors mentioned, with one significant exception: the comments of other federal agencies, in combination with other factors, were the most frequently mentioned reason for NEPA-related postponements. Such comments by themselves, however, played a negligible role. Second, the influence of controversy and judicial decisions was also minimal, either alone *or* in combination with other factors—which is a striking contrast to the Corps experience. External pressures collectively did play an important role, but in most SCS cases these pressures consisted of adverse comments of state and local

Table 5–6

Frequency of Mention, Causes of Reported Modifications of SCS Watershed Projects in Response to NEPA, as of October 1971

	% Cancelled (n = 0) (7)		% Postponed (n = 44) (48)		% Significantly Changed (n = 22) (23)	
Cause of Modification						
Internal re-evaluation	—	(57)	43	(44)	61	(65)
Federal agency comments	—	(–)	48	(13)	27	(30)
State/local comments	—	(29)	34	(33)	22	(61)
Public controversy	—	(43)	11	(50)	9	(43)
Judicial decisions	—	(29)	—	(25)	—	(4)
Other	—	(14)	—	(2)	—	(–)

Note: Numbers of State Conservationists reporting = 38, or 76% of the total. Comparable figures from the Corps are noted in parenthesis, from Table 4–7. Since several causes were sometimes mentioned, columns do not sum to 100%.
Source: October 1971 Survey.

agencies rather than public controversy. Judicial decisions did not play any role, since the SCS did not experience any until 1972. Third, and finally, all factors other than internal re-evaluation were less effective, and in two out of three cases significantly less effective, in achieving significant changes than in achieving postponements.

In short, the principal reasons for NEPA-related modifications of SCS projects appear to have been internal re-evaluation and adverse comments of federal, state, and local agencies, not judicial review or even public controversy. This evidence differs in several respects from the responses given by Corps officials, as will be discussed further below.

These conclusions must be advanced cautiously, since the absence of data on the causes of nearly one-third of the SCS' "significant changes" leaves an important uncertainty in the data. Some possibilities can be inferred: five of these seven projects, for instance, had not yet been authorized, which suggests internal re-evaluation as a likely cause. The same five, however, were also located in one of the states in which SCS projects were under the most strenuous external pressures, including not only opposition from other federal and state agencies but also public controversy and the first lawsuit to be filed against the SCS under NEPA. While internal re-evaluation and external pressures therefore seem to be most likely causes, however, the survey data themselves leave this question uncertain.

As in the case of the Corps, too, twice as many projects were merely postponed as were significantly changed, and the ultimate disposition of these projects, as well as others postponed for re-evaluation under *Watersheds Memorandum 108*, remained uncertain. Re-evaluation might well lead to further revisions to make them less damaging to the environment, and several "probable" revisions of this nature were mentioned in the survey responses, but there was no certainty that this would happen, and the SCS itself stated that many projects were classified in Group 3 for reasons other than their environmental impacts.[i] Moreover, revisions might well be limited to particularly *controversial* projects, or projects from which the SCS might have other reasons for wishing to withdraw its support, rather than extending to all projects whose objectively identifiable impacts were of comparable severity.

Budget, Staff, and Structure

In discussing the Corps, we noted that budget increases had been requested in most general investigations and in a few authorized projects, that some districts had requested new staff members to carry out responsibilities arising from NEPA, and that many districts (though not all) had established new organizational units at the district level—environmental resource "sections" or "branches" —for the same purpose. We further noted that while the numbers of new personnel requested fell far short of unofficial estimates of the numbers needed to discharge its NEPA obligations adequately, budgets and personnel *were* being increased as well as reallocated in order to begin meeting these new environmental responsibilities.

In contrast to the Corps, the Soil Conservation Service requested *no* increases in its staff or budget to fulfill responsibilities arising under NEPA, and it made no formal changes in its administrative structure at the field level. The failure to request staff or budget increases appears to have resulted from a policy position of the Department of Agriculture as a whole rather than strictly from the SCS, since SCS field offices almost certainly wanted and could have used additional staff. SCS witnesses testified that just the administrative costs associated with NEPA had totalled roughly $93,000 in fiscal year 1971, or 2 percent of its total watershed planning budget,[81] but despite the stated willingness of Congressmen to entertain requests for additional funds for these purposes, the policy of the U.S.D.A. was to absorb all such costs within its existing budget.[82]

The effect of this policy on U.S.D.A. programs was to place any new NEPA-related activities in direct competition with existing priorities. Under fixed constraints on budget and staff, any resources devoted to these new activities would have to be reallocated directly away from existing ones rather than being cushioned by new additions. In short, the Corps used increases in funding and personnel to reduce potential conflicts between environmental analysis and more traditional activities; but the Department of Agriculture, by holding re-

---

[i]In all, 43 projects and portions of 23 more were classified in Group 3 by the SCS; of these only 9 were reported postponed in the survey responses, and only 6 were reported significantly revised. See Table 5-3.

sources constant, *maximized* these conflicts. A likely and possibly intentional result was to minimize the amount of change in priorities that might take place in response to the new law.

At the Washington level, the SCS indicated in February 1971 its intention to establish a "watersheds environmental quality committee," whose charge would include reviewing and recommending "appropriate changes in policy and in planning and design criteria to insure the preservation and enhancement of environmental values in watershed projects."[83] As of September 1973, however, the committee still had not been established, and in response to congressional inquiries, the SCS Administrator asserted that conditions had "changed significantly" since the committee was proposed and that he did not want to "create another level of review which requires still more time and overlaps activities and reviews already being carried out," in view of the fact that the Congress and the Council on Environmental Quality were also re-examining the environmental impacts of stream channelization.[84]

This explanation is not convincing, since if the SCS *wanted* to take fuller account of the environmental impacts of its actions, it needed a focal point *within* its own organization to make recommendations for change, irrespective of the findings of the Congress or the CEQ. It seems more likely that the SCS simply did not want to give greater weight to environmental considerations, either in the projects themselves or in the organizational structure through which such projects would be developed and reviewed.

As a result, the SCS did not institutionalize environmental policy in identifiable units of its organizational structure; rather, it *avoided* the creation of such units, thus sustaining the existing flows of both power and ideas within its organization against any new internal coalescence of environmental advocates. In this respect, like others mentioned earlier, the response of the SCS differed from that of the Corps, which created identifiable units at every level of its organizational structure to perform environmental analyses and reviews and recommend changes.

Discussion

In reflecting upon the response of the Soil Conservation Service to NEPA, it is useful to refer briefly back to the language and legislative history of the act itself, and to the purposes stated for it by its authors.

The principal concern of NEPA's authors was the human environment as a whole, and particularly the life-support systems upon which human life and welfare depend. Their principal innovation to express that concern was a series of so-called "action-forcing provisions," which were intended to insure that all federal officials would realize the implications of their proposed actions upon that environment before taking action. Moreover, they sought to insure careful advance review of such actions, by requiring that statements of the consequences be circulated to all other appropriate agencies for comment and be made available to political leaders and interested citizens.

NEPA was *not* intended principally as an instrument of pollution control, nor of fish and wildlife conservation, nor of any other single "environmental protection mission" such as soil conservation. It sought, rather, an overt accounting and objective evaluation of *all* such consequences: a new philosophy of public administration, in effect, to replace the traditional practice of project justification by reference to a single narrowly defined mission. The human environment was too important, and too complex in its interdependencies, to be managed by fragmented pursuit of subgoals. "Disjointed incrementalism" must yield to greater integration and coordination of federal activities, if the quality of the human environment were to be sustained.[85]

During the first two years after NEPA's enactment, the SCS apparently either ignored, or at least failed to recognize these underlying purposes of NEPA. In each dimension of its response discussed above, it basically evaded the "action-forcing procedures" that were intended to insure achievement of those purposes.[86] It did not broaden either its mission-oriented horizons or its criteria for water project evaluation. It did not appreciably broaden the range of impact variables, or environmental conditions, that should be considered in weighing the relative merits of alternative proposals. It avoided preparation of NEPA's environmental impact statements wherever possible, by applying the law only selectively to projects already under consideration as well as by defining the impacts of others as "insignificant," and by modifying still others until compromises were reached at least with objections of fish and wildlife agencies. Finally, it did not even attempt to create a more overt and objective basis for decision among its water projects, but retained instead its traditional justificatory documentation and client-centered orientation.

In short, the SCS treated NEPA simply as a new tactical attack on one category of its activities—stream channelization—by an old "special interest" foe, the fish and wildlife lobby. In so doing, it failed to address the relationship between its activities and the more fundamental concerns reflected in the law; and it failed even to implement the procedural conditions that might permit those concerns to surface in an incremental fashion, in the absence of some further stimulus.

The preparation and review of environmental statements was potentially an educative process, if taken seriously by the agency's headquarters. Through this process, agencies that accepted the opportunity could foster new approaches to project analysis and evaluation, which would be better adapted to the complexities of the present human environment than traditional procedures for project justification. The prerequisite for such innovation, however, was some form of encouragement, or reward, or at least permissiveness on the part of agency headquarters. In the case of the Corps, for instance, a relatively small cluster of policy staff members—in the Chief's Office, in the Office of the Secretary of the Army, and in the Corps' Institute for Water Resources—shaped the agency's paper policies concerning NEPA's implementation; yet once these policies were on paper, they provided at least an opportunity for innovators if not a mandate for everyone. This prerequisite seems to have been lacking in the Soil Conservation Service, or at least in its Watersheds Planning Division.

1972-1974

In the case of the Corps, events between 1972 and 1974 tended to reinforce the general directions of change that had been adopted (at least rhetorically, in official statements by agency headquarters) during 1970 and 1971; and NEPA seemed to have contributed to a climate in which new programmatic directions were being developed, though the extent and longevity of these changes were not yet clear. The overall pattern thus appeared to reflect gradual evolution at the headquarters level, accompanied by some signs of innovation and priority shifts in the more responsive districts, with relatively little change in others.

In the case of the Soil Conservation Service, a similar extension of the analysis reveals evidence on the one hand of more rapid evolution than previously in its official guidelines, but also evidence of more rigid constraints on broader programmatic changes.

External Forces

The year 1972 opened with several important changes in the political environment of the SCS watersheds program. As in the previous period, however, these changes were not all in the same direction; and the actions that followed were similarly mixed.

The initial change was the Soil Conservation Service's first defeat and injunction in a NEPA lawsuit, in the Chicod Creek case mentioned above. This complaint had been filed in November 1971, and the first court hearing on it was held January 5, 1972; on March 16 the court enjoined any further actions on the project until completion of an environmental impact statement, and gave the SCS thirty days to prepare such a statement.[87] The SCS complied, and submitted a draft statement on April 14 and a final statement on July 13, but the injunction was continued while the court sought to determine the adequacy of the statement. On February 3, 1973, it ruled that the statement was inadequate on six items. As of the middle of 1973, this case as well as two others alleging failure of the SCS to comply with NEPA were still awaiting final resolution by the courts.[88] In short, beginning in 1972, the SCS was confronted for the first time with the kind of legal pressure, though on a much more limited scale, that had been applied to the Corps since 1970.

A second change was the gradual evolution of the NEPA guidelines of both the Council on Environmental Quality and the Department of Agriculture. The Council issued a "memorandum" that amounted to guideline revisions in May 1972, and issued draft and final revised guidelines respectively in May and August 1973; the U.S.D.A. issued guideline revisions in early 1972 and again in November 1973 (draft) and May 1974 (final).[89] To the extent that the SCS was waiting for its parent department to act rather than taking the lead itself, these revisions may have provided the policy framework for which it had been waiting, within which it could establish its own guidelines in greater detail.

A third change was the enactment in August 1972 of the Rural Development Act of 1972, Public Law 92–419. The stated purpose of this Act was "to provide for improving the economy and living conditions in rural America," and one of its principal methods for accomplishing this purpose was to amend the Small Watersheds and Flood Prevention Act of 1954 (Public Law 566).

Section 201(b) of this Act allowed federal assistance for projects of *land* conservation and utilization as well as water. Section 201(d) permitted sponsoring organizations to use *federal grants from other programs*, rather than strictly local funds, to secure necessary lands, easements, and rights-of-way—a change that might both increase and effectively conceal the federal costs of projects so financed. Section 201(e) expanded the range of federal cost sharing to include fish and wildlife development, recreational development, groundwater recharge, water quality management (stream-flow regulation only, with review by the EPA), and land conservation and utilization. Finally, Section 201(f) permitted federal payment of 50 percent of the cost of water storage for present municipal and industrial use and permitted loans for such future use that would be both free of repayment until the water was first used and free of interest for the same period or for ten years, whichever came first.

The overall effect of these amendments was to broaden significantly the range of purposes toward which P.L. 566 projects could be directed and to increase sharply the permissible federal share of the costs of such projects. By implication, the SCS was thus offered a major expansion of its mission, in terms both of authorized project purposes and of federal cost-sharing provisions.

The Rural Development Act also included several provisions that potentially affected the SCS Watersheds Program, though they were not directly applicable to it. Section 302 directed the Secretary of Agriculture to carry out a new program of land inventory and monitoring for community development, guidance of urban growth, agricultural protection, and environmental quality management. Section 603 directed him to promote the purpose of "rural development" as well as agriculture and to "provide leadership and coordination within the executive branch" on this subject. Finally, Section 605 permitted the Secretary to enter into long-term (ten-year) contracts with agricultural producers for agricultural conservation plans, to be approved by the local soil and water conservation districts.[j] This last provision established what was in effect a nationwide version of the SCS' Great Plains Conservation Program, permitting the Secretary to enter into long-term contracts (ten years) of federal cost sharing with agricultural producers to carry out self-developed agricultural conservation plans.

Several reports and position papers on matters related to SCS and the environment also appeared between 1972 and 1974, each of which contributed to the visibility of the SCS watersheds program though none was a major political force in itself. A contract study of stream channelization, prepared by Arthur D. Little, Inc., for the Council on Environmental Quality, was published in draft form in March 1972, but it was subjected to such intense criticism that it was sent back for extensive reworking and reappeared in considerably revised form in March 1972.[90] As of 1974, no apparent use had been made of it.[91] A detailed and caustic critique of the SCS' channelization review under *Watersheds Memorandum 108* was also issued by the Bureau of Sport Fisheries and Wildlife in April 1972,[92] and in November 1972, a report by the General Accounting Office concerning the implementation of NEPA included criticism of impact statements on channelization projects as well as on other sorts of actions.[93]

In June 1973, the report of the National Water Commission was released, which included criticism of channelization's environmental consequences and downstream effects,[94] and in September 1973, the Reuss subcommittee issued its report on channelization that summarized the conclusions and recommendations that had emerged both from its 1971 hearings on the subject (discussed above) and from a brief sequel in March 1973.[95] This latter report was strongly critical of the "overuse" of channelization by federal agencies and of their accompanying failure to adequately consider its adverse environmental effects. The report also recommended that the SCS involve the public more fully in the early stages of its watershed planning process, that the SCS publish in the *Federal Register* all of its operating principles that had the force of regulations, as well as its more general policies concerning water resource development, and that the agency comply explicitly with the impact statement requirements established by NEPA rather than evading them by mitigating certain impacts and then declaring the others "insignificant."

Finally, in September 1973 President Nixon issued the *Principles and Standards for Planning Water and Related Land Resources*, which had been prepared by the Water Resource Council (discussed in the preceding chapter, but applicable to the SCS as well),[96] and the Congress enacted the Water Resource Development Act of 1973, also discussed above, which directed the SCS as well as the Corps to give full consideration to *nonstructural* alternatives.[97]

---

[j]Other sections of the law dealt with rural industrial development, subsidies for rural water and waste disposal planning, agricultural credit, rural development research, and other topics.

One further change in the SCS environment was the retirement in 1972 of Hollis Williams, SCS Deputy Administrator for Watersheds, and his replacement by William Davey. Both men were SCS professionals of long standing, but as his testimony (quoted earlier) indicated, Williams as an individual was outspokenly defensive of the agency's traditional practices against any criticism by environmentalists or fish and wildlife interests. Davey might be expected to have both less personal inclination and, as a new Deputy Administrator, less political power to emulate such an aggressive stance.

SCS Policies and Regulations

The SCS' guidelines and procedures were significantly improved between 1972 and 1974, and these improvements suggested a major shift in that agency's official posture towards the procedures established by NEPA. Taken as a whole, SCS policies prior to 1972 reflected a desire to avoid involvement with NEPA as much as possible, but SCS policies from 1972 to 1974 displayed an apparent decision to embrace and apply it, at least insofar as its procedural requirements were concerned. It is significant that in statements made to congressional investigators during 1974, the Council on Environmental Quality identified the Corps' impact statements as among the *best* produced by federal agencies; but it identified those of the SCS as among the *most improved*.[98]

The NEPA-related directives during this period included at least three "Advisory Watersheds Memoranda" concerning detailed statements for previously authorized projects, and one concerning such statements for watersheds projects generally; two revisions of the *Watershed Protection Handbook*; five "Environment Memoranda," concerning particular points of policy and procedure; revised guidelines for the preparation of environmental impact statements; and a codification in the *Federal Register* of the agency's policies and procedures for water resource programs, including incorporation of environmental considerations.[99]

In early 1972, the Secretary of Agriculture revised the departmental guidelines for implementation of NEPA, which event probably provided some of the impetus for the changes in SCS guidelines that followed.[100] Like previous departmental policies, the revision was quite general, and on many topics it simply relayed the language of the CEQ guidelines and recent judicial decisions verbatim. It was more detailed than the earlier version, however, and included more specific examples of "major actions" and "significant effects" in an appendix; it directed that "all reasonable alternatives must be thoroughly studied and discussed" and that benefit-cost analyses be attached to the impact statements; and it established a policy that the detailed statements be used "as a significant part of procedures to monitor, evaluate and control activities for the protection and enhancement of the quality of the environment on a continuing basis."[101]

Shortly after this departmental revision, the SCS issued a notice to its field offices that directed sweeping changes in the sections of its *Watershed Protection Handbook* that dealt with preparation of environmental statements.[102] Many of these changes stressed the integration of environmental analysis with other analyses and decision points. For instance, *Notice 1-19* directed that the collection of environmental data commence with the preparation of the application and that preapplication assistance include baseline inventory as well as rough evaluation of impacts. It also modified the flow of project documentation to insure that the environmental statement would be reviewed concurrently with the proposed work plan, and it modified the work plan content itself so as to permit efficient preparation of both it and the impact statement. Finally, it directed that cumulative and regional impacts, as well as impacts on sites of historical, archaeological, or scientific interest, be explicitly considered in the impact statement.

Additional changes were directed by three advisory memoranda during 1972. The first of these, issued in April, directed that draft and final detailed statements be prepared and signed by the State Conservationists, though they were still to be circulated by the Washington office (rather than the states) unless otherwise authorized by the SCS Administrator. A revision of this memorandum, two months later, directed that the State Conservationists themselves circulate the statements for review, as soon as they were notified that the official copy had been transmitted to the Council on Environmental Quality, and it contained more detailed emphasis on discussion of cumulative impacts of projects.[103] A second revision, in September 1972, continued the decentralization of impact statement preparation by delegating prepublication review to the Regional Technical Service Centers rather than the Washington office and by directing the State Conservationists rather than Washington to prepare the "notice of availability" of the impact statements for publication in the *Federal Register*.[104]

Each of these changes in itself was minor. Taken together, however, they indicated the agency's gradual relinquishment of closely centralized control over the EIS process, thereby delegating responsibility for their preparation and defense more and more from Washington to the technical and field staff. These changes eliminated one of the major differences between SCS practice and that of the Corps, which from the start had delegated EIS responsibility to its District Engineers.

During the latter half of 1972, the SCS Administrator also issued at least five "Environment Memoranda" dealing with particular issues of policy and procedure; some specifically related to NEPA procedures, and others dealing with more general issues of environmental policy. *Environment Memorandum-9* required announcement of all draft and final impact statements in the *Federal Register. EM-10* required that all substantive letters of comment on draft statements be appended to the final statement and that such letters concerning statements already submitted be made available also. *EM-12* established detailed guidelines for SCS review of other agencies' impact statements, including twelve major criteria defining the scope of SCS jurisdiction and expertise with regard to other agencies' actions,[105] and *EM-13* established an SCS policy of recognizing dedicated natural areas as a land use, thus permitting SCS technical assistance in the location and maintenance of such areas.[106]

In June 1973, a particularly significant document was circulated to all State Conservationists and Regional Technical Service Centers. Identified as *Advisory WS-26*, this memorandum transmitted a nine-page list of critical comments and suggested improvements in SCS environmental statements for watershed projects.[107] The memorandum also enclosed portions of several recently prepared impact statements that "are not considered perfect but *do* reflect some desirable qualities that may be useful to you in the preparation of your own statements."[108]

This memorandum was probably the most detailed and informative guidance that the SCS had yet issued to its staff concerning the preparation of impact statements. First, it identified deficiencies, and made recommendations for correcting them, rather than merely stating general principles, and it included examples. Second, it included significant new requirements concerning statement content. Among other things, it required discussion of ecological habitat and functions rather than merely species lists; it required documentation of all factual claims, by footnote or bibliography; it provided more detailed guidance concerning the range of causative actions whose impacts should be considered, including operation and maintenance measures; and it specified a broader and more detailed range of impacts to be discussed, including impacts on water quality and six other "most common" categories of impacts. Third, it required that potential adverse effects even of land treatment measures be discussed, in contrast to previous assumptions that land treatment was inherently beneficial, and while it gave particular attention to the section on "alternatives," it noted that "this section is still giving as much trouble as any section in the environmental statements being received."[109] Finally, it included illustrative lists of the sorts of probable impacts that should be discussed (18 associated with land treatment measures, and 21 associated with structural measures), and it attached portions of three environmental statements as illustrations.

The greatest value of *Advisory WS-26* was that it provided feedback and examples, rather than merely general principles and exhortation. In this respect it was similar to the Corps' circular dated September 1970, which also included a critique of the detailed statements submitted up to that time as a basis for further guidance. Two important differences, of course, were that the SCS memorandum was not issued until nearly three years later and that it came only after many of the criticisms had been levelled at SCS statements repeatedly by sources outside the agency, including the Council on Environmental Quality.

One possible impetus for the preparation of this memorandum was the recent release of proposed revisions in the guidelines of the Council on Environmental Quality, which had been published in the *Federal Register* in draft form in May 1973. As Chapter 3 indicated, these revisions were quite extensive. They were far more detailed than previous versions, and they hinted at a growing and more explicit concern on the part of the Council that the substance as well as the procedures of NEPA be implemented. On the other hand, the Council had made detailed suggestions for improvement in SCS impact statements two years previously, yet SCS had not adopted these suggestions at the time.[110] A more likely explanation, therefore, was the March 1975 *Chicod Creek* decision, which had ruled that SCS impact statement inadequate in at least half a dozen particulars.

Major SCS guideline revisions were issued in June 1974, and these included several changes in focus and emphasis, as well as codifying changes that had been made previously by memoranda discussed above.[111] As a whole, these guidelines required a process that was far more objective, more detailed, and more committed to the spirit of NEPA than earlier ones.

At the outset, they articulated the mission of the SCS in a new and broader form, which gave equal weight to three related goals:

Quality in the natural resource base·for sustained use;
Quality in environment to provide attractive, convenient and satisfying places to
    live, work, and play; and
Quality in the standard of living based on community improvement and ade-
    quate income.[112]

Consistent with this emphasis, they directed that environmental values receive the same consideration as economic, social, and engineering values and that SCS assistance be withheld from applicants who failed to meet NEPA requirements. The impact statement was expanded to include impacts on social and economic factors and on minority groups and civil rights goals, as well as on the physical and biological environment.

Second, more explicit guidance was provided concerning the types of actions that would and would not normally require preparation of detailed statements and concerning the range of alternatives that should be considered and discussed.[113] Considerable new thought was evident in the guidelines for discussing "tradeoffs between short term effects and long term productivity"; this section was now to include discussion of land use trends, cumulative impacts, long-term resource capabilities, and the relationship between the time horizon of the proposed action and the trends in resource problems and needs.[114] The treatment of this particular section of the EIS had never been clearly articulated by the CEQ, and the SCS definition of it appears to have been a significant innovation in its interpretation.

Third, the 1974 revisions also indicated a policy change from the passive posture of providing information, to the active solicitation of public involvement in the agency's planning process. Where earlier guidelines had left citizen participation programs to project sponsors, with no active role for the SCS itself, the 1974 revisions devoted an entire section to public involvement, and this section included identification of four different categories of "publics that should be actively sought out by the SCS."[115] The guidelines directed that the *State Conservationist* identify and maintain a list of these publics, rather than just the applicant, and that he document the process of public involvement in the development of each proposal, including detailed notes of all discussions and meetings ("in some cases, verbatim transcripts may be appropriate").[116] Further, they specified that *joint* hearings with the applicants be held if necessary, depending upon local interest, controversy, magnitude of the proposed action, and applicable laws.

The motivation for this change may well have been defensive, much as the Corps three years earlier sought public involvement in order to deal with objectives early rather than at the end. Whatever the motivation, however, the effect was to increase opportunities for interjection of information, alternatives, and preferences from a wider range of constituencies at earlier stages of planning. This was a valuable change, and one fully consistent with the spirit of NEPA.

The SCS issued three further instructions on environment-related matters during 1974. The first was a supplement or "Subpart B" to the June guidelines, issued in September, which provided additional guidance concerning impacts on archaeological and historic sites, endangered species, scenic beauty, and co-ordination with the Environmental Protection Agency. These guidelines were to be consolidated with the June revisions later in 1974 and republished at that time as an Environment Memorandum (with corresponding changes in the *Watershed Protection Handbook*).[117]

Second, the SCS issued for trial use a new *Environmental Assessment Procedure*, which its staff had been developing during the previous year.[118] This *Procedure* included several useful features, particularly the definition of clear indicators and measurement units for each category of impacts, and a format that permitted direct comparison of the impacts of all alternatives on each indicator in turn. It thus provided a major improvement in the SCS' display of impact predictions, and a relatively simple procedure for aggregating those predictions (weighting by specialists and by multi-disciplinary teams).[k]

Third, the SCS issued procedures for implementation of the *Principles and Standards for Planning Water and Related Land Resources*, which had been prepared by the Water Resource Council and signed by the President the preceding September.[119] These procedures represented a major revision of the SCS' project evaluation process, integrating the dual objectives of national economic development and enhancement of environmental quality, and displaying also the effects of each proposal on regional development and social well being. They incorporated the agency's recent emphasis on public involvement; they established

---

[k]After impacts of each alternative on a resource use had been predicted, a specialist and then a multi-disciplinary team would rank the significance of each impact on a five-point scale (unsuited, poor, fair or neutral, good, excellent), and a summary sheet of these rankings on all resource uses would be prepared as an aid in decision making.

"environmental quality enhancement" as a co-equal objective with economic development; and they required that the alternatives include at least one that "emphasized the environmental quality objective."

The intended relationship between these procedures and the *EAP* was not clearly stated, but the two appeared to be complimentary rather than redundant. The *EAP* was descriptive and predictive of the effects that would occur under each alternative; the *Planning Procedures*, in contrast, established an evaluative process for classifying these effects as benefits or costs to each of the two objectives (economic development and environmental quality).

In summary, then, SCS guidelines from 1972 on showed significant and steady improvement, to the extent that by 1975 they were in most respects equivalent to those of the Corps. One qualification that must be added to this assessment, however, is that the Soil Conservation Service never fully abandoned its "case-by-case" approach to projects authorized prior to the enactment of NEPA. The 1974 guideline revisions did direct that, as a general rule, impact statements should be prepared for all projects requiring congressional approval, controversy, or stream channel modification, and they required that "negative declarations" be published in all cases in which impact statements were not prepared, briefly explaining the basis for the decision.[120] In reviewing previously authorized projects, however, they allowed each State Conservationist to make his own judgment of these factors, weighing them against construction costs, degree of completion of planned work, local financial commitments, degree of public involvement, and how much consideration had already been given to environmental issues during project formulation.[121]

Moreover, the SCS maintained this policy even in the face of the sort of legal pressure that led the Corps to near-universal application of NEPA. Faced with the Chicod Creek decision in 1972, it sought to confine the decision to the Chicod case instead of taking it as a precedent for other similar projects. By mid-1974, in its testimony before the House Appropriations Committee, it was still claiming to be "waiting for the courts to decide" concerning the "retroactivity" of NEPA to such projects, while blaming NEPA for consequent delays in these projects.[122]

The results of this process, according to SCS testimony in mid-1974, were that 50 impact statements were completed or underway for previously authorized projects; 67 more *would* be prepared; 342 projects would receive "negative declarations"; and 57 cases were still under discussion. The stated criterion in these cases was the existence of controversy, rather than the magnitude of environmental impacts *per se.*[123]

Environmental Analysis and Evaluation

Along with the evolution of its policy guidelines, several changes were also evident during the period 1972 to 1974 in the SCS' commitment to environmental analysis of its proposed actions. It is important to recognize that like the guidelines, none of these changes were themselves substantive, and they therefore might or might not lead to outcomes that were more supportive of "environmental policy" than the results that would otherwise have occurred. But to the extent that the procedures called for by NEPA *were* a valid means to its environmental policy ends, these changes amounted to movement, however modest, in the direction of those ends.

One such change has already been mentioned above; namely, the SCS' decision to take upon itself the responsibility for identifying and communicating with groups affected by its actions. Several others should also be noted, however.

First, in 1973 the SCS began contracting out to private firms for environmental analyses on a far greater scale than in previous years. The Corps had been contracting out on a major scale ever since NEPA's enactment, but prior to 1973 the SCS had let only about one-half million dollars' worth of contracts per year for such analyses. During Fiscal Year 1974, however, it reportedly let 186 contracts totalling $2.4 million—nearly a five-fold increase over its previous level.[124] Since the SCS had lacked the manpower to perform many detailed environmental analyses itself, this increase in contracting suggested (though it did not guarantee) a significant improvement in the numbers and detail of such analyses on SCS projects.[1]

Second, in 1973 the SCS also inaugurated a series of ecological training programs, which were intended to "update" the thinking of many of the agency's top program staff on such topics as ecological principles, environmental law, and procedures for environmental impact assessment.[125] The first "round" of this program was a series of three three-week short courses, each involving approximately thirty-five "top program people" from around the country (such as watershed planning party leaders), all of whom had at least ten years' experience. The second round was another series of three sessions, in this case one-week seminars for top-level policy officials: State Conservationists, directors of Regional Technical Service Centers, Washington-level division chiefs, and other "responsible federal officials" within the meaning of NEPA. The third round was a series of three more sessions, each lasting two weeks, for persons in positions of staff leadership in each SCS state office, and SCS officials hoped to run a fourth round in the future if the budget permitted it.

---

[1]The practice of contracting out for environmental analyses has mixed implications as an indicator of response to NEPA. It might permit more detailed and more technically proficient analyses, and perhaps more comprehensive and systematic collection of data than the agency's staff would have time for, and it might thus improve the factual basis of the environmental statement. This was not necessarily true, however, and the quality of many contract studies has been far less than one might hope for. At the same time, delegation of the environmental analysis to a contractor might diminish the effectiveness of NEPA's requirements as an educational device within the agency, removing from its staff the necessity of confronting, and learning to understand and adequately balance, the environmental issues themselves.

In all, these sessions were expected to involve over 400 SCS personnel, most of them persons with significant responsibility in the organization. While such training sessions could not be expected to provide panaceas in the face of deeply ingrained personal and professional values and political forces, they could have great benefit in furthering the educative and "consciousness-raising" purposes of NEPA. They also provide one additional indicator of the SCS' decision during this period to take those purposes seriously.

Third, and most suggestive of possible substantive changes, SCS testimony during this period repeatedly stressed the criterion of *viability* as its ultimate basis for setting priorities among proposed actions. The clearest statement of this principle was given by the SCS Administrator in response to congressional questioning during 1973, in which he stated that priority would be given to projects that "would seem to be most certain to move ahead in an expeditious manner":

Not necessarily . . . the benefit-cost ratio. More on the likelihood of a viable plan being developed, there being no holdup on some particularly important environmental issue, with the local people in a position to acquire the land easements and rights of way . . . . the ones that have the least difficulty, and that would be most certain to result in a plan that could actually begin construction.[126]

These statements suggest that as in the earlier case of the Corps, the use of the courts and direct pressures by groups outside the agency's clientele, as a credible threat to delay if not halt the agency's actions, was a key variable in the agency's decision to apply NEPA's procedures to activities in progress. Corroboration for this suggestion may be found in other parts of his testimony, in which he referred repeatedly to the current broadening of public involvement in SCS watershed planning and to the effects of this involvement:

Increased public concern and awareness is resulting in plans which are responsive to a wider range of interests . . . In order to avoid long extensive costly delays by having projects in litigation, it has seemed prudent to us and to local people in many cases to try to develop the environmental statement and to try to make the adjustment rather than experience this delay . . . . So I think it is incumbent upon us to take all steps that we possibly can to resolve these issues with all groups.[127]

The new commitment to apply environmental analysis and public involvement procedures did not necessarily guarantee changes in proposed actions, of course: the Chicod Creek project, for instance, had not been significantly modified by mid-1974 despite the application of NEPA's procedures and two years of litigation. Moreover, giving priority to *noncontroversial* projects did not necessarily mean building *better* projects—it might simply mean building projects in areas where environmentalist opposition was less effective. But whatever these results, the SCS' policy change did suggest both modest effectiveness on the part of intervenors in SCS project planning and the failure of the agency's attempts to "stonewall" against the application of NEPA's procedural requirements to its previously approved projects.

Watersheds Program

While the SCS' guidelines and procedures continued to evolve, however, its watersheds program as a whole showed less evidence of change and some signs that major changes in mission and priorities would not be permitted.

The period 1972 through 1974 included two record-breaking years for the volume of watershed project construction under the Public Law 566 program. Fiscal Year 1972, following President Nixon's 1971 Agriculture Message, included fifty new construction starts rather than the usual thirty-five, and was described by SCS official as "the most productive year to date for the watersheds construction program."[128] Fiscal Year 1974 included forty project completions, which made it in SCS' words "the most productive installation year in the history of the watersheds program,"[129] and Fiscal Year 1975 was to include forty-five new construction starts.[130] Fiscal Year 1972 also included forty new planning authorizations, and Fiscal Years 1973 and 1974 included sixty each.[131] The testimony of SCS witnesses at the appropriations hearings repeatedly stated their pride at setting such a record of construction during an era of environmental concern and their commitment to continued output of watershed projects while meeting the procedural requirements of NEPA.[132]

The mention of this burst of activity is not intended to imply that all such projects should have been stopped because of conflicts with NEPA, but only that production was accelerated on precisely that group of projects—those authorized before NEPA's enactment but not yet completed—that might be most vulnerable to questions about their consistency with that law's purposes. Supporters of the P.L. 566 program would probably emphasize that many of these projects were in fact environmentally beneficial and that speeding their installation was thus a positive contribution to NEPA's substantive implementation. This may have been true in many cases, but the purpose of NEPA's procedures was to insure that such judgments of the environmental merits of these projects were based upon objective analysis and documentation rather than merely traditional assumptions, and such analysis could hardly be served by accelerating their installation. It seems likely that the agency's congressional guardians were more interested in pushing these older projects through before they were challenged, and in proving that they themselves were still a more powerful political force than the "environmentalist" lobby, than they were in re-examining such projects from the perspective of NEPA.

The role of the House Subcommittee on Agriculture Appropriations was particularly significant here, since it has both the sole power to initiate the SCS' appropriations legislation and a long history of protective oversight of that agency's activities. The subcommittee's long-time chairman, Representative Jamie Whitten, was an author of the Small Watersheds Act of 1954 (Public Law 566); he was also one of the handful of Congressmen to vote against enactment of NEPA. In 1970, when the Council on Environmental Quality and the Environmental Protection Agency were created, he expanded the jurisdiction of his Subcommittee on Agriculture Appropriations to include the Environmental and Consumer Protection budgets as well. As a result, he acquired not only the power to foster and promote agricultural programs, but also the power to control or at least intimidate the agencies that might seek modification of those programs, and he used both these powers visibly and effectively.[133]

Not only did construction continue and increase during this period in the SCS's traditional watershed activities, however, but certain changes in priorities that should have occurred did not. Numerous changes in the SCS' mandate were authorized by the Rural Development Act of 1972 and the Water Resource Development Act of 1973, many of which were environmentally beneficial in their impact, but virtually none of these changes had been implemented by the end of 1974. The failure of these changes to occur provides further insights into the political forces that sustained continuation of the SCS' traditional activities against potential modifications.

The Rural Development Act of 1972 authorized a series of significant changes in the activities of the Soil Conservation Service as well as in those of other agencies of the Department of Agriculture. Among other things, it authorized a new program of land use inventory and monitoring, and it permitted federal cost sharing in SCS P.L. 566 projects for water quality management, fish and wildlife and recreational development, groundwater recharge, municipal water supply, and land conservation, and permitted the use of other federal funds for land rights that were previously strictly local expenses. It also authorized a nationwide program of long-term contracts with individual farmers for agricultural conservation activities, after the fashion of the SCS' Great Plains Conservation Program.

Any of these activities could have become important new priorities for the Soil Conservation Service, and several could serve the same function for the SCS watersheds program that the Urban Studies Program served for the Corps; namely, to permit a shift in the agency's program toward activities more consistent with environmental policy priorities, and away from those that served narrower and more traditional clienteles at the expense of those priorities.

By the end of 1974, however, the SCS had been allowed to implement only a handful of these new authorities, including none of those that might significantly redirect its watersheds program. It did receive departmental delegations of authority to use other federal funds to purchase land rights and to implement the water quality management objective. The latter had little practical effect, however, since it was subject to approval by the Environmental Protection

Agency, and EPA had a standing policy of discouraging the use of streamflow regulation for water quality management.[134] The SCS also received $1.5 million for Fiscal Year 1975 to develop a new land inventory and monitoring program, as called for in the Rural Development Act, though this did not directly affect the watersheds program.[135] The reasons for these limited changes appear to lie in the larger history of relations between the Administration and the House Committee on Appropriations, and while they go far beyond the National Environmental Policy Act, they are obviously important to an understanding of the political forces that shape stasis and change in the SCS watersheds program.[136]

The Water Resource Development Act of 1973 also included new authority for the SCS watersheds program: Section 73 of this law directed full consideration of *nonstructural* means of flood damage reduction, including such measures as flood-proofing of structures, flood plain acquisition, and relocation of flood plain activities, and it permitted federal payment of up to 80 percent of the costs of such measures, which is the average rate of cost sharing for structural measures.[137] As of mid-1974, however, the SCS had not yet been authorized to implement this mandate either, reportedly because the Office of Management and Budget was insisting upon the establishment of a uniform approach through the Water Resource Council.[138] SCS staff members stated a desire to implement this mandate and a belief that it would be an important element of water resource planning in the future, but like the Rural Development Act provisions, they did not yet have authority to implement it.

Conclusion

The response of the Soil Conservation Service to NEPA, like that of the Corps, resists reduction to any single generalization or conclusion. It included indications of change, albeit modest ones, such as major improvements in its guidelines and procedures as well as new environmental training programs. It included some potentials for future change, such as development of a new and detailed environmental assessment procedure, issuance of new procedures for water resource planning, and a stated interest in implementing other recently legislated environmental mandates if and when it were authorized to do so. It also included evidence of strong resistance to change, both inside the agency and in its political environment.

Two conclusions do emerge clearly from the evidence above, however. First, substantive changes in the SCS watersheds program were extremely modest during the period we have examined, despite the enactment of several statutory authorities—including but not limited to NEPA—that could have been used to redirect that program more strongly in the direction of environmental policy objectives. Second, even most policy and procedural changes related to NEPA were effected only from approximately 1972 on—more than two years after the law's enactment and considerably later than similar actions on the part of the Corps. The similarities and differences between the agencies' response will be discussed further in the chapter that follows.

As in the case of the Corps, the response of the SCS to NEPA was still unfolding in 1974, and becoming increasingly intertwined with later events and pressures. Many of the SCS' activities were already supportive of NEPA's purposes; NEPA's requirements had had at least a short-term inhibiting effect on some of those that were not.

The very uncertainty still surrounding both agencies' long-term responses, however, underscores the central characteristic of NEPA's effects: its procedural requirements were *not* a self-enforcing means to the fulfillment of its environmental policy ends, except when reinforced by an agency's desire to change and by complimentary changes in the agency's political environment. The "action-forcing provisions" did not themselves force substantive action, though they did provide new tactical opportunities in the political arena to those who wished to bring about administrative change.

In this regard, what NEPA did not accomplish is as significant as what it did. It did not change the Soil Conservation Service' programmatic priorities, though it did increase the risk of unproductive paperwork and delay if controversial practices (such as channelization) were proposed. Equally important, it did not provide positive incentives that might outweigh the rewards of the agency's present priorities. It did not increase the SCS' options for environmentally beneficial action, nor did it broaden the agency's range of potential clients, nor did it alter the political forces to which the agency was most directly accountable such as its congressional oversight committees.

What NEPA did accomplish was to increase the threat of wasted effort and delay associated with *controversial* actions, and to provide an *opportunity* for redirection of priorities to agencies that were desirous and capable of doing so. This broader redirection, however, could occur only in the presence of additional authority to increase the agency's positive options: for instance, to give equal consideration and funding for nonstructural flood control and to finance broader SCS involvement in land use inventory and monitoring.

In the absence of such further mandates, and of more fundamental changes in the SCS' political environment, the net effect of NEPA on the SCS Watersheds Program appears to have been relatively marginal. It produced some negotiated reduction in environmentally controversial activities, some increases in environmental analysis and research, and some retraining of key personnel, but little change in the agency's programs and priorities as a whole. If public attention should subside, a future "shaking down" of NEPA's requirements might well result even in elimination of the "burdensome" procedures that permitted effective challenge to controversial actions.

6

A Comparative Evaluation

What can we learn from these two case studies? Comparison of the responses of the Corps and the Soil Conservation Service to NEPA suggests important insights about the underlying differences between administrative agencies that engage in similar activities and about the effectiveness of a general mandate such as NEPA for changing the behavior of such agencies. How well did NEPA work? *How* did it work, and how did it not work? How much variation might there be in its effectiveness in different agencies? Two case studies do not provide final answers to these questions, but they do reveal enough points of comparison to suggest tentative conclusions about the efficacy of NEPA and about the results that can be expected from such legislation in the future.

Points of Comparison

The preceding chapters focussed on five principal dimensions of each agency's response to NEPA: policy interpretations, procedures, impact statements, projects, and overall programs. In each of these dimensions, important points of comparison are evident; and taken together, these comparisons suggest fundamental differences in the agencies' *patterns* of response that must be explained.

Policy Interpretations

First, the Corps and the SCS interpreted NEPA differently in their official policy statements and guidelines, even in such basic matters as its applicability to previously initiated actions and the meaning of "significant" environmental impacts. The Corps interpreted NEPA as a *new mandate* to be reflected in its plans and decisions, while the SCS, at least until 1974, interpreted it as a *reiteration* of its *existing* objectives and mandates.

The Corps took the position that NEPA created a new objective for federal water resource development activities that authorized the Corps to consider a broader ranger of effects than had been considered in previous practice under the criteria of Senate Document 97. It directed recognition of environmental quality as a new objective for water resource planning, as well as consideration of it in the evaluation of all Corps projects henceforth, and it requested new funds and personnel to carry out these new responsibilities.

131

The SCS, in contrast, interpreted NEPA as a reinforcement of its traditional mission and policies. For at least two years after the enactment of the law, it directed no change in the range of considerations that were to enter into its water resource planning process, and it requested no increases in funds or personnel to carry out the mandates of NEPA, even though its water resource projects consisted of many of the same impact-producing activities, and were justified by the same predominantly economic criteria, as those of the Corps.

It is true, of course, that NEPA reinforced the goal of conserving soil and water, and urged precisely the sort of harmonious relationship between human activities and their biological and physical resource base that the SCS had been established during the "dust bowl" era to achieve. But in taking this policy position, the SCS ignored the crucial differences that had since arisen between this physical conservation mission of the agency as a whole, and the fundamentally economic mission of its Small Watersheds Program. It thus failed to take the position of policy leadership in implementing NEPA that one might have expected of it.

Moreover, the SCS failed to recognize conflict between the policy and goals established by NEPA, and the single-minded pursuit of *any* one mission, even soil and water conservation. The SCS has a tradition of expertise on agricultural soil erosion and runoff, but according to its own testimony, very little even on such closely related subjects as water quality management and downstream effects of stream channel modification. NEPA thus required broader vision even on the part of conservation agencies such as the SCS, but while Corps guidelines recognized this need and exhorted its staff to take an holistic view of the human environment, the SCS interpreted NEPA as simply a reinforcement of its existing mission.

The Corps and the SCS also differed significantly in their attitude towards the public involvement implications of NEPA. The Corps' policy statements and guidelines linked the preparation of NEPA's "detailed statements" to procedures for early and continuing public involvement in water resource project planning, including active solicitation of reactions and objections at early stages in its administrative processes. SCS policies, in contrast, encouraged a flow of information about proposed projects from its client "local sponsoring organizations" to the public, but until 1974 they did not require any active role on the part of the SCS in public involvement activities, nor did they encourage or even permit early public review of environmental impact statements themselves.

The Corps delegated responsibility for the preparation, public disclosure, and defense of environmental impact statements to its District Engineers from the start, and it required that these activities precede the submission of their recommendations to Washington. Its guidelines stressed early and continuous liaison with all interested sectors of the public, in order to raise and answer potential objections as early as possible, and they required that public meetings and other vehicles for such liaison be incorporated throughout the process of project planning.

The SCS, in contrast, required *local sponsors* to carry out a public *information* program throughout the course of planning, but it did not accept a responsibility itself for informing and involving the public, nor did it require even the sponsors to do more than inform them; and it made its "detailed statements" public only at the final stage of project review formalities, after tentative agreement had already been reached on a final work plan both in the field and in Washington. Not until its 1973 and 1974 guideline revisions did the SCS direct that impact statements were to be prepared and made public in the field, and that SCS officials were themselves to "actively seek out" and involve different sectors of the public in their project planning activities.

Procedures

Second, both agencies' interpretations of the law centered almost exclusively upon its procedural requirements rather than its policy goals and in particular upon procedures for the preparation of impact statements rather than for implementing Section 102 as a whole. Within this context, however, they moved at very different speeds in integrating NEPA's requirements into their administrative processes. The SCS lagged considerably behind the Corps not only in recognizing a new policy mandate in NEPA, but even in implementing its procedural requirements.

Both the Corps and the SCS centered their attention almost exclusively on the requirement for "detailed statements of environmental impacts" and virtually ignored most other provisions of the law. The Corps adopted "environmental quality" as a new objective of its water resource development program, while the SCS asserted that environmental quality was consistent with its previous objectives, but neither developed any guidance on the achievement of the goals specified in Title I of NEPA, such as stewardship for future generations, achieving the widest possible range of beneficial uses without degradation, preservation of diversity and of the national heritage, achieving balance between population and resource use, enhancing the quality of renewable resources, and maximizing recycling of depletable resources. Nor did the Council on Environmental Quality give any appreciable emphasis to these goals, or even to NEPA's other procedural requirements (such as developing methods for consideration of unquantifiable amenities and values).

It is clear from the law's language and legislative history that its policy content was intended to be central, and that its procedural requirements were intended as instruments to those policy ends. Yet the overwhelming preoccupation of both agencies was with just one of those instruments, the "detailed statement," as though the preparation of this document in a form adequate to pass internal review and to survive a court test were an end in itself. For instance, neither agency provided any formal guidance for compliance with Section 102 (2) (B), which required the development of procedures and methods for giving "appropriate consideration to unquantifiable values," nor did either develop any guidance concerning the applicability of the law's policy goals. The water resource activities of both agencies have important implications for the achievement of such goals; yet neither they nor the Council on Environmental Quality developed guidelines to address these subjects.

Given that both agencies (and others) were preoccupied with NEPA's procedural requirements, however, they differed sharply in the speed with which they implemented those requirements. The Corps responded immediately and affirmatively to the new law's procedural provisions and made early and sustained policy commitments to their implementation. The SCS, in contrast, sought to avoid implementation of these requirements wherever possible for two to three years after the law's enactment, and only in 1973 and 1974 did its procedures begin to approach the level of implementation that had been directed in the Corps two to three years earlier. Even in the face of the Corps' guidelines and repeated revisions of them—which were readily accessible if the SCS had wished to emulate them and which had been publicly praised in testimony by the Council on Environmental Quality—and in the face of strong criticism of its own implementation record by the CEQ, the SCS took nearly four years to reach the level of procedural guidance that the Corps' guidelines had attained two to three years before.

This difference in the timing of adaptation to NEPA stands out clearly in examination of the two agencies' guidelines and presents a rather curious contrast between them. One would expect stronger leadership from a "conservation" agency, and more tardiness and recalcitrance from "development-oriented" engineers; yet in this case the opposite occurred. The Corps' guidelines were the vanguard of federal agencies' implementation efforts and provided examples of interpretation that were later hailed by CEQ and adopted by other agencies. Its actions changed more slowly, but its policies and procedures were exemplary.

In contrast, the SCS *waited out* this process rather than seeking leadership of it and issued detailed guidance only after most significant interpretations and innovations had been established elsewhere—and after the SCS itself had been confronted with an effective lawsuit. The stated attitude of SCS officials was that NEPA "had needed a shakedown period," that CEQ guidelines prior to August 1973 had been "too fuzzy," and that there had been too much "overreaction to individual decisions" of the courts rather than waiting for patterns of precedent to be established.[1]

The SCS apparently was content to keep a low profile during the initial period of experimentation, to follow along and adopt the "standardized" interpretations and requirements that emerged from this period, but not to seek a role of experimental or innovative leadership in implementing the law. Even in 1974, the principal form of leadership that the SCS appeared likely to exhibit was in *diminishing* the visibility of NEPA's procedures: at least three SCS officials expressed the view during this period that "the pressures for implementation of NEPA are beginning to moderate, so now we can shake the process down, eliminate the burdensome parts, and integrate it into our planning."[2]

Environmental Impact Statements

The environmental impact statements prepared by the Soil Conservation Service during the initial years after NEPA's enactment were generally comparable, in length and in quality of content, to the majority of those prepared during the same period by the Corps of Engineers. Few clear differences could be discerned, for example, in the average quality of these statements, although the Corps' *best* statements were distinctly more sophisticated than any of those prepared by the SCS. In general, the impact statements prepared by both agencies lacked detail and lacked careful measurement in the presentation of adverse environmental impacts; they lacked both factual detail and objectively balanced discussion of a range of alternatives; and they consistently substituted undefended claims and judgments for factually supported conclusions.

Despite similarity in their statements' content, however, five important differences between the two agencies were evident in the manner in which these statements were prepared and used. First, the Corps ordered that environmental statements be prepared for all its backlogged projects, beginning with those for which a major decision point was imminent, while the SCS ordered statements prepared only on a case-by-case basis and thus wrote far less statements than the Corps (though the quality of these statements was not noticeably better as a result).

The Corps directed that impact statements be prepared for all pending projects on which *any* major federal action remained to be taken and that any doubt should be resolved in favor of preparing the statement. It did not require any substantive review of the projects' environmental merits in the course of preparing such statements, but it did require that all its pending projects be brought into compliance with the letter of NEPA's procedural requirements. The SCS, in contrast, directed that impact statements be prepared for previously initiated actions only on a case-by-case basis, thereby leaving great discretion to its field officials to weigh the benefits and costs of doing so, and it implicitly allowed its officials to exempt actions from EIS requirements by mitigating their impacts sufficiently to satisfy fish and wildlife agencies that there would be no further "significant impacts."

Second, the SCS did not even attempt to establish consistent criteria for deciding which projects should be the subjects of environmental statements and which should not—in short, for identifying which types of actions were likely to have "significant environmental impacts" and which were not.[3] Instead, it focussed on environmental *"acceptability"* and directed its activities to negotiating compromises, on a case-by-case basis, between project sponsors and the fish and wildlife agencies who were the principal opponents of many channelization projects. Such an approach might result in improved projects only where no other kinds of adverse environmental impacts might be involved, and even then, only in cases where the fish and wildlife agencies had the power to negotiate hard bargains and make them stick. This approach clearly subverted the educative purpose of the environmental impact statement requirements, which was to make the staff of the SCS itself more sensitive to the full range of impacts of their actions.[4] The Corps, in contrast, directed that impact statements be prepared for *all* water projects in a specific list of categories, both new and old, and that a statement be prepared if there was any doubt one way or the other.

Third, the SCS, unlike the Corps, generally did not undertake further studies or more basic research projects to try to *find out* more about the environmental impacts of its actions. Immediately upon the enactment of NEPA, the Corps requested substantial increases in study funds for nearly all its proposed projects, specifically to undertake further environmental studies to fulfill the mandate of NEPA; and it also allocated sums through its in-house research arm, the Institute for Water Resources, to undertake more long-range studies of environmental impacts of various types of Corps activities, which might lead to improved guidelines and regulations in the future.[5] The SCS, in contrast, did not request budget increases for such studies; and as a result, according to testimony of the Council on Environmental Quality, new environmental studies generally were not undertaken.[6]

Fourth, the SCS took far less pains than the Corps to discuss and respond to the comments made on its draft environmental statements by other agencies and individuals. Most final statements published by the Corps from 1971 on included not only summaries of the key points of comments submitted, but also point-by-point discussion and responses to them by the agency, thereby identifying any changes made in the statement or project as a result of such comments as well as reasons for the Corps' disagreement with the comments' allegations in instances where it disagreed. SCS final statements during 1971 began to include summaries of the comments, rather than merely stapling the comments to the back of the statement as an appendix, but most failed to discuss or respond to these comments or to make changes in their statements or actions as a result.[7] In short, the SCS apparently failed not only to discuss and respond to such comments; it demonstrated little interest in using or learning from these comments at all, despite the fact that many were quite detailed and raised questions that deserved serious consideration.[a]

---

[a]Compare, for instance, even the 1974 revised draft environmental impact statement for Chicod Creek Watershed, North Carolina, with the comments made by numerous agencies,

Table 6-1

Estimated Effort Required for Preparation of SCS and Corps Environmental Statements, per Project, as of October 1971

	Man-Hours, SCS State Offices[a]	Man-Hours, Corps Districts[b]
Noncontroversial Projects		
Mean	164	443
Median	140	275
Controversial Projects		
Mean	341	1798
Median	200	620
Percent Increase, Controversial Projects		
Mean	108%	306%
Median	43%	125%

[a]N = 23, or 46% of all SCS State Conservationists.

[b]N = 22, or 60% of all Corps District Engineers (From Table 4-4).

Fifth, and finally, survey responses indicated that despite the considerably smaller number of statements it submitted, the SCS also put significantly less effort into the preparation of environmental statements than did the Corps and that it also put less effort than the Corps, and less proportional increase in effort, into the preparation of statements on projects where controversies existed. Table 6-1 shows these data, with the responses of the Corps included for comparison.[b] These indications suggest at least that the SCS was less committed to the NEPA environmental statement process than was the Corps, and that it was less responsive to controversy involving persons or groups other than its clients.

Project Modifications

The effectiveness of NEPA (or of any new policy mandate) must ultimately be measured not by the policies, procedures, and organizational structures through which it is translated, but by its influence upon the substantive activities that are those organizations' outputs. These two case studies suggest that relatively few significant substantive changes took place in the water resource projects of either agency as a direct consequence of NEPA, though there is reason to suspect that

organizations, and individuals on its earlier draft. Many of the comments are not even addressed, and some of those that are mentioned are answered superficially and without factual support.

[b]Note that as in the case of the Corps data (Table 4-4), the medians diverge markedly from the means, thereby revealing the presence of a small number of extremely high estimates or wild guesses. The medians therefore are probably more reliable estimates.

considerably more change may have resulted indirectly from its influence. Moreover, the causes of these changes, the mechanisms through which NEPA exerted its influence, differed significantly between the two agencies.

NEPA was reported to have had some substantive effect upon only about 6 percent of each agency's authorized projects, and in 60 to 70 percent of these cases the effect was simply postponement, rather than cancellation or significant change. It is possible that these percentages would increase over time, as the agencies' efforts turned to projects that were less fully planned at the time of the law's enactment, but with the passage of time such changes might have to be attributed more and more to intervening variables in the larger flow of events, rather than to the direct influence of NEPA.

The indirect effects of NEPA, however, appear to have been more widespread, though the evidence of such changes is necessarily softer, more inferential, and more intricately intertwined with the influence of other forces and events. The data of Tables 4–8 and 6–1, for instance, revealed disproportional influence of NEPA's requirements upon both the allocation of staff effort and the modification of projects in districts that had been subjected to NEPA-related controversy and litigation. The Corps' willingness to incorporate public views early in the planning of projects and the SCS' adoption of "viability" as a criterion for setting priorities among projects both suggest important indirect influences of NEPA upon project-by-project planning and evaluation that are likely to be considerably more pervasive and significant than its direct effectiveness against projects that were already highly developed at the time of the law's enactment.

At least as interesting as the absolute numbers of projects affected by NEPA, however, are the differences between the configurations of factors to which the two agencies' officials attributed these modifications (see Tables 5–5 and 5–6). These configurations show that pressures from sources external to the agency were in each case the principal force driving implementation of the law, but that the sources and effectiveness of these pressures differed considerably.

In the case of the Corps, external pressures were strong and reasonably unified, and they emanated principally from the vanguard of the "environmental movement" and the courts. The political pressures on the SCS from the environmental movement were weaker, including only a handful of lawsuits, and were more vigorously neutralized by counterpressures from the agency's traditional supporters in the Congress. Virtually the only concerted pressures on the SCS came from the fish and wildlife agencies and their constituencies, traditional foes of the SCS' stream channelization activities, who seized upon NEPA's interagency review requirements as a new tactical instrument of opposition to those activities.

Three points stand out clearly in Tables 5–5 and 5–6. First, "internal reevaluation" was the *sole* cause of more postponements and changes in SCS projects than in Corps projects, although it was a contributory cause of roughly the same number of modifications as in the Corps. In other words, this factor was mentioned no more often by the SCS than by the Corps, but other factors were mentioned less often by the SCS, particularly in instances of "significant change." The mandate of *Watersheds Memorandum 108* may again have been an important factor here, since it explicitly required internal re-evaluation of all the agency's potentially most damaging projects, and may thus have strengthened the respondents' perception of the significance of internal re-evaluation.

Second, "external pressures" were dramatically less effective on the SCS than on the Corps, both alone and in conjunction with internal re-evaluation. Judicial decisions played no role at all during this period (the first lawsuit against the SCS was not even filed until November 1971), and public controversies were mentioned in only one-tenth of the SCS' postponements and changes (in contrast to nearly half of those reported by the Corps). Corps respondents had credited external pressures with a role in nearly three-quarters of all project modifications, in each of the three categories (cancelled, postponed, significantly changed), including six out of seven of the projects cancelled. In contrast, no projects were cancelled by the SCS, because of external pressure or any other reason, and external pressures either alone or in conjunction with internal re-evaluation figured in only a meager 13 percent of the reported postponements and in none of the significant changes.

External pressures did play a significantly stronger role in conjunction with federal agency comments, as will be discussed further below, but the pattern that was so evident in the case of the Corps, in which an overwhelming number of the project modifications were attributed to these pressures either directly or in conjunction with internal re-evaluation, was not evident in the reports of the SCS.

Third, a significant number of the SCS' project modifications were attributed to two configurations that were not even mentioned by Corps respondents: the combination of *federal agency comments* with "external pressures," on the one hand, and, with "internal re-evaluation" on the other. Federal agency comments on their own had a negligible impact, but in conjunction with internal re-evaluation, they were responsible for nearly 20 percent of all postponements, and in conjunction with external pressures, they were responsible for one-quarter of all postponements and nearly one-tenth of all significant changes. As Table 5-6 showed, these comments were in fact the most frequently cited cause of all SCS project postponements and the second most frequently cited (though a distant second, behind internal re-evaluation) cause of all significant changes.

The nature of these federal agency comments, and their role in the new configurations, becomes clear from an examination of the comments that were actually submitted on SCS environmental statements during 1970 and 1971. With the exception of a handful of cautionary comments from the Department of Health, Education and Welfare concerning potential sanitation problems, the *only* detailed (and frequently critical) federal comments on SCS projects came from the Department of the Interior and its Bureau of Sport Fisheries and Wildlife. Moreover, these federal agency comments were buttressed by adverse comments from state and local agencies in five out of the six project revisions in which they were mentioned, and state and local comments were supported by adverse comments from federal agencies in all five cases in which they occurred.

All these facts, in short, suggest that the primary source of pressure for modifications in SCS projects was *not* the new "environmentalist" groups, which operated directly on the agencies through the news media and the courts, nor even the agencies that were responsible for pollution control and environmental protection generally. Rather, it was the traditional coalition of fish and wildlife agencies and their constituents, who opposed SCS channelization projects principally because of their effects on fish and wildlife values and expressed their views principally through the traditional channels of interagency review and comment.

Program Changes

Finally, the program priorities of the SCS, in contrast to those of the Corps, did not show any evidence of redirection during the four years following NEPA's enactment. The Corps, it will be recalled, initiated the Urban Studies Program during this period, as well as the pilot "environmental reconnaissance inventories," three prototype projects for nonstructural reduction of flood damages, and considerable experimentation with new techniques for involving the public in its activities. These did not significantly deflect the mainstream of the Corps water program during this period, but they did demonstrate the Corp's ability to bend and adjust its priorities in response to new pressures and constituencies. There were no apparent analogs for these activities in the programs of the SCS, except perhaps the newly funded program of land use inventory and monitoring, and the SCS watersheds program continued on its previous course virtually untouched by the enactment of NEPA.

The only evidences of change in the SCS watersheds program during this period were, first, its modification of some channelization activities to reduce the objections of fish and wildlife agencies and, second, its testimony that priorities were now being based upon project "viability"—a change that might reflect the projects' geographic locations and political controversiality as much as their relationship to environmental policy goals. It is likely that a similar criterion of "viability" was applied to Corps projects during this period, but unlike the SCS, the Corps succeeded in acquiring new missions to serve areas where its traditional activities were less welcome. There was an equal or greater need for the skills of the SCS in urbanizing watersheds, but while a few SCS offices did begin to respond to this need, the watersheds program as a whole retained its traditional agricultural image and orientation rather than overtly redirecting its priorities.

In suggesting these differences in the extent of their substantive change, it is important to note that the Corps and the SCS did not start from the same base point in relation to environmental goals. The Corps was an engineering agency, which had gradually been permitted to include some environmentally oriented purposes in its projects. The SCS, in contrast, was an agricultural conservation agency, a type of environmental protection organization, a few of whose activities appeared to serve parochial purposes of its clients at the expense of broader environmental policy goals. One could reasonably argue, therefore, that the SCS did not need to change as much as the Corps, and that this difference mitigates the criticism implied in the comparison.

The difficulty with this argument, however, is not that it is incorrect but that it misses a more significant point. The SCS may have required less corrective action than the Corps in order to harmonize its activities with environmental goals, but it failed to assert the leadership in pursuit of those goals that should have been forthcoming from an environmental protection agency. In principle, the SCS' traditional expertise made it far more competent than the Corps to lead in the implementation of environmental goals, but it nevertheless failed to adopt a position of leadership in the implementation of NEPA while the Corps did so.

Explanations

Perhaps the most significant point in the comparisons above is not any one of them singly, but the fact that taken together, they formed patterns of response that were distinctly different from agency to agency. Moreover, these different patterns took shape in spite of ostensible similarities in the types of impact-producing activities involved, and in the objectives and criteria by which these activities were evaluated and justified. Each agency's policy statements, structural arrangements, resource allocations, and project decisions are interrelated, though not always fully consistent; taken together, they form patterns of action and inaction that illuminate the goals that the agency implicitly serves.

The Corps' immediate acceptance of NEPA's mandate in its official statements, its application of the law's procedures to projects in progress, its structural changes and budget requests, its increasingly detailed internal guidelines, its linkage of environmental assessment with new public involvement mandates—these formed one pattern of response. The SCS' assumption of no new mandate, its substantive review of one category of projects while avoiding broad application of NEPA's procedures *per se*, its narrower identification of environmental impacts with fish and wildlife, its lack of structural or budgetary change, its less vigorous approach to public involvement—these formed a very different pattern.

It is unlikely that these differences were haphazard, since they both arose and were sustained in spite of the obvious similarities in the two programs' "major federal actions" and evaluation criteria, and in spite of each agency's knowledge of the other's response. One can only conclude that differences between the two agencies' organizational and political environments exercised telling influence upon their behavior and led them to create deliberately different patterns of interpretation and implementation in response to the same legislative mandate.

One must ask, however, *why*? *Why* did the Corps, at least on paper, move so quickly to accept NEPA as a mandate for change, to link it to public involvement procedures, and so forth? *Why* did the SCS demonstrate so little commitment, let alone leadership, in its implementation prior to 1973 and 1974? One would have expected the reverse: the Corps was supposed to be a bastion of recalcitrant engineers, which would accept an environmental mandate only grudgingly, while the SCS was a conservation agency supposedly dedicated to leadership in resource protection. Despite controversies over a few activities, the SCS *was* an "environmental" agency of forty years' experience, which presumably could have set a high standard for the implementation of a law such as NEPA. For some reason, however, it did not; it treated NEPA as merely a tactical attack on the practice of stream channelization by its old fish and wildlife adversaries and as a justification for its other traditional activities, rather than as an opportunity or mandate for future leadership.

The Corps' early and visible response may be explained in at least three ways, and these explanations are more likely complementary than mutually exclusive. First, despite its reputed power and the strength of its pro-development public works lobby, the Corps was particularly visible and vulnerable to the political forces demanding implementation of environmental policies. Several other agencies engage in similar activities, including the SCS, and numerous others take actions whose environmental impacts may be even more damaging than those of the Corps.[c] Yet few are as widely known as the Corps, and few if any serve as such central and ongoing political symbols of engineered modification of natural resource systems.

Because Corps projects are strictly federal actions, moreover, they can easily be singled out for attack as symbols of federal intrusion on behalf of economic "special interests"—in contrast, for instance, to programs of federal technical and financial assistance to local applicants—and they can frequently be stopped simply by withdrawal of a governor's or Congressman's support, if not by citizen outcry directly.

It is hardly surprising, therefore, that when the enactment of NEPA established a new symbolic policy of environmental protection, the Corps was widely

---

[c]Agencies engaged in similar activities include the Bureau of Reclamation, Soil Conservation Service, Tennessee Valley Authority, and Federal Power Commission; examples of others with equally damaging impacts include other units of the Department of Defense, the regulatory programs of the Department of Agriculture and the Environmental Protection Agency (if standards are set too low), and the U.S. Agency for International Development.

chosen as an initial target for challenge by environmental interest groups. NEPA was a symbol of public consensus against narrowly economic or mission-oriented criteria, and the numerous early judicial decisions halting Corps projects (at least temporarily) became symbols themselves of the apparent effectiveness of new "public interest" citizen groups in challenging traditional "big government" activities. This explanation is strongly corroborated by the importance ascribed to external pressures in the survey responses.

The second likely explanation is that the Corps was more *able* to change than many other agencies. The Corps is a nationwide agency, and it is a relatively large agency with a substantial budget for the planning and design of its actions. It also has a long history of multiple-purpose activity and has adjusted its priorities gradually over time as more and more missions were assigned to it. It has a substantial backlog of actions among which it can set priorities, and it possesses considerable administrative autonomy, subject to congressional concurrence, which permits it to make adjustments in these priorities.

For all these reasons, the Corps had a wider range of flexibility than many other agencies and more potential activities among which it could choose if some were challenged or blocked. An agency whose entire livelihood is threatened is almost certain to react defensively; an agency that has other options or opportunities may instead simply change its priorities, without feeling a threat to its existence. The Corps' continued existence was never seriously threatened by NEPA, even though some egos were bruised by effective challenges to specific projects. As an agency, therefore, it simply adjusted its priorities somewhat in response. This explanation is particularly consistent with the new programs undertaken by the Corps during the same period, such as the urban wastewater studies.

Finally, a third explanation of the Corps' response is simply that it was *ready* to change and consequently viewed NEPA as a strategic opportunity as well as a tactical threat: a threat to many of its proposed projects from the new "environmentalist" lobby, but also an opportunity for further broadening of its activities, constituencies, and project evaluation criteria.

The Corps' projects were already under attack—the Cross Florida Barge Canal, for instance, which became one of the most celebrated NEPA cases, was already in litigation when NEPA was enacted, and NEPA violations were simply added to the complaint later—and in a broader context, the Corps had already experienced a long history of political and legal warfare with many of the groups whose "preservationist" wagons were now hitched to the rising "environmentalist" star. NEPA was therefore an obvious tactical threat, since it provided major new leverage to groups opposing many of its projects.

At the same time, however, NEPA also provided a strategic *opportunity* to the Corps on another front, against the insistence of the Office of Management and Budget that its projects be justified by narrowly economic criteria. No agency wants its image to be symbolic of callous destruction in an era of rising environmental concern and in fact the Chief's Office had already considered environmental quality as a potential new objective for Corps activities for some years prior to the enactment of NEPA.

It was noted earlier that the narrowly economic criteria for evaluation of water projects were largely a product of Budget Bureau insistence, not of Corps preference. In the years immediately preceding NEPA's enactment, the Corps had already taken a strong hand in the drafting of the Water Resource Council's "Principles and Standards," which proposed establishment of environmental quality as a separate objective one to two years before NEPA was enacted.[8] At the time NEPA was enacted, however, this draft was bogged down in lengthy bargaining with the Budget Bureau and was not officially approved (in revised form) until 1973.[9] In the meantime, NEPA provided an opportunity to affirm the principle that environmental quality *was* a new mission of the Corps, supplemental to and distinct from its traditional economics oriented priorities.

The strategic value of this environmental objective to the Corps was not limited to image improvement, however. In addition to countering its "black hat" image, this response offered at least two more tangible benefits in its traditional political battles. First, it would free the agency from the tough and quantifiable economic criteria by which OMB was able to exercise control over it, since this economic objective might then be balanced against one or more additional objectives that were less clearly defined. Second, it could logically lead to authority for projects whose economic costs were greater than their economic benefits—so long as the Corps could claim that their benefits to "environmental quality" more than made up the difference.

Accordingly, the Corps seized upon NEPA immediately as a basis for the policy that environmental quality *was* now a new objective of the agency's activities, to be recognized and fully considered in the planning and justification of all its projects.

Whatever mixture of these explanations is appropriate, the Corps clearly did show evidence of change in response to NEPA. These changes were far more evident in policy statements and experiments than in day-to-day activities, and it continued to receive periodic wrist slaps from the courts. Some of the signs, however, suggested that at least the foundations were being established for more pervasive adaptation: in particular, the acceptance of new environmental protection-related missions, the recruitment of environmentally oriented professional personnel who might gradually acquire seniority and effective roles in Corps decisions, the establishment of new units both for environmental resources and for comprehensive urban studies, and the substantial reallocation of study budgets toward environmental studies, urban studies, and public involvement programs.

The SCS, in contrast, viewed NEPA as a much narrower tactical threat from a more limited constituency and ignored its strategic potential. For the SCS, NEPA was a threat only to its water resource projects, not to its other more traditional and more widespread programs on behalf of soil conservation, and even at that, it was a threat directed almost exclusively at its stream channel excavation activities by traditional critics of those activities among fish and wildlife interests and their patron agencies. The SCS therefore emphasized the complementarity of NEPA's purposes to its traditional and strategic mission of soil conservation and glossed over the inconsistencies between those purposes and its water resource program under Public Law 566.

At least five reasons may help to explain this response. The first three all concern the SCS' *vulnerability* to pressures for change; the fourth concerns its *ability* to change; and the fifth concerns its *readiness* to change.

First, the SCS was not as vulnerable as the Corps to the charge that its activities were environmentally destructive. Most of its activities were in fact directed toward the protection of an environmental resource, namely, productive soils. The watersheds program worked in a different fashion—trading federal financing of water control structures for private commitments to conservation farming practices on lands above the structure—but this program was only one of the agency's major activities, and even within this program many projects undoubtedly were more beneficial than adverse in their environmental impacts.

As a result, pressures on the SCS had to be more precisely targeted than on the Corps, upon particular projects or upon one particular category of actions such as stream channel excavation. Unlike the Corps, the SCS as a whole did not provide a credible political symbol of environmental destruction, and it thus was less vulnerable to nationwide pressures by the environmental lobby except on the issue of channelization.

Second, the SCS was less visible than the Corps to the predominantly urban and suburban environmental interest groups. Its soil surveys were widely known, but its watershed activities took place predominantly in rural areas for the benefit of predominantly agricultural client groups, with relatively little interest or concern by most other citizens—again excepting the long-standing opposition of fish and wildlife organizations to the practice of stream channelization. Until the Chicod Creek lawsuit, virtually the only organized opposition to SCS activities was this traditional coalition of fish and wildlife agencies and their constituents, and their opposition was voiced through traditional channels of interagency review rather than through broadly based controversy and lawsuits.

In sharp contrast to the Corps, the SCS was under no direct pressure from the courts during 1970 and 1971; the first legal complaints of NEPA violations against SCS watershed projects were not lodged until mid- and late 1971.[10] Moreover, while numerous decisions favoring environmental litigants against federal *projects* were delivered during this period (such as those involving the Corps), decisions involving federal *assistance programs* favored environmental litigants in only two temporary instances prior to August 1971 and went against them in half a dozen.[d] This trend began to change during the latter half of 1971, but too

[d]Decisions favoring environmental litigants were *Texas Committee v. United States*, 1 ERC 1303 (W.D. Texas, February 5, 1970), *dismissed as moot* (5th Circuit, August 25, 1970); and *Gibson v. Ruckelshaus*, 3 ERC 1028, 1 ELR 20337 (E.D. Texas, March 1, 1971), *reversed and remanded*, 3 ERC 1370 (5th Circuit, August 9, 1971). Decisions against environmental litigants during this period included *Pennsylvania Environmental Council v. Bartlett*, 315 F. Supp. 238 (M.D. Penna., April 30, 1970), *affirmed* 3 ERC 1421 (3rd Circuit, Decem-

late to provide a source of pressure on the SCS during most of the period we have discussed.[e]

In short, the SCS generally had a "low profile" during the first two years after NEPA's enactment, which shielded most of its work—with a single major exception, stream channelization—from the sort of frontal attack on its priorities and traditional practices to which the Corps was subjected.

Third, the SCS Watersheds Program was under pressures from various Committees of the Congress during this period, but these pressures were more mixed in their signals than those on the Corps, and the forces pressuring it for change were less powerful than those pressuring it to continue firmly ahead with business as usual.

Congressional pressures for change in the SCS watersheds program came exclusively from outside its own oversight committees, principally from the Conservation and Fish and Wildlife Committees.[f] Perhaps the most significant point about these pressures was the obvious interrelationship of NEPA with long-standing traditional controversies between contending interest groups. Both these committees called the SCS watersheds program officials before relatively hostile hearings during 1970 and 1971, and the implementation of NEPA was a major issue in all these hearings. In each case, however, even in hearings explicitly devoted to oversight of the implementation of NEPA, the *focus* of inquiry was the more traditional conservationist issue of protecting fish and wildlife resources, rather than the broader issue of NEPA's environmental policy.[11] To these committees and their constituencies, NEPA obviously was not principally a policy statement or philosophical mandate, but a new political instrument for use in old struggles.

---

ber 1, 1971); *Bucklein v. Volpe*, 2 ERC 1082, 1 ELR 20043 (N.D. Calif., October 29, 1970); *Northwest Area Welfare Rights Organization v. Volpe*, 2 ERC 1704, 1 ELR 20186 (E.D. Wash., December 3, 1970); *Ely v. Velde*, 321 F. Supp. 1088 (E.D. Virginia, January 22, 1971), *reversed* 3 ERC 1280 (4th Circuit, November 8, 1971); *Echo Park Residents Committee v. Romney*, 3 ERC 1255 (C.D. Calif., May 11, 1971); and *Citizens to Preserve Foster Park v. Volpe*, 3 ERC 1031, 1 ELR 20389 (N.D. Indiana, August 8, 1971).

[e]Decisions favoring environmental litigants against federal assistance programs in late 1971 included *San Antonio Conservation Society v. Texas Highway Department*, 2 ERC 1872, 1 ELR 20379 (5th Circuit, August 5, 1971); *Goose Hollow Foothills League v. Romney*, 3 ERC 1087 (D. Oregon, September 9, 1971); *Nolop v. Volpe*, 3 ERC 1338 (D. South Dakota, November 11, 1971); and the reversal of *Ely v. Velde* on November 8, 1971, as cited in the previous footnote. The first decision against the Soil Conservation Service itself followed not long thereafter, with a temporary injunction against the Chicod Creek project in March 1972 (*NRDC v. Grant*, 341 F Supp. 356, E.D. North Carolina, March 1972).

[f]It is worth recalling in this regard that NEPA was sponsored and overseen in the House of Representatives by the Subcommittee on Fish and Wildlife Conservation of the Committee on Merchant Marine and Fisheries, one of the two committees (along with the Subcommittee on Conservation and Natural Resources of the Committee on Government Operations) that most regularly attacked the SCS for the impacts of stream channelization on fish and wildlife resources.

Ensuing events, moreover, showed clearly that these pressures for change were neither expressions of majority congressional opinion, nor even a viable political force against the SCS' supporters in its own oversight committees. First, immediately after the hearings on stream channelization held by Congressman Reuss' Subcommittee on Conservation, a subcommittee of the House Public Works Committee held hearings to investigate "delays and excessive paperwork" in public works programs, targeting on environmental impact statements among other examples, and it used these hearings as an opportunity for the SCS to complain publicly about its treatment in the channelization hearings.[12] Second, Congressman Jamie Whitten, an author of the Small Watersheds Act and chairman of the subcommittee overseeing the SCS' appropriations, inserted language into the conference report on agriculture and environmental appropriations to require discussion of economic as well as environmental impacts in EIS's.[13] While this language seemed gratuitous, even redundant with the language of NEPA, its insertion could easily be interpreted as restoring an emphasis on economic objectives and thus neutralizing the implication of NEPA that change in priorities was called for. Third, the efforts of channelization opponents to block or delay funding for it on the floor of the House were soundly defeated.

As in the case of the Corps, the SCS' legislative oversight committees did require it to prepare environmental statements on project proposals for which legislative authorization was pending at the time NEPA was enacted, and this requirement did force the SCS to begin writing such statements within the first year after the law was passed. Unlike the case of the Corps, however, the Committee did not wait for the statements before proceeding: by the time the statements were submitted, the Congress had already authorized the projects, thereby underscoring the committees' disinterest in the statements as anything more than a ritual paperwork exercise.[14]

In short, while the Corps was permitted to adjust its procedures and priorities somewhat in response to environmentalist pressures, the SCS was actively protected against such pressures by its congressional patrons.[g] Both the legislative and the appropriations committees overseeing the SCS were aggressively dedicated to continuation of its traditional watersheds program and priorities, and we may assume that they were supported in that dedication by the agriculture and public works lobbies. The fish and wildlife coalition had no political leverage on the SCS that was even remotely comparable to this in its effectiveness. The Conservation and Fish and Wildlife Subcommittees were both relatively minor ones in the congressional hierarchy; they had no general oversight authority over the SCS; and they could be supported only weakly by the prin-

---

[g]One possible explanation for this difference is that the agencies' overseers in the Congress (as well as some in the Office of Management and Budget) were sympathetic to the Corps' "image problem," but (correctly) did not think that the SCS had such a problem; and that they therefore were more permissive towards requests for new funds and authorities from the Corps than from the SCS.

cipal environmental agencies (CEQ and EPA) since these agencies' budgets were also controlled by the Subcommittee on Agriculture Appropriations.

Fourth, the SCS was more constrained than the Corps in its ability to redirect its watersheds program. In addition to the congressional constraints mentioned above, the Service's range of authorized purposes was narrower than that of the Corps and lacked such categories as navigation, power production, and recreational reservoir management, as well as others authorized by the Rural Development Act but not yet delegated for implementation. Its field of potential clients and constituencies therefore was correspondingly narrower. In addition, its projects were subject to statutory ceilings of size and cost; it had less funds available than the Corps for environmental analyses within the planning budget for each project; and it had no authority to conduct more basic research on topics relevant to its activities. Finally, it had less autonomy within the Department of Agriculture than the Corps possessed within the Department of Defense, and less autonomy from its clients in that its projects involved federal assistance to local sponsoring organizations rather than direct federal implementation. For all these reasons, the SCS had considerably less flexibility to adjust its watersheds program than did the Corps, despite the fact that its mission was ostensibly closer to the purposes of NEPA than the Corps' was.

The fifth possible explanation for the SCS' tardy response is that unlike the Corps, it may have been neither ready for nor interested in a major redirection of policy or priorities, at least prior to 1973. It was comfortable in its traditional activities; it was under no serious pressure or threats to change; it was doing what its congressional committees wanted it to do and what its officials took pride in; and it was not suffering from the "image problem" of environmental destruction for which the Corps was under attack.

The SCS *was* subject to the same narrowly drawn evaluation criteria as the Corps and might therefore have had a similar interest in establishment of environmental quality as an objective of water resource planning. However, the benefit-cost issue was not as central to the SCS as it was to the Corps, perhaps because the SCS' program was less threatening to the federal budget than that of the Corps (and constraints other than the Office of Management and Budget thus had greater significance). Moreover, environmental quality already *was* the principal objective of most of the SCS' activities, while it was not for those of the Corps. The SCS therefore had little external impetus to implement NEPA promptly, and in the absence of such impetus, and in the presence of hostility to the new law from its congressional patrons, it chose to follow rather than to lead in the law's implementation.

These five arguments all provide plausible explanations for the tardiness of the SCS' implementation of NEPA. The other question that must be addressed, however, is *why did the agency then adopt a more positive position in 1973 and 1974?* Would not the same arguments hold good during this later period? How can one explain the fact that the SCS did alter its stated policies significantly during these years, though perhaps not many of its activities themselves?

One plausible explanation is that the SCS became more vulnerable to pressures for change during the latter period. Channelization may not have been the agency's primary activity, but it had been receiving more adverse publicity for several years—from the environmental lobby, from at least two congressional committees that had been holding extensive hearings on the practice, and from the public generally.[15] This adverse publicity was in fact tarnishing the "environmentalist" image of the SCS and overshadowing its positive activities in many people's minds. The Chicod Creek lawsuit, moreover, demonstrated that the SCS *was* vulnerable to legal pressures under NEPA and could be subjected to costly delays—costly to the SCS, and even more so to its clients—if it failed to comply conscientiously with NEPA's requirements.

While these forces still lacked power to force change in the agency's priorities, they did exert an effective inhibiting influence on particular projects, and demonstrated that the agency was not invulnerable in this regard. This pressure also strengthened the position of those in the agency who wished to embrace new environmental priorities, but had previously been prevented from doing so.

At the same time, the boundaries of NEPA's interpretation were becoming more distinct, possibly with the effect of reducing the agency's anxiety concerning the extent of change that might be demanded. The new Deputy Administrator, coming freshly into this situation without necessarily the same degree of commitment as his predecessor to earlier priorities, may well have decided to try to restore the agency's image of environmental leadership. This explanation seems plausible to the extent that the agency's own recalcitrance or unreadiness was the principal force blocking earlier change.

A contrasting and equally plausible explanation, however, is that the changes that appeared to be taking place in the SCS during 1973 and 1974 were merely symbolic rather than substantive, rhetorical rather than real. The agency's policy statements and guidelines had changed, to be sure, but the nature of its activities had not, and its output of these activities actually increased (with the possible exception of channelization). The Chicod Creek decision demonstrated the agency's vulnerability to attacks for *procedural* noncompliance, but the broader pattern of judicial opinion demonstrated equally the reluctance of the courts to challenge the substantive content of proposed actions.[16]

It is possible, therefore, that the agency permitted symbolic changes (perhaps to restore its environmental image) only after credible threats to its activities themselves had been surmounted. By 1973, the channelization hearings had come and gone without major legislative change, judicial interpretation of the law was stabilizing, popular pressures were beginning to moderate: the SCS had *weathered* the environmental issue and could now afford to make symbolic changes in its guidelines and procedures, as well as some incremental substantive changes in personnel training programs, with the assurance that its programs themselves would not be significantly affected. Political behavior is frequently characterized by agreement on particular actions that are assumed to contribute to divergent ends, and it may thus be quite consistent that environmentalists sought compliance with NEPA's procedures as a means to NEPA's substantive ends, while others permitted that compliance as an intended substitute for the implementation of those ends.

Conclusion

Both organizational and political differences between the Corps and the SCS contribute important elements to an explanation of the differences between their responses to NEPA. Neither of these dimensions is complete in itself; both are essential, and both played roles at least as strong as the language and legislative history of NEPA in shaping the agencies' responses to the law. The Corps *is* a larger agency than the SCS, with more autonomy, more resources, and more flexible options among priorities and constituencies; and as an engineering agency, it was probably more conscious of the disparity between its traditional objectives and those of NEPA than was the SCS. At the same time, however, the two agencies are also embedded in overlapping but different clusters of political constituencies—the one, public works, and the other, primarily agriculture—and they differ significantly in their salience both to environmental interest groups and to the public generally. These forces also shaped the agencies' responses, and indeed have probably contributed to shaping the differences between their organizational environments themselves over a longer period of time.

If one wishes to understand and predict administrative agencies' responses to a new legislative mandate, therefore, it is not sufficient to look merely at the language and legislative history of the law, important though these are. To the extent that there is any room for interpretation in the statute, agencies may be expected to interpret it in different ways depending upon the threats and opportunities that it raises in their organizational and political environments.

Nor is it sufficient to look merely at the organizational arrangements and administrative processes of the agencies that must implement the law, important though these are also. These arrangements may illuminate important areas of constraints upon the agency's response, but they are not themselves reliable indicators of that response: they are, rather, intermediate variables for explaining responses to legislated policy, influencing those responses but influenced themselves by the pressures of the agency's political environment.

An adequate explanation requires attention to both the language of the law and the organizational arrangements through which it must be implemented, but more than these, it requires understanding of the political forces influencing each agency's behavior over time. During the brief period of these case studies, NEPA did appear to have altered slightly the balance of power among the forces contending in the Corps' political environment, but it did not appear to have had this effect in the case of the SCS. The extent to which this effect would continue over a longer time period, and the advantages and limitations of the NEPA mechanism generally as an instrument of administrative change, are the subject of the final chapter that follows.

7

Values and Limitations of the NEPA Mechanism

The purpose of the National Environmental Policy Act, in the words of the Senate committee report on it, was to establish a "clear statement of the values and goals which we seek . . . a set of resource management values which are in the long-range public interest and which merit the support of all social institutions . . . in short, a national environmental policy."[1] The report argued that such a policy was necessary, in view of the accelerating spread of pollution, crowding, and other forms of environmental degradation; that it was an unavoidable responsibility of the Congress, since "only there could competing political interests be adequately represented and accommodated";[2] and that it must be implemented within the activities of all agencies of the federal government, since "environmental programs are presently administered by 63 Federal agencies located within 10 of the 13 departments as well as 16 independent agencies of the executive branch."[3]

The NEPA Mechanism

In order to insure implementation of this policy, the authors of NEPA devised an innovative mechanism intended to link the law's policy principles to the day-to-day, action-by-action, incremental decisions that are the reality of government life—and that are also, they recognized, a principal source of cumulative environmental degradation. This mechanism was a series of procedural requirements, described as "action-forcing provisions," that included both general directives concerning the development of environmental information and alternatives in all agency activities and a specific requirement for documentation and review of environmental impacts for all "major" actions that might have "significant" impacts.

The authors apparently presumed that this mechanism would work through the "force of fact":[4] if environmental information could be placed before each official in the decision process along with the traditional information about proposed actions and their alternatives, it would influence the decision in the direction of NEPA's policy goals. Rational officials would tend to choose environmentally better actions in preference to environmentally worse ones, but they could not be expected to do so unless information concerning these consequences was brought to their attention.

An important conclusion of the case studies above, however, is that the "detailed statement" turned out to be not a single "action-forcing mechanism," but the pivotal document of *three* such mechanisms. These mechanisms were, respectively, the "upward" approval process for a proposed action within the originating agency (and to higher authorities above it), the "horizontal" process of review and comment by other agencies having "jurisdiction or special expertise," and the "downward" availability of the statement and agency comments for *public* review, comment, and legal action. Each of these mechanisms functioned in a somewhat different fashion than the others: the first, by bringing new and more complete information to the attention of officials responsible for federal actions; the second, by increasing the circulation of information among agencies that had divergent missions as well as different bodies of expertise; the third, by increasing opportunities for *ad hoc* objection to action proposals by individuals who opposed them. These mechanisms also differed in the effectiveness of their contributions to the achievement of NEPA's purposes, both generally and in each agency, as we shall discuss further below.

A second important conclusion is that the third of these mechanisms—the review of environmental statements by individuals outside the federal administrative structure, with its accompanying opportunity for *ad hoc* involvement and legal action—was by far the most effective "action-forcing mechanism" driving continued implementation of NEPA's mandate during the first few years of the law's existence. Inserted by the Senate at the last minute before the conference on the bill, never debated on the record or subjected to hearings, and effectuated in practice by citizen energy and judicial receptivity, it was this provision that most forcefully and pervasively compelled agency officials to respond to the new law's charge. The external pressures on the agencies that resulted were important in themselves, in their injection of new constituencies and interest groups into the orbit of the agencies' attention; and they were made enormously more effective than could have been predicted, by the unexpected receptiveness of the judiciary to citizen petitions for review of administrative actions.[5]

Perhaps the most important result of these external pressures was not that they succeeded in challenging individual actions, but that they apparently provided the necessary prerequisite to achieving some more general changes in agency procedures and behavior. Many actions were not changed in spite of heavy applications of pressures and lawsuits by environmental interest groups and *ad hoc* citizens action organizations—indeed, the number of such confrontations that were ultimately successful represents an extremely small fraction of the agencies' activities. But few if any agencies voluntarily made strong commitments to the implementation of NEPA's procedures, let alone its purposes, in the *absence* of such pressures, and the two agencies we have examined clearly did not. While the source of these pressures varied from agency to agency, the importance of their presence in some effective form cannot easily be disputed.[a]

---

[a]An apparent exception to this statement was the early policy adopted by the Corps concerning NEPA's expansion of its authorities. Even in this case, however, statements by Corps officials implied that the expectation of increased external pressures was also an important reason for the change.

This conclusion is particularly interesting inasmuch as preenactment statements by the bill's sponsors concentrated so heavily on the first mechanism—the provision of environmental information for internal agency decisions—apparently on the assumption that if only better environmental impact information were brought to the attention of officials making decisions, the "force of fact" would selectively favor actions that were environmentally preferable.

The second mechanism—interagency review and comment—had been included simply to assuage Senator Muskie's concern that the environmental protection agencies have opportunities to review other agencies' judgments concerning environmental impacts, though it also addressed the coordination problem that had been raised in the 1968 Daddario report. However, this mechanism was only occasionally successful in countering the tendency of agencies to limit their conflicts by long-term accommodations.[6] All three of these mechanisms were valuable, but clearly the principal force driving NEPA's implementation during this period was the threat of *ad hoc* external challenge by environmental interest groups and citizen opponents.

In short, NEPA's "action-forcing" mechanism has proven itself an extraordinarily successful innovation, at least to the extent of insuring that a new range of information was incorporated into proposals for federal action, but it achieved that success principally by providing a new channel of effective access, through which concerned individuals could both review such proposals and their impacts and then make their views known. Its direct effect was to raise a credible threat of challenge to any potentially controversial federal action, thus insuring that officials proposing such actions would at least think through ahead of time what sorts of impacts might invite challenge. More generally, it contributed incalculably to a climate of broader forethought about the possible impacts of government actions, sensitizing both agency officials and the general public to the diverse consequences that could result from proposed actions.

For all the changes in procedures and in general awareness, however, there is not yet much systematic evidence of direct change in substantive activities as a result of NEPA, either in individual actions or particularly in fundamental federal priorities for action. To the extent that environmental impacts could be ameliorated by *design* changes, beneficial progress was occurring; to the extent that they required *site* changes, some changes were also taking place; but to the extent that they resulted inherently from certain types of government actions, such as the construction of dams, highways, and nuclear power plants, little if any substantive change in priorities was occurring except as a function of budgetary, political, and other considerations broader than the procedural requirements of NEPA.

In addition, an important uncertainty that is not resolved here is the fate of the substantial number of actions *delayed* by NEPA, such as those that were reported "postponed" during the period studied. In some of these cases, postponement might indicate active re-evaluation and perhaps future "significant revisions" making them more responsive to NEPA's purposes. In other cases postponement might be merely a temporary delay, perhaps until the environmental issue "cooled off" and the proposal could be reactivated without significant change. A third possibility is that some of these proposals were so effectively blocked by opposition to environmentally damaging features of them that the agencies postponed them indefinitely—that is, abandoned them—in favor of other and less controversial projects.[b]

The evidence presented above does not show the distribution of these three possibilities. If the last possibility should in fact be true in a significant number of cases, however, several important implications would follow from it.[c] First, the effectiveness of external opposition would obviously be even greater than it appears in the conclusions above. Second, however, such opposition would have to be reasonably stable over time rather than merely a "fad" phenomenon, lest cases that appeared to verify the third possibility prove to be merely instances of the second. The maintenance of such mobilized opposition is costly and difficult, particularly on behalf of "consumer" values such as environmental quality as against actions having economic benefits to motivate organized action, as Olson has noted.[7]

Finally, if agencies *were* responding to public pressure by turning from more to less controversial actions, then it is crucially important that such agencies *have a wide scope of activities available to them*, in order that they might be able to turn to activities more compatible with new demands.[d] As

---

[b]This is not intended to suggest that the solutions advocated by external pressure groups were necessarily optimal, or that "sufficient effectiveness" means veto power over any project that does not suit the preferences of intervenors. The point is that postponement, unless it is for the purpose of active re-evaluation to meet new policy goals, is inefficient from the perspectives of both the agency and the intervenors in contrast to a decision to proceed with or change the action. The achievement of postponements thus is not in itself evidence of an effective mechanism, unless the postponement amounts to de facto abandonment or results in substantive re-evaluation and in revision if warranted.

[c]One hopeful sign is that the Corps was given authority in 1973 to request "deauthorization" of inactive projects, and by the end of 1974 it had exercised this authority for the first time by sending up a list of several hundred projects that it proposed to deauthorize unless there was objection. Neither the nature of these projects nor the Congressional response to the deauthorization request has yet been carefully documented, but this device at least appears to have potential for removing some obsolete and undesireable proposals from circulation.

[d]If an agency's jurisdiction is limited to water resource development, for instance, either by law or by its political or professional environment, it may always be expected to promote water resource development as a solution to as many problems as possible. Water resource development may or may not be the best solution to these problems, either individually or collectively; yet if that is the limit of the agency's jurisdiction, that will tend to be the limit of its search for alternative solutions. Such "functional" planning jurisdictions thus tend to generate proposals that are optimal for the *agency's* purpose, followed by a "fishing expedition" to discover and add on any additional benefits that might be attributed gratuitously to them.

If such an agency has broad geographic jurisdiction, it may at least be able to adjust its priorities so as to favor proposals that are well matched to their political environments over those that are controversial. Such changes may or may not be "substantive" in the sense of

noted above, differences in the availability of such alternative activities help to explain the differences in policy response to NEPA by the Corps, which has relatively diverse possibilities for action, and by the SCS, whose possibilities were more closely circumscribed.

Limitations of the NEPA Mechanism

If the behavior of the agencies showed that external pressures were *necessary* for the achievement of significant administrative change, however, it did not insure that the forms those pressures took between 1970 and 1974 were *sufficient* to its achievement. Indeed, the paucity of substantive changes suggests that these forms were *not* sufficient, including even recourse to the courts; and this prima facie evidence is supported by identification of certain inherent problems in the working of NEPA's "action-forcing mechanisms" during the same period.

A central and crucial characteristic of the NEPA mechanism was its dependence upon *procedural instruments* for the achievement of substantive policy goals. Such instruments have strengths, chief among which is the sensitivity of both agencies and courts to procedural correctness in the administrative process; but they also suffer from important limitations. Chief among these limitations is their inability to directly change either the agencies' decisions or the makers of those decisions.

The procedures established by Section 102 of NEPA were intended to be instruments, not ends in themselves. Yet virtually all agency guidelines through 1974 were devoted to implementation of the procedure rather than of NEPA's substantive policies. Great scrutiny has been devoted to whether or not impact statements discuss every category of impact that might be considered significant; but no action has yet been rejected because it failed to "approach the maximum attainable recycling of depletable resources," or because it failed to promote the achievement of NEPA's other stated goals and objectives. The fascination of both administrative agencies and courts with NEPA's procedural requirements has so far neglected, if not obscured, the policy purposes that the procedures were intended to serve.

As a result, there has been a growing gap between the usage of environmental statements as new documents accompanying routine forms of agency action—dams, nuclear reactor licenses, highway links, and so forth—and the increasingly compelling need for an environmental perspective in truly major

---

favoring NEPA's goals, but they do at least reflect responsiveness to changes in popular preferences.

The point here, however, is that even geographic changes in priorities require agency jurisdictions broad enough to permit such changes. Barring outright reduction of an agency's activities, which would both threaten the agency's survival and require Congressional action, substantive change requires the availability to the agency of alternative activities, more compatible with new demands, to which it may turn.

federal policy decisions, such as those setting the fundamental directions for food and energy use, resource consumption, pollution, and population.

An important lesson from this experience is that administrative agencies are quite capable of implementing new procedural requirements without necessarily making the changes in their substantive actions that the procedures were intended to bring about.

The other limitation of NEPA's procedural mechanisms is their failure to significantly affect the mission-oriented organization of administrative planning and decision making in the federal government. The U.S. government is characterized by great fragmentation of both agencies and oversight committees along "mission" lines and by the absence of any strong integrative institution that could insure coordination of these missions. One of the problems that led to the development of NEPA, in fact, was the increasing incidence of conflict among these various missions. While NEPA's procedures provided for greater illumination of these conflicts, however, its procedures did not provide new mechanisms for the resolution of them.

A second and equally important characteristic of the NEPA mechanism concerns its dependence upon the instruments of *controversy* and *judicial review* as forces for administrative change. By the end of 1974, both of these instruments appeared less successful as long-term strategies for achieving administrative change than as short-term tactics, and this conclusion has important implications for future environmental policy actions.

The use of *ad hoc* controversy appears to have been moderately effective in cases where three conditions obtained:

1. Design changes rather than outright cancellation of a proposed action were an acceptable outcome to opponents.
2. Delay was an effective source of pressure on the agency (e.g., significant costs would be incurred by inaction).
3. Controversy was backed by a credible threat of litigation (well-organized and well-financed opposition, justiciable issue, and likelihood of successful opposition in the courts).

Many situations lacked strong combinations of these characteristics, however, and all suffered from certain underlying problems in the instruments of controversy and judicial review *per se*.

First, controversy and judicial review both operate as after-the-fact recourses at the end of the administrative process. These limitations were mitigated in the case of NEPA only by a waiting period to allow comments and reactions to the EIS before proceeding. Judicial review does not occur until administrative action is final and all administrative remedies have been exhausted, and controversy is not easily aroused until there is a specific proposal to attack. Such recourses therefore could not insure systematic consideration of environmental goals throughout the development and screening of action proposals. At best, they could raise a sufficiently threatening specter to encourage defensive documentation earlier in the process, but such actions aimed at avoiding the threat would not necessarily result in positive pursuit of NEPA's goals.

Second, controversy and judicial review are costly, both in money and in emotional commitment, time, and effort. They can therefore be relied upon to mobilize effective public support only in the most flagrant of cases, and even then only among constituencies with sufficient sophistication to become politically involved and with sufficient financial resources to hire legal and technical representation. Many action proposals were never challenged for these reasons, though their environmental impacts might be at least as serious as those of actions that did become controversial.

For similar reasons, many actions that were successfully challenged tended to be site-specific, project-type actions, whose location and implications were sufficiently obvious to provide a rallying symbol for opponents and victims. It is more difficult to mobilize effective opposition to actions that touch people's lives less directly—yet it is precisely these actions that often have the most widespread implications for the human environment. Examples might include budget allocations for military research and development, weather modification programs, genetic recombination experiments, subsidies for super-tanker construction, enforcement policies for pollution regulations, and government procurement practices.

Third, controversy and judicial review frequently are unable to compel change in the underlying policies, missions, and criteria upon which choices among action proposals are based. Administrative agencies are notoriously adept at "covering themselves" procedurally against legal challenge without necessarily changing their criteria for taking action, thus making a costly charade of "action-forcing" procedural requirements. Environmental interest groups can derive little satisfaction from delaying strip mining proposals on a few tracts in Montana on procedural grounds, until they are able to effectively challenge the policies upon which those proposals are based, such as the "Project Independence Blueprint." The delays may be useful or even necessary as tactics, but they are doomed to eventual frustration unless they are embedded in broader strategies of effective challenge to basic policy directions.

Fourth, controversy and judicial review have limited impact on the long-term coalitions of politically powerful individuals whose values shape administrative decision processes. NEPA's instruments assisted new actors to inject themselves into administrative processes on an *ad hoc* basis to challenge particular action proposals, but they did not significantly alter the channels and actors through which each agency's normal rewards and punishments flow. These include the line of command and authority within the agency, the staff of the Office of Management and Budget, and the agency oversight and appropriations committees of the Congress. Over the long term, it is these systems and actors that most deeply influence government policy making, not *ad hoc* challenges to specific actions; yet NEPA's instruments had little effect on these systems except to the extent that the cumulative weight of individual controversies made the political process somewhat more sensitive to controversial types of impacts.

Fifth, and finally, controversy and litigation are limited by their reliance upon negative sanctions and threats for the achievement of their purposes. They function inherently as adversary rather than cooperative processes, and their principal weapon is the power to delay proposed actions at significant cost to the agency. Frequently the agency official's only reward for his efforts is the avoidance of lawsuits or public embarrassment. The achievement of environmental goals may require a continuing threat of *ad hoc* opposition, but it also requires positive *rewards* for the pursuit of these goals, comparable to the personal satisfaction and peer-group approbation that officials normally receive for successful implementation of their traditional missions. NEPA's mechanisms did not provide these rewards.[e]

For all these reasons, instruments of *ad hoc* external pressure do not appear to provide an adequate substitute for properly functioning administrative processes, though they do provide an essential recourse against the malfunctioning of them. By whatever means, information concerning environmental goals and consequences must be infused into the total administrative process, in such a way that their proper consideration becomes self-regulating—subject, of course, to the permanent threat of external challenge, though less often, one hopes, the need for its actuality.

Conclusion

NEPA's "action-forcing mechanisms" have been extraordinarily effective in raising the level of debate over the consequences of proposed actions, but not yet very effective in resolving these debates. They have forced procedural action throughout the federal executive branch to document the impacts of proposed actions, but much less substantive action to implement NEPA's policy goals. They have been successful beyond any apparent expectations of their authors in drawing attention to environmental problems and issues, in a vivid and case-by-case fashion, but they have not yet resulted in coherent and consistent environmental policy making. While major battles are fought between opposing

---

[e]One problem, of course, is the disappointment of some agency officials that environmental interest groups often do not support them even when they do make changes, but instead continue to oppose them just as strongly at every opportunity. Their hopes may have been unrealistic, but it is hardly surprising that they then tend to feel more kindly towards others who support rather than condemn their professional activities, and who cooperate with them rather than confronting them. For an interesting study of this see Daniel A. Mazmanian, "Citizens and the Assessment of Technology," paper delivered at the 1974 Annual Meeting of the American Political Science Association, Chicago, August–September 1974.

interest groups over particular issues, major policy decisions continue to be made with only limited understanding or concern for long-term man–environment relationships.

From the perspective of 1976, NEPA so far has barely scratched the surface of the interplay among populations, resources, and environments that is so clearly the crux of the most serious man–environment problems we face. Yet it has proven an unusually potent expedient, and it may well have been the best instrument that its sponsors in the Congress could have created at the time. NEPA's purposes could not have been enacted by frontal challenge to the missions of existing agencies—those missions were and are supported by powerful constituencies not only in the agencies but in lobbies of beneficiaries and in the congressional committee structure. Faced with the realities of mission-oriented, politically powerful constituencies, NEPA's sponsors had to seek by indirection what could not have been achieved by confrontation: to set in motion new forces of procedure and information flow that might result in new political pressures and administrative results. The case studies above suggest that their strategy was partially but by no means totally successful during the first five years of NEPA's implementation.

NEPA will undoubtedly be reviewed periodically, in view of the continuing expense and threat that it imposes upon the executive agencies. It could undoubtedly be improved: there is no merit either in delay or in expensive *ad hoc* studies for their own sakes, if a more efficient means can be found to insure the achievement of NEPA's purposes. However, the paramount consideration in any modification of NEPA must be to keep intact its instruments of review and recourse, while devising further means of increasing its effectiveness and efficiency.

Reviewable, predecision statements of impact and alternatives have proven an important reform in the governmental process, on both rational and democratic grounds: rational, in that they permit independent scrutiny and verification of the analytic basis for government decisions; and democratic, in that they provide broader access to knowledge of government agencies' intentions. In both these respects they are important in themselves, as well as helping somewhat to further NEPA's policy goals. They also continue a trend toward rationality and accountability in government that were fostered by such previous reforms as the Administrative Procedures Act and the Freedom of Information Act.[8] Such progress should not be lightly discarded.

At the same time, further steps are needed to bring about the achievement of NEPA's policy goals, since impact statements have not yet been closely linked to those goals. A logical step would be to give more direct emphasis to the law's policy mandate and to the implications of this mandate for each agency's activities. With the continuing (and in some cases, worsening) of problems in the relationships between human activities and the environmental resources affected by them, we may hope, though we may not assume, that such efforts will be forthcoming. Another step is the extension of similar requirements to other units of government, a step that has already occurred in twenty-two states, several hundred units of local government, and several other nations and international organizations.

NEPA's impact statement mechanism was, to borrow the punch line from a familiar anecdote, the two-by-four that got the government mule's attention. It remains to be seen, however, where that stubborn creature of habit will go from here.

A depressing but not unlikely scenario is that either by direct attack or by gradual "bureaucratic nibbling,"[9] the agencies and their supporters will do away with NEPA's action-forcing mechanisms and thus with the necessity of dealing with its substantive policy. NEPA's mandate poses a direct challenge to fundamental patterns of agency behavior, which Lindblom and others have summarized as fragmenting complex problems among multiple units, allowing each unit to pursue its own mission and to rely upon later actions by other units for sequential correction, and preferring incremental rather than radical changes in policies and other decisions.[10] It may be difficult for such a challenge to survive indefinitely against such deeply ingrained norms; or if it does, it might do so only because it has been proceduralized and trivialized to the point that its continued existence is irrelevant to the politics of decision making.[f]

---

[f]Efforts have already been made to weaken or eliminate NEPA's impact statement requirements, both generally and in arguments to exempt particular classes of actions, and one may expect such efforts to continue as long as NEPA has any effectiveness. Such efforts in fact provide an important indicator of the mechanism's value, since it is only worth a political battle if its presence or absence has politically significant consequences.

These efforts have taken two principal forms. The direct form is a plea to the Congress to exempt certain actions or classes of actions from further requirements for procedural compliance with the impact statement provisions, on the grounds either that the class of actions "doesn't fit" within the NEPA framework, or that some "crisis" exists that is too important to permit the delays that would allegedly be involved in fulfilling those requirements. So far, most such efforts have succeeded only in discrete cases: water quality permits, a few nuclear reactors, and the Trans-Alaska Pipeline were exempted, and Housing and Urban Development block grants were turned over to local officials for preparation of impact statements, but no general weakening amendments to NEPA have yet been enacted.

The more indirect form of attack has been couched in terms of "reducing bureaucratic red tape." Congressman Wright's 1971 hearings of that name provide one example of this approach; similar intentions may be suspected in statements that NEPA's requirements should be "shaken down" and the "burdensome parts eliminated" (e.g., SCS statements quoted in Chapter 5). This argument is subtler and more difficult to counter, in part because impact statements *do* increase agencies' paperwork load. It also appeals to people's desire to trust that their government will work efficiently in "the public interest," and to the widespread myth that government agencies do function as mechanical instruments of representative democracy rather than as self-interested political organisms. The case studies above, however, suggest that such trust is misplaced. The reality of organizational behavior is more complex, and changing it does require new rewards and threats from each agency's political environment. Administrative efficiency is a valuable goal, but must always be subsidiary to the achievement of more fundamental social purposes—in this case, the environmental policy objectives established by NEPA.

This argument also has not yet resulted in any modification of NEPA, but one may

A more optimistic scenario, on the other hand, is that in the context of continuing environmental problems, the implementation of NEPA's procedures may prove to be merely the chaotic but necessary first step towards serious implementation of its policies. The preparation of impact statements by itself has not forced, and will not force, this outcome, but the policy principles that NEPA espoused and the climate of awareness that its "action-forcing provisions" have fostered may yet prove it a profoundly important change in the philosophical basis for administrative decision making.

---

expect continuing efforts by the agencies to "streamline the burdensome aspects" of NEPA's requirements as they integrate those requirements into their standard operating procedures. While such efforts are not necessarily bad, continuing scrutiny will be necessary to insure that the action-forcing mechanisms themselves are not streamlined out.

Appendix

Appendix

The National Environmental
Policy Act of 1969*

An Act to establish a national policy for the environment, to provide for the establishment of a Council on Environmental Quality, and for other purposes.

Be it enacted by the Senate and House of Representatives of the United States of America in Congress assembled, That this Act may be cited as the "National Environmental Policy Act of 1969."

Purpose

Sec. 2. The purposes of this Act are: To declare a national policy which will encourage productive and enjoyable harmony between man and his environment; to promote efforts which will prevent or eliminate damage to the environment and biosphere and stimulate the health and welfare of man; to enrich the understanding of the ecological systems and natural resources important to the Nation; and to establish a Council on Environmental Quality.

Title I

Declaration of National Environmental Policy

Sec. 101. (a) The Congress, recognizing the profound impact of man's activity on the interrelations of all components of the natural environment, particularly the profound influences of population growth, high-density urbanization, industrial expansion, resource exploitation, and new and expanding technological advances and recognizing further the critical importance of restoring and maintaining environmental quality to the overall welfare and development of man, declares that it is the continuing policy of the Federal Government, in cooperation with State and local governments, and other concerned public and private organizations, to use all practicable means and measures, including financial and technical assistance, in a manner calculated to foster and promote the general welfare, to create and maintain conditions under which man and nature can exist in productive harmony, and fulfill the social, economic, and other requirements of present and future generations of Americans.

---

*42 U.S.C. §4321 *et seq.*, 83 Stat. 852, P.L. 91-190.

(b) In order to carry out the policy set forth in this Act, it is the continuing responsibility of the Federal Government to use all practicable means, consistent with other essential considerations of national policy, to improve and coordinate Federal plans, functions, programs, and resources to the end that the Nation may—

(1) Fulfill the responsibilities of each generation as trustee of the environment for succeeding generations;

(2) Assure for all Americans safe, healthful, productive, and esthetically and culturally pleasing surroundings;

(3) Attain the widest range of beneficial uses of the environment without degradation, risk to health or safety, or other undesirable and unintended consequences;

(4) Preserve important historic, cultural, and natural aspects of our national heritage, and maintain, wherever possible, an environment which supports diversity, and variety of individual choice;

(5) Achieve a balance between population and resource use which will permit high standards of living and a wide sharing of life's amenities; and

(6) Enhance the quality of renewable resources and approach the maximum attainable recycling of depletable resources.

(c) The Congress recognizes that each person should enjoy a healthful environment and that each person has a responsibility to contribute to the preservation and enhancement of the environment.

Sec. 102. The Congress authorizes and directs that, to the fullest extent possible: (1) the policies, regulations, and public laws of the United States shall be interpreted and administered in accordance with the policies set forth in this Act, and (2) all agencies of the Federal Government shall—

(A) Utilize a systematic, interdisciplinary approach which will insure the integrated use of the natural and social sciences and the environmental design arts in planning and in decisionmaking which may have an impact on man's environment;

(B) Identify and develop methods and procedures, in consultation with the Council on Environmental Quality established by title II of this Act, which will insure that presently unquantified environmental amenities and values may be given appropriate consideration in decisionmaking along with economic and technical considerations;

(C) Include in every recommendation or report on proposals for legislation and other major Federal actions significantly affecting the quality of the human environment, a detailed statement by the responsible official on—

(i) The environmental impact of the proposed action,

(ii) Any adverse environmental effects which cannot be avoided should the proposal be implemented,

(iii) Alternatives to the proposed action,

(iv) The relationship between local short-term uses of man's environment and the maintenance and enhancement of long-term productivity, and

(v) Any irreversible and irretrievable commitments of resources which would be involved in the proposed action should it be implemented.

Prior to making any detailed statement, the responsible Federal official shall consult with and obtain the comments of any Federal agency which has jurisdiction by law or special expertise with respect to any environmental impact involved. Copies of such statement and the comments and views of the appropriate Federal, State, and local agencies, which are authorized to develop and enforce environmental standards, shall be made available to the President, the Council on Environmental Quality and to the public as provided by Section 552 of title 5, United States Code, and shall accompany the proposal through the existing agency review processes;

(D) Study, develop, and describe appropriate alternatives to recommended courses of action in any proposal which involves unresolved conflicts concerning alternative uses of available resources;

(E) Recognize the worldwide and long-range character of environmental problems and, where consistent with the foreign policy of the United States, lend appropriate support to initiatives, resolutions, and programs designed to maximize international cooperation in anticipating and preventing a decline in the quality of mankind's world environment;

(F) Make available to States, counties, municipalities, institutions, and individuals, advice and information useful in restoring, maintaining, and enhancing the quality of the environment;

(G) Initiate and utilize ecological information in the planning and development of resource-oriented projects; and

(H) Assist the Council on Environmental Quality established by title II of this Act.

Sec. 103. All agencies of the Federal Government shall review their present statutory authority, administrative regulations, and current policies and procedures for the purpose of determining whether there are any deficiencies or inconsistencies therein which prohibit full compliance with the purposes and provisions of this Act and shall propose to the President not later than July 1, 1971, such measures as may be necessary to bring their authority and policies into conformity with the intent, purposes, and procedures set forth in this Act.

Sec. 104. Nothing in section 102 or 103 shall in any way affect the specific statutory obligations of any Federal agency (1) to comply with criteria or standards of environmental quality, (2) to coordinate or consult with any other Federal or State agency, or (3) to act, or refrain from acting contingent upon the recommendations or certification of any other Federal or State agency.

Sec. 105. The policies and goals set forth in this Act are supplementary to those set forth in existing authorizations of Federal agencies.

Title II

Council on Environmental Quality

Sec. 201. The President shall transmit to the Congress annually beginning July 1, 1970, an Environmental Quality Report (hereinafter referred to as the "report") which shall set forth (1) the status and condition of the major natural, manmade, or altered environmental classes of the Nation, including, but not limited to, the air, the aquatic, including marine, estuarine, and fresh water, and the terrestrial environment, including, but not limited to, the forest, dryland, wetland, range, urban, suburban and rural environment; (2) current and foreseeable trends in the quality, management and utilization of such environments and the effects of those trends on the social, economic, and other requirements of the Nation; (3) the adequacy of available natural resources for fulfilling human and economic requirements of the Nation in the light of expected population pressures; (4) a review of the programs and activities (including regulatory activities) of the Federal Government, the State and local governments, and nongovernmental entities or individuals with particular reference to their effect on the environment and on the conservation, development and utilization of natural resources; and (5) a program for remedying the deficiencies of existing programs and activities, together with recommendations for legislation.

Sec. 202. There is created in the Executive Office of the President a Council on Environmental Quality (hereinafter referred to as the "Council"). The Council shall be composed of three members who shall be appointed by the President to serve at his pleasure, by and with the advice and consent of the Senate. The President shall designate one of the members of the Council to serve as Chairman. Each member shall be a person who, as a result of his training, experience, and attainments, is exceptionally well qualified to analyze and interpret environmental trends and information of all kinds; to appraise programs and activities of the Federal Government in the light of the policy set forth in title I of this Act; to be conscious of and responsive to the scientific, economic, social, esthetic, and cultural needs and interests of the Nation; and to formulate and recommend national policies to promote the improvement of the quality of the environment.

Sec. 203. The Council may employ such officers and employees as may be necessary to carry out its functions under this Act. In addition, the Council may employ and fix the compensation of such experts and consultants as may be necessary for the carrying out of its functions under this Act, in accordance with section 3109 of title 5, United States Code (but without regard to the last sentence thereof).

Sec. 204. It shall be the duty and function of the Council—

(1) To assist and advise the President in the preparation of the Environmental Quality Report required by section 201;

(2) To gather timely and authoritative information concerning the conditions and trends in the quality of the environment both current and prospective, to analyze and interpret such information for the purpose of determining whether such conditions and trends are interfering, or are likely to interfere, with the achievement of the policy set forth in title I of this Act, and to compile and submit to the President studies relating to such conditions and trends;

(3) To review and appraise the various programs and activities of the Federal Government in the light of the policy set forth in title I of this Act for the purpose of determining the extent to which such programs and activities are contributing to the achievement of such policy, and to make recommendations to the President with respect thereto;

(4) To develop and recommend to the President national policies to foster and promote the improvement of environmental quality to meet the conservation, social, economic, health, and other requirements and goals of the Nation;

(5) To conduct investigations, studies, surveys, research, and analyses relating to ecological systems and environmental quality;

(6) To document and define changes in the natural environment, including the plant and animal systems, and to accumulate necessary data and other information for a continuing analysis of these changes or trends and an interpretation of their underlying causes;

(7) To report at least once each year to the President on the state and condition of the environment; and

(8) To make and furnish such studies, reports thereon, and recommendations with respect to matters of policy and legislation as the President may request.

Sec. 205. In exercising its powers, functions, and duties under this Act, the Council shall—

(1) Consult with the Citizens' Advisory Committee on Environmental Quality established by Executive Order No. 11472, dated May 29, 1969, and with such representatives of science, industry, agriculture, labor, conservation organizations, State and local governments and other groups, as it deems advisable; and

(2) Utilize, to the fullest extent possible, the services, facilities and information (including statistical information) of public and private agencies and organizations, and individuals, in order that duplication of effort and

expense may be avoided, thus assuring that the Council's activities will not unnecessarily overlap or conflict with similar activities authorized by law and performed by established agencies.

Sec. 206. Members of the Council shall serve full time and the Chairman of of the Council shall be compensated at the rate provided for Level II of the Executive Schedule Pay Rates (5 U.S.C. 5313). The other members of the Council shall be compensated at the rate provided for Level IV of the Executive Schedule Pay Rates (5 U.S.C. 5315).

Sec. 207. There are authorized to be appropriated to carry out the provisions of this Act not to exceed $300,000 for fiscal year 1970, $700,000 for fiscal year 1971, and $1 million for each fiscal year thereafter.

Approved January 1, 1970.

Notes

Notes

Chapter 1
Federal Agencies and Environmental Policy

1. *Congressional Record*, February 18, 1969; reprinted in U. S. Congress, Senate Committee on Interior and Insular Affairs, *National Environmental Policy*, Hearing on S. 1075, April 16, 1969, Washington, D.C., 1969, pp. 24-25.

2. Public Law 91-190, Section 101 (A) (83 Stat. 852 *et seq.*; 42 U.S.C. 4321).

3. Cf. A. Myrick Freeman et al., *The Economics of Environmental Policy* (New York: John Wiley and Sons, 1973), pp. 64-80.

4. For fuller discussion of this point, see Richard N.L. Andrews, "Three Fronts of Federal Environmental Policy," *Journal of the American Institute of Planners* XXXVII (July 1971), pp. 258-66; also Richard N.L. Andrews, *Environmental Policy and Administrative Change*, Dissertation, University of North Carolina, Chapel Hill, 1972, chapter 2.

5. Charles A. Reich, "The Law of the Planned Society," *Yale Law Journal* LXXV (July 1966), pp. 1264-65.

6. Cf. Francis E. Rourke, *Bureaucracy, Politics, and Public Policy* (Boston: Little, Brown Co., 1969), p. 1; also Mancur Olson, Jr., *The Logic of Collective Action* (New York: Schenken Press, 1968).

Chapter 2
Legislative History of NEPA

1. S. 2549, the Resources and Conservation Act (1959); S. 2282, the Ecological Research and Surveys Act (1966); and S. 2805, "to authorize the Secretary of the Interior to conduct investigations . . . and to establish a Council on Environmental Quality" (1967). For a meticulously detailed history of federal environmental policy, issues, and legislation during the 1960s, see Ronald L. Shelton, *The Environmental Era: A Chronological Guide to Policy and Concepts, 1962-1972*, Dissertation, Cornell University, Ithaca, N.Y., 1973.

2. U.S. House of Representatives, Committee on Science and Astronautics, *Managing the Environment*, Serial S, Washington, D.C., 1968, pp. 24, 30.

3. *A National Policy for the Environment. A Report on the Need for a National Policy for the Environment; An Explanation of Its Purpose and Content; An Exploration of the Means to Make It Effective; and a Listing of Questions Implicit in Its Establishment*, A Special Report to the Committee on Interior and Insular Affairs, United States Senate (Together with a Statement by Senator Henry M. Jackson), 90th Congress, 2d Session, July 11, 1968, reprinted in U.S. Congress, Senate Committee on Interior and Insular Affairs, *National Environmental Policy*, Hearing on S. 1075, April 16, 1969, Washington, D.C., 1969, pp. 30–45.

4. Ibid., *passim.*

5. U.S. Congress, Senate Committee on Interior and Insular Affairs, *Congressional White Paper on a National Policy for the Environment*, Serial T, Washington, D.C., 1968.

6. *National Environmental Policy*, Hearing on S. 1075, p. 1. The reason for omitting reference to a national environmental policy was probably to forestall any controversy over committee jurisdiction between Jackson and Senator Edmund Muskie's Subcommittee on Air and Water Pollution of the Committee on Public Works, whose jurisdiction included nearly all previous environmental legislation. A similar maneuver later took place in the House of Representatives in order to keep the bill in the jurisdiction of a committee favorable to its purposes.

7. Ibid. Administration witnesses at this hearing opposed creation of a statutory Council on Environmental Quality on the grounds that the President had already established a Cabinet-level council for the same purpose. They hinted, however, that the President would welcome a congressional policy statement on the environment. The record suggests that the Administration agreed not to oppose creation of the CEQ in return for inclusion of the policy statement. Professor Caldwell, mentioned above as author of the Committee's background report on national environmental policy, suggests an additional reason for creating the statutory CEQ: what was needed was a new political and evaluative viewpoint on environmental policy, not the sort of technical and scientific approach that would be provided to the Cabinet council by the existing Office of Science and Technology. See Lynton K. Caldwell, *Environment: A Challenge to Modern Society* (Garden City, N.Y.: Natural History Press, 1970), pp. 222–23; also Geoffrey Wandesforde-Smith, "National Policy for the Environment," in Richard A. Cooley and Geoffrey Wandesforde-Smith (eds.), *Congress and the Environment* (Seattle: University of Washington Press, 1970), pp. 221-22.

8. *National Environmental Policy*, Hearing on S. 1075, Appendix 2, p. 207.

9. See Lynton K. Caldwell, "Environment: A New Focus for Public Policy?" *Public Administration Review* XXIII (September 1963). The concept of these "action-forcing provisions," which were the principal innovation em-

bodied in the Act, was authored by Professor Caldwell, who was not only the earliest academic prophet of the environment as a new focus for public policy, but also a consultant and a source of ideas and advice to Senator Jackson throughout the development of NEPA.

Caldwell's testimony at the Senate hearing provided the basis for Senator Jackson's amendment:

. . . I would urge that in the shaping of such [national environmental] policy, it have an action-forcing, operational aspect. When we think of policy we ought to think of a statement which is so written that it is capable of implementation; that it is not merely a statement of things hoped for; not merely a statement of desirable goals or objectives; but that it is a statement which will compel or reinforce or assist all of these things, the Executive agencies in particular, but going beyond this, the Nation as a whole, to take the kind of action which will protect and reinforce what I have called the life support system of this country . . . . a statement of policy by the Congress should at least consider measures to require the Federal agencies, in submitting proposals, to contain within the proposals an evaluation of the effect of these proposals upon the state of the environment . . . [*National Environmental Policy*, Hearing on S. 1075, p. 116].

10. U.S. Congress, *National Environmental Policy Act of 1969*, Senate Committee Report 91-296, July 9, 1969, Washington, D.C., 1969.

11. Ibid., p. 14.

12. Ibid., p. 9. As noted above, this echoes the testimony of Professor Caldwell.

13. Ibid., pp. 3, 9. This section of the bill was stricken before enactment, though some of its provisions were retained in other sections.

14. Ibid., p. 10.

15. Id.

16. H.R. 6750. Assignment of the Senate bill to a committee could have led to its demise in a jurisdictional dispute between the Merchant Marine and Fisheries Committee, which was sympathetic to NEPA and was in fact developing similar legislation, and Congressman Wayne Aspinall's Interior and Insular Affairs Committee, which was the House counterpart in jurisdiction (but not in its attitude towards NEPA) of Senator Jackson's committee.

17. U.S. Congress, *Council on Environmental Quality*, House Report 91-378, July 11 and 19, 1969, Washington, D.C., 1969, p. 9.

18. *Congressional Record*, September 23, 1969, p. H 8285.

19. Ibid., p. H 8284. The jurisdictional jockeying between Dingell and Aspinall has already been mentioned, as well as Aspinall's lack of support for the purposes of NEPA as proposed by the Senate. As a senior committee chairman and member of the House Rules Committee, Aspinall was in a position to exact a price from Dingell for the Rules Committee's permission to let the bill come to the floor for a vote; and that price was the acceptance of his amendments.

20. Ibid.

21. Id.

22. J. Clarence Davies III, *The Politics of Pollution* (New York: Pegasus, 1970), pp. 67, 71–72.

23. *Congressional Record*, October 8, 1969, pp. S 12117–12147.

24. Ibid., pp. S 12117–18.

25. *Congressional Record*, October 8, 1969, pp. S 12110–11.

26. See Lynton K. Caldwell, "The National Environmental Policy Act: Status and Accomplishments," in *Natural Resources and National Priorities: Proceedings of the 38th North American Wildlife and Natural Resources Conference*, Washington, D.C., March 18–21, 1973. This interpretation is supported in a retrospective explanation of the law's purposes by Professor Caldwell.

27. U.S. Congress, *Conference Report on S. 1075*, House Report 91–765, December 17, 1969, Washington, D.C., 1969, p. 3, and *Congressional Record*, December 17, 1969, p. H 12635.

28. *Congressional Record, loc. cit.*

29. *Congressional Record*, December 23, 1969, p. H 13094.

30. The National Environmental Policy Act of 1969, Public Law 91–190; 83 Stat. 852 *et seq.*; 42 U.S.C. 4321–4347.

31. Ibid., Section 101.

32. Ibid., Sections 102–105.

33. Ibid., Sections 201–207.

34. *National Journal* IV (February 26, 1972), p. 34.

35. *Congressional Record*, December 23, 1969, pp. H. 13094–13096.

36. Caldwell, "NEPA: Status and Accomplishments," *op. cit.*

Chapter 3
Executive Environmental Policy

1. James L. Sundquist, *Politics and Policy: The Eisenhower, Kennedy, and Johnson Years* (Washington, D.C.: The Brookings Institution, 1968), p. 323; see also Ronald L. Shelton, *The Environmental Era*, Dissertation, Cornell University, Ithaca, N.Y., 1973.

2. Shelton, *The Environmental Era*; see also Lynton K. Caldwell, *Environment: A Challenge for Modern Society* (Garden City, N.Y.: Natural History Press, 1970).

3. See Geoffrey Wandesforde-Smith, "National Policy for the Environment," in Richard A. Cooley and Geoffrey Wandesforde-Smith (eds.), *Congress and the Environment* (Seattle: University of Washington Press, 1969), p. 221,

and also Shelton, *The Environmental Era*. Shortly after his election in 1968, Nixon established a task force chaired by Russell Train to guide his initial policy positions in this area; it recommended that he appoint a special assistant for environmental affairs and establish a "President's Council on the Environment" to be chaired by the Vice President. Nixon ignored the first recommendation, however, and his Executive order creating the recommended Council was issued only after Senator Jackson's hearings on NEPA and was with the exception of a single radio-television address during his 1968 campaign, the only official Presidential pronouncement on the subject prior to 1970.

4. See U.S. Council on Environmental Quality, *Environmental Quality—1971*, Washington, D.C., 1971, pp. vii–viii, for his words: "This process [required by NEPA] has fostered a wide range of basic reforms in the way Federal agencies make their decisions . . . It is critically important that these new environmental requirements not simply produce more red tape, more paperwork and more delay. Nor is there any reason why this should happen. In fact, efficiency and responsiveness of Government is enhanced when environmental considerations are an integral part of decision-making from the time when a project is first considered and not merely added as after-thoughts when most matters have already been decided. . . The National Environmental Policy Act has given a new dimension to citizen participation and citizens' rights . . . We must also work to make government more responsive to public views at every stage of the decision-making process."

5. See for instance Shelton, *The Environmental Era*, pp. 483–84.

6. CEQ, *Environmental Quality—1971*, p. xi.

7. Quoted in *National Journal* III (December 25, 1971), p. 2535. The content of the President's pledge itself is less important than its symbolic stance and its implication that the environmental lobby was "going too far" and must be restrained by the administration.

8. See, for instance, *National Journal* IV (1972), pp. 827–29, 1586, and 1621–32, for evidence of this policy change, including Nixon's support of attempts to weaken NEPA by amendment; a legislative initiative to "streamline" powerplant licensing procedures; emphasis on industry-government cooperation rather than environmental regulation in his 1972 Special Environmental Message; veto of the Water Pollution Control Act amendments; and introduction of environmentally hazardous energy initiatives desired by industry, including expanded oil leasing on the outer Continental Shelf, accelerated development of the Liquid Metal Fast Breeder Reactor, and opposition to any attack on the oil depletion allowance.

9. The President's State of the Union Message on Natural Resources and the Environment, February 15, 1973. See U.S. Council on Environmental Quality, *Environmental Quality—1973*, Washington, D.C., 1973, Appendix E.

10. See CEQ, *Environmental Quality—1973*, Appendix F, for the six pro-

posals: accelerated leasing of the outer Continental Shelf, immediate authorization of the Trans-Alaska Pipeline System (TAPS), prototype leases of western lands for oil shale production, vastly expanded leasing of lands for strip mining of coal, accelerated development of the Liquid Metal Fast Breeder Reactor, and a slow-down in state implementation of secondary air quality standards.

11. Ibid., Appendix F. In Nixon's words: "I urge that the highest national priority be given to expanded development and utilization of our coal resources, . . . carefully meeting the primary, health-related standards, but not moving in a precipitous way toward meeting the secondary standards [of the Clean Air Act] . . . ." Other evidence of this priority during 1973 included a directive to Secretary of the Interior Rogers Morton in April to exert maximum effort in obtaining immediate authorization of the Trans-Alaska Pipeline System, the casting of a tie-breaking vote by Vice President Agnew to exempt TAPS from further review under NEPA, advocacy of other energy-related exemptions from NEPA, and the reduction of the President's message accompanying the annual report of the Council on Environmental Quality (which had been a seven- to eleven-page statement of goals and policy in each previous year) to a routine three-page cover letter. See, for instance, *National Journal* V (1973), pp. 553, 666, 1078, and 1722–30.

12. See, for instance, *National Journal* V (1973), pp. 1911–15; also see *Sierra Club Bulletin* LIX (May 1974), p. 18.

13. State of the Union Message of President Richard M. Nixon, January 30, 1974.

14. See, for instance, *Sierra Club National News Report* VI (March 29, 1974) p. 1, and *Sierra Club Bulletin* LIX (May 1974), p. 18.

15. See *Sierra Club National News Report* VI (June 14, 1974), p. 1.

16. Executive Order No. 11514, *Federal Register* XXXV (March 5, 1970), p. 4247.

17. Ibid., Section 2(b).

18. Ibid., Sections 3(d), 3(f), 3(h), and 3(i). Note that the congressional conference committee on NEPA had deleted Senate-approved language that would have allowed the Council to "review and approve" agency procedures for considering unquantifiable values, thereby leaving it only the power to "review and *appraise*" agency programs (NEPA Section 204(3)). The Executive order's mandate to "coordinate" federal programs appears to expand this authority.

19. U.S. Senate, Committee on Interior and Insular Affairs, *National Environmental Policy*, Hearing on S. 1075, April 16, 1969, Washington, D.C., 1969, pp. 116–17. See also Frederick R. Anderson, *NEPA in the Courts* (Baltimore: Johns Hopkins Press, 1973), pp. 11–12.

20. See Anderson, *NEPA in the Courts*, pp. 12–13, and Richard A. Liroff,

"The Council on Environmental Quality," *Environmental Law Reporter* III (1973), p. 50052. In fact, OMB's few official directives pursuant to NEPA show little interest even in implementing the law in the course of its own activities. See discussion later in this chapter. Also, the deliberate assumption of this role by the Council is demonstrated by the fact that its chairman, Russell Train, was the person who drafted the Executive order.

21. Executive Order No.11514, Section 3(h).

22. U.S. Council on Environmental Quality, "Interim Guidelines," *Federal Register* XXXV (April 1970), may also be found in Council on Environmental Quality, *Environmental Quality—1970*, Washington, D.C., 1970, Appendix G.

23. Interim Guidelines, No. 7(b). The Muskie bill was enacted in April 1970 (Public Law 91-224, the Environmental Quality Improvement Act of 1970, 42 U.S.C.A. 4372-4374).

24. Interim Guidelines, No. 4(b).

25. Interim Guidelines, Nos. 9(c) and 10(b). When questioned about the exemption of these documents from public disclosure, CEQ Chairman Train argued that while the Council urged full disclosure of these draft statements, such disclosure could not be required since the "draft statement" concept had been created only by the CEQ guidelines rather than by the statute. See U.S. Congress, House Committee on Merchant Marine and Fisheries, *Administration of the National Environmental Policy Act*, Hearings, Serial 91-41, Washington, D.C., 1971, Part 1, pp. 53-54.

26. See Council on Environmental Quality, *102 Monitor* I (February 1971), p. 52. Ninety-three "draft statements" had been received by the Council prior to February 1, 1971, compared with 274 final statements. Revisions in the guidelines published in 1971 made them mandatory for nearly all actions, however.

27. *Administration of NEPA*, Serial 91-41. The hearings were conducted by Congressman John Dingell's Subcommittee on Fisheries and Wildlife Conservation of the House Committee on Merchant Marine and Fisheries, NEPA's parent committee in the House of Representatives.

28. Ibid., Part 1, pp. 54, 59. Ironically, the Atomic Energy Commission was scathingly denounced by a court seven months later for making a "mockery" of the Act (see *Calvert Cliffs Coordinating Committee v. Atomic Energy Commission*, 2 ERC 1779 [D.C. Circuit, July 23, 1971]).

29. See ibid., Part 1, p. 64. In Train's words: "The moment you require it as a matter of law, you have given a right which is enforceable in the courts by way of injunctive proceedings against any act of any executive at any time that might conceivably have an environmental impact . . . . It seems to me you are creating a monster which you might not be able to deal with."

30. See ibid., Part 1, p. 67. The threat is expressed in the following exchange:

MR. DINGELL: . . . The question is who is going to see to it that this Executive order is carried out. Is the Council on Environmental Quality going to do it?
MR. TRAIN: Yes.
MR. DINGELL: Or is this committee going to have to do it?
MR. TRAIN: It is the responsibility of the Council.
MR. DINGELL: Well, then I would suggest to you, Mr. Train, that it would be well for you to give this committee full information as to how you propose to change your guidelines so that this Executive order is carried out.

31. See ibid., Part 1, p. 64. Another exchange between Dingell and Train illuminates this point:

MR. DINGELL: . . . you still have not told me how this interpretation you have been making of this statute will not [sic] prevent the adverse commentary of the agencies with special jurisdiction and expertise, the impact statement, and the announcement of the decision reaching the public the same day.
MR. TRAIN: No, under our present procedures, that is perfectly possible.

32. *Supra*, note 30.

33. *Federal Register* XXXVI (1971), p. 7724. For the January proposed revisions, see *Federal Register* XXXVI (1971), p. 1398.

34. Ibid., Nos. 1 and 2.

35. Ibid., No. 3.

36. Ibid., No. 10(b).

37. Ibid., Nos. 10, 7, and 7(b). The latter requirement (EPA comments on water quality impacts) amounted to a step away from the Council's earlier literal acceptance of the Muskie-Jackson "Explanation," and the reason for this step was not clear. It may have been an attempt to provide additional information or review power to the administrator of the newly created EPA, or a product of bad experience with state certification under the Interim Guidelines. It did not result from a judicial decision, since this issue was not construed by the courts until seven months later, and it does not appear to have resulted from enactment of the Clean Air Act (42 U.S.C. 1857), which contained provisions for mandatory comment by the EPA Administrator on all environmental impacts within his jurisdiction, since the CEQ guidelines appeared in its January proposed revisions while the other guideline revisions implementing the Clean Air Act were not added by the Council until the April final version.

38. For texts of the memos, as well as those discussed below, see U.S. Congress, Senate Committees on Public Works and on Interior and Insular Affairs, *National Environmental Policy Act*, Joint Hearings, Serial 92-H32, March 1972, Washington, D.C., 1972, pp. 39-58. Several of the other memos were primarily

informational; for example, a memorandum of May 14, 1971, merely listed the agencies that were expected to prepare detailed procedures for NEPA implementation; a July 30 memo alerted the agencies to key points of the recent *Calvert Cliffs* decision (*supra*, note 28) and to its possible implications for their procedures; and a memo of December 3 provided extracts of major judicial decisions bearing on eight major issues which the agencies' procedures must address. Two other memos, dated August 5 and September 23, were simply reminders concerning the deadlines established by the Council for revision of the agencies' procedures.

39. Ibid., p. 42.

40. Ibid., pp. 45–47.

41. For text, see Council on Environmental Quality, *102 Monitor* II (June 1972), pp. 1-21.

42. See Liroff, "The Council on Environmental Quality," pp. 50054-54; see also discussion of OMB policy, *infra*. The Council may have resorted to "memoranda" and "recommendations" rather than guideline revisions *per se* in order to avoid the controversial "quality of life reviews" that had recently been ordered by the Office of Management and Budget, whereby all proposed regulations dealing with environmental protection (among other subjects) would be subject to review and comment by OMB and other agencies before their publication.

43. *Federal Register* XXXVIII (August 1, 1973), p. 20550-62, Section 3(a).

44. U.S. Congress, *Administration of the National Environmental Policy Act*, House Report 92-316, Washington, D.C., 1972), p. 44, and *National Journal* VI (February 9, 1974), pp. 206-07.

45. H.R. 92-316, p. 44.

46. *National Journal* V (February 10, 1973), pp. 238-42, and Liroff, "The Council on Environmental Quality," p. 50060; see also *National Journal* V (February 3, 1973), p. 173, and *National Journal* VI (February 9, 1974), pp. 206-07. The number of positions was held constant in FY 1975 at 50; the budget request was increased by $60,000 over FY 1974, from $2.46 to $2.52 million.

47. Liroff, "The Council on Environmental Quality," pp. 50059-60.

48. Source of these criteria: personal interviews of Council staff by the author.

49. See *Weekly Compilation of Presidential Documents*, January 25, 1971, p. 81, for an example of such judicious choice of issues: the Council's widely publicized recommendation to the President that he halt construction of the Cross-Florida Barge Canal, which he did in January 1971. First, this project had great symbolic significance nationwide as a threat to the Everglades National Park. Second, there was active and vigorous local opposition to it, includ-

ing scientists as well as laymen, which had already led to a lawsuit (in fact, the project was enjoined by the court within the same week that the President ordered it halted). Third, it was a major project of the Corps of Engineers, itself perhaps the principal public symbol of "environmental destruction" among the federal agencies, to which a setback would serve as an example to others of Presidential commitment to environmental policy. Fourth, its cost to the federal budget was high, and its expected benefits marginal anyway. Finally, it was a Democratic project, which had been proposed repeatedly for decades without success until it was activated as a result of a campaign commitment by President Kennedy. It thus provided an ideal opportunity for a major symbolic action by President Nixon. Significantly, it was an isolated example of such Presidential commitment, which was not repeated by President Nixon in response to other Council recommendations (such as the SST, the Amchitka Nuclear Tests, and others). As noted above, however, the President's authority to halt this action unilaterally was questionable, and his action was declared illegal in 1974 (see *Environmental Defense Fund v. Corps of Engineers*, No. 71-652-Civ-J [M.D. Florida, February 4, 1974]). For the text of the Council's recommendations, see U.S. Congress, House Committee on Appropriations, *Public Works for Water and Power Development and Atomic Energy Commission Appropriation Bill, 1972*, Hearings, March 1971, Washington, D.C., 1971, Part 1, p. 633.

50. For recent discussion of the structure and activities of OMB, see *Science* CLXXXIII (January 18, 1974), pp. 180-84; ibid. (January 25, 1974), pp. 286-90; and ibid. (February 1, 1974), pp. 392-96. Its policies are particularly significant because of strenuous attempts by Nixon throughout his Administration to politicize it and to make it an effective instrument of his priorities.

51. Office of Management and Budget Bulletin, No. 71-3 (August 31, 1970) and No. 72-6 (September 14, 1971), and OMB Circular A-19 (July 31, 1972).

52. See *National Journal* (October 27, 1973), p. 1594, for the comment that "certain agencies were unpopular with OMB throughout the Nixon Administration—the Bureau of Reclamation, the Corps, and the National Oceanic and Atmospheric Administration."

53. OMB Circular A-19, Paragraph 7(d)(2).

54. Liroff, "The Council on Environmental Quality," pp. 50054-55. See also Thomas E. Cardinal, "Comment: The National Environmental Policy Act of 1969 and Its Implementation: A Socio-Political-Legal Look at the 'New Environmental Planning'," *Journal of Urban Law* L, pp. 465-85, at p. 482.

55. Note that when OMB circulated such proposed regulations for review, they were sent not only to other federal agencies (whose actions were the targets of CEQ guidelines), but also to bodies such as the National Industrial Pollution Control Council in the Department of Commerce, which was made up of industrial executives whose corporate activities were among the chief targets of all

categories of "quality of life" regulations, health, and consumer protection as well as environmental quality. See footnote d.

56. Comment, "CEQ Proposes New Guidelines for NEPA," *Environmental Law Reporter* III (May 1973), p. 10056.

57. For text of this memorandum, see Frederick R. Anderson, *NEPA in the Courts*, pp. 131–32, footnote 325.

Chapter 4
NEPA and the Army Corps of Engineers

1. 2 Stat. 137: 4 Stat. 22, 32; 10 Stat. 56; 39 Stat. 950, 33 U.S.C. 701.

2. 49 Stat. 1570; 58 Stat. 887; 48 Stat. 401, 16 U.S.C. 661.

3. U.S. Office of Management and Budget, *The Budget of the United States Government, Fiscal Year 1972*, Washington, D.C.: U.S. Government Printing Office, 1971, pp. 288–91.

4. U.S. Congress, Senate Committee on Public Works, *Civil Works Program of the Corps of Engineers: A Report to the Secretary of the Army by the Civil Works Study Board*, Committee Print, Washington, D.C., 1966, pp. 56–58. This report also notes the intention of the Corps to increase the number of officers assigned to civil works from 114 to 427 over a six-year period, to provide more of its officers with that form of training.

5. 49 Stat. 1571. The Corps' continuing authorities include 33 U.S.C. 426(g), beach erosion; 33 U.S.C. 701(s), flood control; and 33 U.S.C. 577, navigation projects. These authorities contain ceilings on the amounts that may be expended on any one project, and in practice most projects so constructed are quite small by Corps standards (costing an average of about $50,000).

6. See for instance Thomas M. Clement and Glenn Lopez, *Engineering a Victory for the Environment* (Washington, D.C.: U.S. Government Printing Office, 1971), chapter 2, and Elizabeth Drew, "Dam Outrage," *Atlantic* CCXXV (April 1970), p. 54. According to some sources, primary support for such requests frequently comes from local interests which stand to gain economically from Corps projects, such as barge companies, contractors, industrialists and real estate speculators. The requests also are frequently preceded by consultation with the District Engineer as to how such objectives and other local aims may be realized.

7. Authority for review of unfavorable recommendations by committee resolution may be found in 33 U.S.C. 542 and 33 U.S.C. 701.

8. For a synopsis of the average time required for each phase of the process, see Testimony of Major General Frank P. Koisch, in U.S. Congress, House Committee of Public Works, Subcommittee on Investigations and Over-

sight, *Red Tape—Inquiring Into Delays and Excessive Paperwork in Administration of Public Works Programs*, Hearings, June 17, 1971, Serial 92-15, Washington, D.C., 1971, pp. 317-27.

9. Ibid., p. 317.

10. 33 U.S.C. 547. Note that in practice, however, the budget for the pre-authorization planning phase is limited to a percentage (for instance, 10 percent) of the expected total project cost, and as a result, important planning studies may be performed superficially or not at all during this phase and must be done or redone in detail during preparation of the "First General Design Memorandum," after authorization of a project, when design and construction funds are appropriated. At this later stage, however, since authorization has already occurred, analysis must be directed toward alternative designs rather than toward alternative elements of the project or alternative projects.

11. U.S. Army, Corps of Engineers, Planning Manual EM 1120-2-1, "Survey Investigations and Reports, General Procedures" (no date), paragraph 1-139.

12. See Drew, "Dam Outrage," p. 55. The Corps typically describes this as an "independent" review board, since it was established by statute at the turn of the century to exercise an additional review of project worth. However, its conclusions are not binding on the Chief of Engineers, and its seven members are themselves Division Engineers, who might be expected to protect their own projects by not attacking each other's.

Corps officials cite the fact that 53 percent of the projects considered by the board are reported unfavorably by it, but by contrast, 50 percent of these are submitted with unfavorable reports by the District Engineers, leaving only 3 percent actually revised by the BERH. See Northcutt Ely, *Authorization of Federal Water Projects* (Washington D.C.: U.S. National Water Commission, 1971), p. 122.

13. *Red Tape*, Serial 92-15, p. 317.

14. Drew, "Dam Outrage," p. 55; Arthur Maass, *Muddy Waters* (Cambridge, Mass.: Harvard University Press, 1951), pp. 30-31.

15. Arthur Maass, "Public Investment Planning in the United States: Analysis and Critique," *Public Policy* XVIII (Winter 1970), p. 242.

16. See *National Journal* IV (1972), pp. 1846-55; *National Journal* V (1973), pp. 238-42, 705, 1353-58. The Office of Management and Budget has responsibility for releasing funds to the agencies on a schedule commensurate with the timetable for their expenditure. During the Nixon Administration, however, a major controversy arose over the "impoundment" by OMB of Congressionally appropriated funds for reasons of Administration *policy*: to control inflation, to delay or kill programs to which the President was opposed, or to punish Administration opponents. This practice was declared illegal by a series of courts during 1973, but it was a major factor in the pace of construction at least until this time and perhaps thereafter as well.

17. *Red Tape*, Serial 92-15, p. 322.

18. Ibid., p. 327.

19. The Corps' general authorities are contained in 33 U.S.C. sections 426, 540, and 701, which relate respectively to beach erosion, flood control, and navigation. Permissive language in those sections, as well as other statutes such as the National Environmental Policy Act and The Fish and Wildlife Coordination Act, mention additional factors to be considered.

20. See Testimony of Major General Frank P. Koisch, in U.S. Congress, House Committee on Government Operations, Subcommittee on Conservation and Natural Resources, *Stream Channelization*, Hearings, June 1971, Washington, D.C., 1971, Part 2, p. 557, for the testimony of the Corps' Director of Civil Works: "During the late 1950s and all through the 1960s, Congress, the Administration and the executive agencies became increasingly aware and concerned about other things related to water projects, such as recreation, water quality, fish and wildlife, forest resources, and land use. Greater weight and importance were given to these factors in planning. These concerns culminated in the National Environmental Policy Act which established national policy for the quality of the environment."

21. Cf. Public Law 89-90, the Water Resources Planning Act of 1965. Prior to this law, the executive had promulgated such criteria by fiat.

22. Federal Inter-Agency River Basin Committee, Subcommittee on Benefits and Costs, *Report to the Federal Inter-Agency River Basin Committee, Proposed Practices for Economic Analysis of River Basin Projects*, Washington, D.C., 1950.

23. U.S. Bureau of the Budget, *Circular A-47*, Washington, D.C., December 31, 1952.

24. *Policies, Standards and Procedures in the Formulation, Evaluation and Review of Plans for Use and Development of Water and Related Land Resources*, Senate Document 87-97, Washington, D.C., May 29, 1962.

25. U.S. Water Resources Council, "Principles and Standards for Planning Water and Related Land Resources," *Federal Register* XXXVIII (September 10, 1973), pp. 24778-869.

26. 49 Stat. 1750. The law did not, however, define what a "project" included, nor did it specify that all increments or elements of such a project must have benefits greater than their costs.

27. Senate Document 97, sections V(C) (1), V(A) (7), V(B)(1), and V(A) (4). The Water Resource Council's "Principles and Standards" carried this breadth even further, by creating four separate "accounts" to show the benefits and costs of a proposed project respectively on national economic development, environmental quality, regional economic development, and social well-being. These principles were not officially adopted until nearly three years after NEPA's enactment, however, and in the adopted version the latter two accounts

were included only as informational displays rather than as formal objectives of the projects. For the reasons for this change, see discussion in the text concerning the policy position of the Office of Management and Budget towards these criteria.

28. *Stream Channelization*, Part 2, pp. 557, 580. General Koisch's testimony may have failed to give full credit to the agency for some of its innovations and experiments, such as the Susquehanna Basin Study in which a concerted attempt had been made to utilize a multiple-objective framework for planning, and creation of an in-house research arm (the U.S. Army Engineer Institute for Water Resources) to explore new issues and directions for the agency. However, his statement probably does represent fairly the every-day practices of most Corps districts.

29. For discussion of theory and criteria for public expenditures, see generally Robert H. Haveman and Julius Margolis (eds.), *Public Expenditures and Policy Analysis* (Chicago: Markham Press, 1970), and especially its chapter 1, "The Public Sector and the Public Interest," by Peter O. Steiner.

30. Cf. James T. Murphy, "Political Parties and the Porkbarrel: Party Conflict and Cooperation in House Public Works Committee Decision Making," *American Political Science Review* LXVIII (1974), pp. 169-85.

31. For further discussion see Gilbert F. White, "Environmental Impact Statements," *The Professional Geographer* XXIV (November 1972), pp. 304-05. President Franklin Roosevelt directed as early as 1936 that all plans for land drainage and water storage projects be reported to his Natural Resources Committee, for review and comment by other affected agencies. Other mandates included Executive Order No. 9384 (1940); various interagency committees established during the 1940s; the Fish and Wildlife Coordination Act of 1946, amended in 1958; and the Water Resources Planning Act of 1965.

32. According to Maass ("Public Investment Planning," pp. 213-16): "Agencies with limited rather than general interests in river basin development . . . have promoted administrative procedures and in one case legislation that require the principal planning agencies . . . to refer to them for review all proposed plans, so that the limited-purpose agencies can determine whether their interests have received proper attention . . . . In the case of water resource planning this strategem got off to a good start in the late 1930s and the 1940s because the principal planning agencies were themselves more interested in developing certain purposes than others—the Corps of Engineers in navigation and flood control, the Bureau of Reclamation in irrigation and electric energy; and because the technique of benefit-cost analysis was developed in those years in a way that restricted the types of benefits and costs that could be counted, so that most of the benefits and costs of some special purposes were of necessity excluded from the important planning calculation."

33. White, "Environmental Impact Statements," p. 305.

34. See *Red Tape,* Serial 92-15, for hearings which were deliberately staged to dramatize the alleged burdens imposed upon public works planning agencies by the procedural and documentation requirements of NEPA and other recent legislation.

35. U.S. Army Corps of Engineers, EC 1165-2-83, March 3, 1970, "National Environmental Policy Act of 1969"; U.S. Army Corps of Engineers, EC 1165-2-85, April 22, 1970, "Budget Material in Response to the National Environmental Policy Act of 1969 for Authorized Projects"; and U.S. Army Corps of Engineers, EC 1165-2-86, April 30, 1970, "National Environmental Policy Act of 1969."

36. See EC 1165-2-83 for part of its statement: "The spirit and intent of the National Environmental Policy Act will be effectuated by the Corps of Engineers in all of its pre- and post-construction activities . . . . [Section 102 of NEPA is] interpreted to be applicable to survey reports and to requests for funds to initiate construction of previously authorized projects . . . . Pending issuance of detailed instructions presently under preparation, it is essential that each survey report not now essentially completed include a detailed five-point statement as required by Section 102 (2) (C), including required information on the coordination that has been accomplished and analysis of alternatives, as required by Section 102 (2) (D) if appropriate."

37. See EC 1165-2-85, which also reiterated the point of the earlier circular that "a statement will be necessary for all authorized projects not yet under construction"; emphasized the necessity for including environmental statements with upcoming budget material under preparation, and directed that all units give "priority consideration to those projects whose starting time is imminent."

38. See EC 1165-2-86 for the following directive: "In formulating water resource development or management plans, impact on the environment will be fully considered from the very initiation of planning . . . . Preparation of the five-point statement required by the Act will constitute an *integral part of the preauthorization survey process*" [emphasis added].

39. Ibid. These categories were to include proposals for legislation; proposals for project authorization; initiation of construction or land acquisition; budget submissions requesting funds either for initiation of construction or land acquisition, or for continuation of those activities or even operation and maintenance if unresolved conflicts existed; and the issuance of permits likely to have significant adverse effects on the environment.

40. See ibid. for the following quotation: "The public will be informed of the general content of all statements before or at the time that the recommendation or report is furnished to the Council on Environmental Quality . . . . In addition, prior to formulation of recommendations and preparation of the statement, in all cases where public hearings are held, the responsible official will present, in the notice of the hearing and at the hearing, a discussion setting forth

the information, as known to him, upon which his statement will be based . . . . Whenever public announcement of recommendations or reports is made prior to submission of the statement to the Council on Environmental Quality, the announcement will contain an appropriate summary of the proposed statement and comments of other agencies."

41. U.S. Army Corps of Engineers, EC 1120-2-56, September 25, 1970, "Preparation and Coordination of Environmental Statements." (See also U.S. Congress, House Committee on Merchant Marine and Fisheries, *Administration of NEPA*, Hearings, Serial 91-41, Washington, D.C., 1971, Part 2, p. 20.)

42. See EC 1120-2-56 for a discussion of problems and clarification of particular aspects of the statements: for instance, they should describe the project sufficiently to permit independent evaluation; they should not be construed as a further means for supporting project justification; they should include and comment on opposing views; they should include a full and objective appraisal of both beneficial and adverse environmental effects; and they should include effects of regional significance.

43. Ibid., Appendix B. It stated in part: "Impacts shall be detailed in a dispassionate manner to provide a basis for a meaningful treatment of the trade-offs involved. Quantitative estimates of losses or gains . . . will be set forth wherever practicable . . . . A distinction should be observed here, whereby the *impacts* (changes) were initially detailed without making value judgments while at this [later] point are discussed in terms of their *effects* (who or what is affected by the changes) . . . placing some relative value on the impacts described" [author's emphasis].

44. Ibid. At the third or "late-stage" public meeting: "The environmental discussion regarding the proposal and alternatives will be specific and thorough regarding the environmental impacts and effects." Note, however, that there are no required public hearings after the official draft statement is prepared and circulated to other agencies for comment. The public thus would not necessarily have access to expert but opposing viewpoints at the time of the hearings.

45. Ibid. On projects that had been recommended, authorized or under construction prior to NEPA's enactment: ". . . the range of alternatives and the opportunity to study and evaluate them may be more limited. However, to the maximum extent feasible, alternative solutions and opportunities for environmental enhancement, preservation and mitigation will be investigated prior to preparation of the statement."

46. U.S. Army Corps of Engineers, EC 1165-2-91, September 30, 1970, "National Environmental Policy Act of 1969: Operation and Maintenance"; and OM 15-2-1, October 14, 1970, "Chief of Engineers Environmental Advisory Board."

47. U.S. Army Corps of Engineers, EC 1120-2-62, November 18, 1970,

"Personal Involvement of Reporting Officers in Policy Problems and Environmental Considerations."

48. U.S. Army Corps of Engineers, EC 1165-2-500, November 30, 1970, "Environmental Guidelines for the Civil Works Program of the Corps of Engineers."

49. U.S. Army Corps of Engineers, ER 1105-2-507, May 28, 1971, "Preparation and Coordination of Environmental Statements" *Federal Register* XXXVI, June 11, 1971, pp. 11309-18). An engineer circular remains in effect only for a specified time period, while an engineer regulation is binding until explicitly superseded.

50. Ibid, number 5 (e).

51. Ibid, number 8 (b).

52. Ibid. For instance, where the September circular had stated that the preliminary draft statement "may" be made available to interested citizens, paragraph 8(d) of this regulation directs that it "will" be made available to the public while it is under review by other agencies. Similarly, paragraph 10(b) directs that copies of the final statement be made available upon request "on an expedited basis," and paragraph 8(b) authorizes the Division Engineer to order an extra public meeting if environmental impact or controversy becomes apparent after the normal three meetings.

53. Ibid., Appendix C, paragraph 3(f). The principal reason for expansion of the list to include social and economic impacts was a provision of the Rivers and Harbors Act of 1970 (Section 122), which directed the Corps to promulgate guidelines for full consideration of these impacts *along with* "environmental" impacts. See 84 Stat. 1823, Section 122. This mandate will be discussed further below.

54. U.S. Army Corps of Engineers, EC 1165-2-100, May 28, 1971, "Public Participation in Water Resource Planning."

55. Ibid., paragraph 9. Submission of these plans for review by OCE or other higher echelons of the Corps, however, was explicitly voluntary.

56. See ibid., paragraph 5, for Remarks of Lieutenant General F.L. Clarke, Chief of Engineers, before the Short Course on Public Participation in Water Resources Planning, Atlanta, Georgia, February 2, 1971: "In the past we have conducted our planning activities with a relatively small percentage of the people who have actually been concerned, and these were Federal, state and local government officials of one kind or another. Today there are, in addition, vast numbers of private citizens who, individually, or in groups and organizations and through their chosen representatives, are not only keenly interested in what we are doing with the Nation's water resources but who want to have a voice and influence in the planning and management of these resources . . . we cannot and must not ignore (these) other voices . . . ."

This circular, it should be noted, was not the first indication of Corps concern about the need for public participation, but rather the latest in a series of actions that had been taken by the Office of the Chief since enactment of NEPA. A previous circular had been issued on September 1, 1970, which anticipated the requirements of the September 25 circular with respect to the consideration of environmental issues in public meetings during planning (U.S. Army Corps of Engineers, EC 1120-2-55, "Public Meetings in Planning"); the "Environmental Guildelines" of November 30 had included further mention of the need for public participation; a study report on the subject was published in December 1970 (A. Bruce Bishop, *Public Participation in Water Resources Planning*, IWR Report 70-7, Fort Belvoir, Va., 1970); and in February 1971, the OCE had sponsored a "Short Course on Public Participation in Water Resources Planning" for Corps personnel, in Atlanta.

57. Cf. Testimony by CEQ Chairman Train at the 1970 Congressional oversight hearings, *supra*, Chapter 3; see also Richard A. Liroff, "Environmental Administration: NEPA and Federal Agencies," in Stuart Nagel (ed.), *Environmental Politics* (New York: Praeger, 1974), footnote 19 and accompanying text.

58. See Testimony of Major General Frank P. Koisch, in *Administration of the NEPA*, Serial 91-41, Part 1, p. 917, for the explanation of the Corps' Director of Civil Works: "We recognized that because of the nature of our business we couldn't afford to wait any longer than that to get started on our procedures and meet the requirements of the Congress for the 1970 river and harbor bill."

59. Testimony of Major General Koisch, *Administration of NEPA*, Serial 91-41, Part 1, p. 926.

60. Council on Environmental Quality, *102 Monitor* I (January 1972), p. 66. According to a survey of the Corps districts by the author in late 1971, over 600 statements had actually been prepared during this period, but some of these were drafts that were later superseded by final statements (the Council's figures subtract the draft when the final statement is submitted), and others were still under internal review by the Corps and had not yet been released.

61. See *Administration of NEPA*, Serial 91-41, Part 2, p. 20.

62. See U.S. Congress, House Committee on Public Works, *Omnibus River and Harbor and Flood Control Act–1970*, Hearings, October 1970, Serial 91-48, Washington, D.C., 1970. All 85 detailed statements were published as an appendix to these hearings.

63. *102 Monitor.*

64. OMB, *The Budget of the United States Government, Fiscal Year 1972*, pp. 281-91.

65. U.S. General Accounting Office, *Improvements Needed in Federal Efforts to Implement the National Environmental Policy Act of 1969*, Washington, D.C., 1972, Appendix II, p. 63.

66. See *102 Monitor* II–IV (1972–1974). This rate excludes substitutions of final for previously submitted draft statements.

It is crucially important that the Corps decided as it did to apply the law to all its actions, rather than attempting arbitrarily to limit it to "new" actions. The Corps' planning process is over fifteen years long, and even then many actions are taken as a result of restudy of old plans or delayed appropriation of funds rather than being truly "new." Any other policy might therefore have encouraged significant limitation of the law's application.

67. See *Administration of NEPA*, Serial 91–41, Part 1, p. 932. General Koisch testified that "there were statements submitted this year to catch the omnibus bill that were not done at the District level." For other criticisms of them, see EC 1120-2-56, paragraph 3, "Discussion."

68. Leonard Ortolano and William W. Hill, *An Analysis of Environmental Statements for Corps of Engineers Water Projects*, IWR Report 72-3 (Fort Belvoir, Va.: U.S. Army Engineer Institute for Water Resources, 1972). The authors examined 234 detailed statements, of which 27 were draft statements and the remaining 207 represented nearly all the statements that were considered to be in final form as of August 1971.

69. Ibid., p. 104. The treatment of alternatives was generally brief:

Typically, the section of the environmental statement dealing with alternatives consisted of a brief paragraph or two describing some or all of the following: the implications of not building the project; the nature of the "structural alternatives" with or without a discussion of their economic and/or environmental ramifications; and the nature of the "non-structural alternatives," usually with the reasons for not pursuing them.

The implications of not building the proposed project were mentioned in about 85 percent of the statements. Commonly, the alternatives were rejected for being technically infeasible, too costly, or having impacts on the environment that were even more serious than those associated with the proposed project.

70. Ibid., pp. 102-25. On the last point, the report concluded that most such comments were either ignored or treated inadequately, and that nonstructural alternatives were usually dismissed in a single word: "infeasible."

71. Ibid., pp. 111-12.

72. See Ortolano and Hill, *An Analysis of Environmental Statements*, and several other major efforts in this area, including the Environmental Impact Assessment Project of The Institute of Ecology, sponsored by the Ford Foundation; the Public Lands Project at Northwestern University, under the direction of Professor H. Paul Friesema; a study of selected statements by various agencies by the U.S. General Accounting Office; and a study of 200 randomly selected statements by William V. Kennedy and Bruce B. Hanshaw. U.S. General Accounting Office, *Adequacy of Selected Environmental Impact Statements Prepared Under*

the National Environmental Policy Act of 1969, Washington, D.C., 1972, and William V. Kennedy and Bruce B. Hanshaw, "The Effectiveness of Impact Statements," *Ekistics* CCXVIII (January 1974), pp. 19-22.

73. *102 Monitor* I (1971).

74. Ortolano and Hill, *An Analysis of Environmental Statements*.

75. During the fall of 1971, this author conducted surveys of all districts and divisions of the Corps of Engineers and of all State Conservationists' Offices of the Soil Conservation Service. Response rates, which were quite high, ranged from approximately 60 to 90 percent depending on the question; and the results of this survey will be referred to frequently during this and the following chapter.

76. Based on the average effort devoted to preparation of environmental statements for "typical" noncontroversial and controversial projects, in the opinions of the District and Division Engineers surveyed in October 1971. The differences between means and medians reveal the presence of a small number of extraordinarily high estimates, or possibly "wild guesses," which distorted the means upwards; but using either means or medians as a basis, the conclusions are clear.

It is particularly interesting that greater effort was devoted to noncontroversial projects in defendant districts and not just to the projects that were the subjects of litigation as one might expect; for this suggests strongly that at least through the threat of litigation, NEPA *was* forcing an educational process to occur in the field organization of this agency.

77. OMB, *The Budget of the United States Government, Fiscal Year 1972*, pp. 281-91, and U.S. General Accounting Office, *Improvements Needed*, Appendix II, p. 63. The Board of Engineers for Rivers and Harbors reported that 17 to 20 projects had been reported negatively or recalled by the districts after critical environmental review by BERH, and that approximately 20 had been significantly changed as a result of environmental review by BERH. These projects were not identified by name, and it is not clear therefore how extensively these estimates overlap with the districts' responses. Since BERH review occurs prior to congressional authorization, the maximum overlap would be the 14 projects listed as "investigated" or "recommended" in the tables above. Of these 14, only 9 mentioned internal reevaluation as a cause of modification, and only 3 of those 9 attributed significant change to internal reevaluation in the absence of external factors. The role of the BERH thus does not appear to affect the analysis here presented.

78. *State of Delaware v. Pennsylvania New York Central Corporation* (D. Delaware), complaint filed February 13, 1970; *Stewart v. Resor* (E.D. Pennsylvania, No. 70-5551), complaint filed February 24, 1970, temporary restraining order granted February 24, 1970, TRO vacated February 27, 1970; *Society of Northwest Steelheaders v. Corps of Engineers* (E.D. Washington, No. 3362), complaint filed March 11, 1970; *Environmental Defense Fund v. Corps of En-*

gineers (D.D.C.), second amended complaint filed April 9, 1970; *Sierra Club v. Laird* (D. Arizona, Civ. No. 70-78 TUC), complaint filed May 25, 1970; and *Izaak Walton League v. Macchia* (D. New Jersey), complaint filed August 3, 1970.

79. *Sierra Club v. Laird*, 1 ELR 20085 (D. Arizona, June 23, 1970), and *Zabel v. Tabb*, 430 F. 2d 199 (5th Circuit, July 16, 1970). General Koisch of the Corps commented on these decisions: "With the recent favorable court decisions, the policy statement of the Act has given us a firm basis for denying permits that are excessively harmful to the environment. It has provided us, through the impact statement procedure, a better way to discuss and consider environmental detriments in our planning and public participation activities." He added, however, that passage of the Act had also created serious manpower and funding problems for the Corps. See *Administration of NEPA*, Serial 91–41, Part 1, p. 915.

80. The dismissed case was *Sierra Club v. Corps of Engineers*, 2 ERC 1795 (W.D. Wisconsin, 1971), in which the judge ruled that plaintiffs had not demonstrated that the proposed action would cause "irreparable harm"; the permit action was upheld in *U.S. v. Brookhaven*, 2 ERC 1761 (E.D. New York, July 3, 1971). The other six decisions were *Environmental Defense Fund v. Corps of Engineers*, 324 F.Supp. 878, D.D.C. 1971 (Cross-Florida Barge Canal); *Environmental Defense Fund v. Corps of Engineers*, 325 F.Supp. 749, E.D. Arkansas, 1971 (Gillham Dam); *Izaak Walton League v. Macchia*, 329 F.Supp. 504, D. New Jersey, 1971; *Texas Committee on Natural Resources v. Resor*, 1 ELR 20466, E.D. Texas, 1971; *Environmental Defense Fund v. Corps of Engineers*, 331 F.Supp. 925, D. D.C. 1971 (Tennessee-Tombigbee Waterway); and *Kalur v. Resor*, 335 F.Supp. 1, D. D.C. 1971.

While the specific holdings of these decisions varied, two points were made quite clear through them: NEPA must be applied to previously initiated projects so long as any "major federal actions" remained to be taken, and NEPA's detailed statements must not merely be prepared but must contain "adequate" consideration of environmental impacts and alternatives to provide "at least . . . environmental full disclosure." See especially the Gillham Dam decision, 2 ERC at 1267.

For full discussion of the judicial opinions concerning NEPA, see Frederick R. Anderson, *NEPA in the Courts* (Baltimore: Johns Hopkins, 1973).

81. See *Omnibus River and Harbor and Flood Control Act—1970*, H.R. 91-1665, p. 52. As Congressman William Harsha put it, "I think we will need these reports when we are on the House floor dealing with this situation." Passage of this bill is usually timed to precede the biennial congressional elections in order to benefit incumbents, and this pressure may thus have helped force the Corps to gear up for writing detailed statements somewhat more promptly than other agencies.

82. Cf. *Red Tape*, Serial 92–15. These hearings were sponsored by the Subcommittee on Investigations and Oversight, chaired by Representative James Wright (D–Texas). Interestingly, comparison of the testimony of the Corps during these hearings with that of other agencies (such as the Highway Administration and Soil Conservation Service) suggests that the Corps more than the others *did* in fact support implementation of NEPA, that it did not attribute substantial headaches and paperwork to the requirements of detailed statements, and that unlike the others (and unlike Congressman Wright) it was not interested in using these hearings as a platform for political attacks on NEPA.

83. See further discussion *infra*, Chapter 5.

84. *Supra*, Chapter 3, note 49. This directive was eventually declared illegal by the courts, but not until 1974; in the meantime, it served as a form of pressure on the Corps.

85. Among the most important of these precedents were *Wilderness Society v. Hickel*, 325 F.Supp. 422, D. D.C. 1970 (the Trans-Alaska Pipeline decision on the initial detailed statement); *Calvert Cliffs Coordinating Committee v. Atomic Energy Commission*, 449 F.2d 1109, D.C. Circuit 1971; and *Natural Resources Defense Council v. Morton*, 337 F.Supp. 165, D. D.C. 1971. The first of these concerned the adequacy of a detailed statement; the second required (among other things) that detailed statements accompany and be considered with other project documents throughout the normal review process and that they reflect individualized "balancing" of environmental and other considerations; and the third required reasonable discussion of alternatives, even those outside the agency's jurisdiction, in sufficient detail to permit reasoned choice by a reviewer.

86. White, "Environmental Impact Statements."

87. See Joseph J. Brecher and Manuel E. Nestle, *Environmental Law Handbook* (Berkeley, Calif.: California Continuing Education of the Bar. 1970), pp. 107–108; see also *Abbott Laboratories v. Gardner*, 387 U.S. 136 at 148 (1967), and Louis L. Jaffe, *Judicial Control of Administrative Action* (Boston: Little, Brown, 1968), chapter 10.

88. For fuller discussion of this question, see Daniel A. Mazmanian and Jeanne O. Nienaber, "Bureaucracy and the Public: A Case Study of Citizen Participation in the Corps of Engineers," paper presented at the Annual Meeting of the Midwest Political Science Association, Chicago, April 1974.

89. U.S. Congress, Senate Committee on Public Works, *Public Works for Water and Power Development and Atomic Energy Commission Appropriations, Fiscal Year 1972*, Hearings, March 1971, Washington, D.C., 1971, Part 1 *passim*.

90. Survey of Corps Districts by the Office of the Chief of Engineers, September 7, 1971.

91. See U.S. Environmental Protection Agency, Office of Research and Monitoring, *Toward a Philosophy of Planning: Attitudes of Federal Water Plan-*

ners, by Raymond H. Wilson, Washington, D.C., 1973, especially pp. 53–55, 128, 148, 167–71. A revealing study of the attitudes of seventy federal water resource planners, nearly all of whom were engineers and the majority of whom were employed by the Corps, was carried out during 1970 and 1971. Among other things, this study showed that:

1. Most of their views of nature and the environment were pragmatic, rarely going beyond physical attributes; this was particularly true in the Corps.
2. Environmental goals were viewed as increasing in emphasis relative to traditional economic goals, but this trend was less evident in the Corps than in either the Federal Water Quality Administration or the Bureau of Reclamation.
3. Nonsupervisory planners, and persons with less than ten years' service in their agencies, both gave significantly greater emphasis to environmental and resource management goals than to economic goals; and both groups also felt that economic goals had been overemphasized. Supervisory planners, however, and planners with more than ten years' agency service, both emphasized economic goals and felt that environmental and resource management goals had been over-emphasized.
4. Nonsupervisory planners and those with less than ten years' service also believed that water pollution problems would be more serious in the future; this was particularly true of BuRec and FWQA planners. Supervisory planners and planners with more than ten years' service, however, generally believed that such problems would be less serious or unchanged; and this attitude was particularly prevalent in the Corps.

92. October 1971 survey by author.

93. See EC 1165-2-91. At the Washington headquarters level of the Corps, an environmental resources branch has been created in the planning division as early as 1966, long before enactment of NEPA. In addition, the Chief of Engineers established an "Environmental Advisory Board" in October 1970, composed of distinguished environmentalists, and granted it a broad mandate to examine existing and proposed actions of the Corps, to identify problems and deficiencies, and to propose improvements or changes. This Board's function was advisory only, and its members differed in their opinions of its effectiveness (its first chairman, Charles Stoddard, resigned in symbolic protest after one year). It did serve, however, at least as a symbol of the Corps' willingness to listen more closely to environmental interest groups—much as President Nixon's "National Industrial Pollution Control Council" symbolized his particular interest in the opinions of industrialists concerning pollution control—and as a source of some new ideas and suggestions, such as the Corps' pilot "environmental reconnaissance inventory" program. For further discussion of this Board, see Daniel A. Mazmanian and Mordecai Lee, "Tradition be Damned! The Army Corps of Engineers Is Changing, *Public Administration Review XXXV* (March–April

1975), p. 166ff, and Lt. Gen. F.J. Clarke and Roland C. Clement, "Redirection for the Corps: Perspectives," *Water Spectrum* IV (Fall 1972), pp. 1-7.

94. As one author notes: "Typically, the introduction of technical innovative activities into modern organization is by means of segregated units, often called research and development units. Segregating such activities prevents them from affecting the *status quo* to any great extent. The organization does not have to change." See Victor Thompson, "Bureaucracy and Innovation," in William Scott (ed.), *Organization Concepts and Analysis* (Belmont, Calif.: Dickenson, 1969), p. 129. The same point might be made about the Corps' Washington-level research unit, the Institute for Water Resources.

95. Anderson, *NEPA in the Courts*, pp. 287, 288-89.

96. *Scientists' Institute for Public Information v. Atomic Energy Commission*, 2 ELR 20642 (D. D.C. 1972), 3 ELR 20525 (D. D.C., June 1973).

97. Anderson, *NEPA in the Courts*, pp. 286-88.

98. See footnote u of this chapter.

99. *Sierra Club v. Froehlke* (Trinity River-Wallisville Dam), 3 ELR 20248 (S.D. Texas, 1973); but note later appellate decision, *Sierra Club v. Callaway*, 4 ELR 20731 (5th Circuit, August 1974).

100. Anderson, *NEPA in the Courts*, pp. 263-65.

101. Concerning the failure of agencies to implement judicial precedents, see for instance James W. Moorman, "Litigating Environmental Causes With the Government," paper presented at the American Law Institute-American Bar Association Conference on Environmental Law, San Francisco, February 9, 1974. Moorman's central point is that the agencies of the federal executive have in recent years arrogated to themselves a discretion in excess of their legal authority, extending in some cases even to blatant evasion of court orders when these orders countervened their policies.

102. See for instance *Conservation Council of North Carolina v. Froehlke*, 340 F.Supp. 222 (M.D. N. Carolina), affirmed 2 ELR 20259 (4th Circuit, 1972), 3 ELR 30132 (4th Circuit, 1973); *Sierra Club v. Froehlke* (Kickapoo River), 345 F.Supp. 440, 2 ELR 20307 (W.D. Wis., 1972); and *Environmental Defense Fund v. Armstrong* (New Melones Dam), 2 ELR 20604 (N.D. Cal.), 352 F.Supp. 50, 2 ELR 20735 (N.D. Cal. 1972), 3 ELR 20294 (N.D. Cal., 1973).

103. U.S. National Water Commission, *New Directions in U.S. Water Policy*, Final Report: Summary, Conclusions and Recommendations, Washington, D.C., 1973, especially pp. 6-10. The National Water Commission was created by Act of Congress in 1968 to review national water resource problems over a period of five years and to consider also the social and economic consequences of water development. Its recommendations, however, and in particular its recommendation of more widespread use of user charges, were greeted by immediate and substantial resistance by the water development lobby and by many Congressmen. See *National Journal* V (August 4, 1973), pp. 1125-31.

104. U.S. Water Resources Council, "Principles and Standards for Planning Water and Related Land Resources," *Federal Register* XXXVIII (September 10, 1973), pp. 24778-869. The Water Resources Council is an interagency committee created by the Water Resource Planning Act of 1965, whose authority included the review of the standards and criteria established by Senate Document 97 in 1962 and the promulgation of new uniform principles and standards to guide water resource project evaluation.

105. Public Law 93-251, The Water Resource Development Act of 1973 (H.R. 10203, S. 606), Section 80. See further discussion in the text.

106. Mazmanian and Lee, "Tradition Be Damned!"

107. P.L. 93-251.

108. U.S. Congress, House of Representatives, *Water Resources Development Act of 1973 and River Basin Monetary Authorization Act of 1973*, House Report No. 93-541, Washington, D.C., 1973, Sections 73, 2, and 88 (pp. 115-16, 76-82, and 126-27).

109. Ibid., Sections 77, 54-56, and 22.

110. Ibid., Section 1.

111. Ibid., Section 12.

112. Ibid., Section 80.

113. Ibid., Section 6.

114. C. Grant Ash, "Three Year Evolution," *Water Spectrum* V (Fall, 1973), pp. 28-35, at p. 30.

115. For a lengthier list of related policies and guidelines, see U.S. Army Corps of Engineers, "Planning: Preparation and Coordination of Environmental Statements," ER 1105-2-507, *Federal Register* XXXIX (April 8, 1974), p. 12737, Section 3, "References."

116. U.S. Army Corps of Engineers, "Planning: Preparation and Coordination of Environmental Statements," ER 1105-2-507, *Federal Register* XXXVIII (February 16, 1973), p. 9242, and the same (revised), *Federal Register* XXXIX (April 8, 1974), p. 12737. Note that despite the quality of these guidelines, however, Corps projects continued to be halted periodically by the courts for inadequate compliance.

117. Concerning the "Statement of Findings," see also ER 1105-2-509.

118. U.S. Army Corps of Engineers, "Planning: Guidelines for Assessment of Economic, Social, and Environmental Effects of Civil Works Projects," ER 1105-2-105 (December 15, 1972).

119. Public Law 91-611, The Omnibus River and Harbor and Flood Control Act of 1970, Section 122 (84 Stat. 1818). A similar provision was inserted into the Federal Aid Highway Act of 1970. The author of the provision was Congressman Jamie Whitten (D-Miss.), whose public statements indicated a concern that the presumably beneficial effects of public works projects would re-

ceive inadequate attention as NEPA's requirements resulted in greater attention to effects on the natural environment. A major related concern at the time was the threat that more stringent environmental regulatory measures would force marginal firms or industrial plants out of business.

120. ER 1105-2-105. These guidelines set out a detailed sequence of eleven steps comprising the process of "effects assessment": a profile of existing conditions was to be assembled, then these conditions were to be projected forward over the expected lifetime of the proposed project, first without and then with the project; significant effects were then to be identified, described, and displayed and then beneficial and adverse effects were to be evaluated; project modifications were then to be considered, outside feedback was to be sought, and the assessment was then to be used in preparing recommendations, statements of findings, and detailed environmental statements. The guidelines also included an attachment which listed "sample causative factors" and "sample project effects."

121. U.S. Army Corps of Engineers, *Digest of Water Resources Policies and Activities*, EP 1165-2-1 (December 28, 1972). See especially Appendix A, Chapter 3, pp. A-17 to A-21.

122. See among others Drew, "Dam Outrage," Clements and Lopez, *Engineering a Victory*, Maass, *Muddy Waters*, and Walter A. Rosenbaum, *The Politics of Environmental Concern* (New York: Praeger, 1973), chapter 6.

123. For further discussion, see for instance Mazmanian and Nienaber, "Bureaucracy and the Public."

124. The Seattle District. See U.S. General Accounting Office, *Improvements Needed in Federal Efforts to Implement the National Environmental Policy Act of 1969*, Washington, D.C., May 1972, p. 35.

125. Mazmanian and Lee, "Tradition Be Damned!" The four pilot areas inventoried were the states of Washington and Vermont, and the Charleston (South Carolina) and Wilmington (North Carolina) Districts of the Corps. See also U.S. Army Corps of Engineers, "Environmental Reconnaissance Inventory Pilot Test: Fact Sheet" (mimeo), April 20, 1972.

126. See U.S. Army Corps of Engineers, "Wastewater Management Program: Study Procedure," May 1, 1972, and also Mazmanian and Lee, "Tradition Be Damned!" The initial studies were located in Boston, Chicago, Cleveland, Detroit, and San Francisco.

127. Mazmanian and Lee, "Tradition Be Damned!"

128. Ibid. Note that several other technical assistance authorities were also newly delegated to the Corps, including assistance to states in water and related land use planning, supplementing its few previous activities such as flood plain information studies.

129. See "Wastewater Management Program: Study Procedure," Preface.

According to General Roper of the Office of the Chief of Engineers: "I cannot emphasize too strongly the priority which is attached to this program. It should clearly stand out above all other tasks as the highest priority Civil Works Planning program within the Corps of Engineers; and this priority should be reflected in the attention and energies directed toward each of these studies, and to those which follow."

130. P.L. 93–251, Section 80. The three projects were the Charles River Basin, Massachusetts; the Mississippi River at Prairie du Chien, Wisconsin; and the South Platte River below Chatfield Dam, Colorado.

131. Mazmanian and Lee, "Tradition Be Damned!"

132. Id. The Soil Conservation Service provides an illuminating example of the opposite case, as the following chapter will show.

133. P.L. 93–251, Section 80.

Chapter Five
NEPA and the SCS Small Watersheds Program

1. Public Law 74–46, 16 U.S.C. 590 a-f; 49 Stat. 1570.

2. 58 Stat. 887. See also the testimony of Hollis R. Williams, Deputy Administrator for Watersheds, Soil Conservation Service, in U.S. Congress, House Committee on Public Works, Subcommittee on Investigations and Oversight, *Red Tape—Inquiring Into Delays and Excessive Paperwork in Administration of Public Works Programs*, Hearings, June 17, 1971, Serial 92-15, Washington, D.C., 1971, p. 191.

3. Public Law 83–566; as amended, 16 U.S.C. 1001–1008.

4. Public Law 566, Section 1.

5. Ibid., Section 2. See also Robert J. Morgan, *Governing Soil Conservation* (Baltimore: Johns Hopkins Press, 1965), especially pp. 37–40, 221, 321.

6. P.L. 566, Section 4. In addition, the SCS requires that not less than 75 percent of the effective land treatment measures be installed on designated critical sediment course areas, and SCS guidelines require that this portion of the land treatment be installed or provided for prior to installation of the federally funded structural measures (see Soil Conservation Service, *Watershed Protection Handbook*, chapter 104.036b). Note, however, that while the local sponsors of the project have a supposed obligation to effectuate the remainder of these measures, the SCS has no apparent recourse against them if they fail to fulfill it. See Morgan, *Governing Soil Conservation*, pp. 188–89.

7. See for instance U.S. Department of Agriculture, *Assistance Available from the Soil Conservation Service*, Agriculture Information Bulletin No. 345, Washington, D.C., 1970.

8. U.S. Congress, House Committee on Appropriations, *Agriculture-Environmental and Consumer Protection Appropriations for 1972*, Hearings, Washington, D.C., 1971, Part 3, pp. 515-98, 508. For comparison, the budget of the Corps for the same year was $1.3 billion, of which $780 million was for construction (see previous chapter).

9. See *Agriculture . . . Appropriations for 1972*, Hearings, Part 3, p. 497, for 1971 testimony by SCS officials: *"When it is determined* that a plan will provide substantial benefits from flood prevention or agricultural water management, consideration is given to all other phases of the conservation, development, utilization, and disposal of water. This includes such purposes as municipal and industrial water supply, recreation, and fish and wildlife" [emphasis added] . See also testimony of SCS officials, in U.S. Congress, House Committee on Government Operations, Subcommittee on Conservation and Natural Resources, *Stream Channelization*, Hearings, June 1971, Washington, D.C., 1971, Part 2, p. 521.

10. P.L. 566, Sections 2, 5(4); and 12.

11. P.L. 566, Sections 3-5.

12. Ibid., Sections 2, 5(4); and 12. Regarding the review of these projects, note that SCS projects are not subject to the review provisions of the Fish and Wildlife Coordination Act, unlike projects of the Corps and the Bureau of Reclamation. Instead, Section 12 of P.L. 566 as amended requires the SCS only to "notify" the Secretary of the Interior of its intention to assist a sponsoring organization in preparing a work plan, and to allow the Interior Department to participate in that process if it wishes to do so at its own expense. While Interior's recommendations must be "considered" prior to work plan approval, however, they need not be adopted unless they are not only "technically and economically feasible" but also "acceptable and agreed to" by both the local sponsors and the SCS. For more detailed discussion, see U.S. Congress, House Committee on Government Operations, *Stream Channelization*, House Report 93-530, Washington, D.C., 1973, pp. 46-53; also U.S. Congress, House Committee on Merchant Marine and Fisheries, Subcommittee on Fisheries and Wildlife Conservation, *Administration of the National Environmental Policy Act*, Hearings, December 1970, Serial 91-41, Washington, D.C., 1971, Part 1, p. 994.

13. For the text of an opinion of the Solicitor for the Department of Agriculture, see *Stream Channelization*, Hearings, Part 5, pp. 2945-46:

All activities of the soil conservation districts are carried out in the name of the district which is not a federal agency but a local unit of government organized under state law. The Soil Conservation Service cooperates with districts by extending technical advice, material and other assistance, but the work of a district is its own responsibility and undertaking. A district's activities can in no way to be considered those of a Department or Agency of the United States.

See also *Stream Channelization*, H. Rept. 93-530, p. 49.

14. Morgan, *Governing Soil Conservation*, pp. 203–14. Morgan states that these committees tend to be "insulated from urban society, largely self-perpetuating, and focussed almost exclusively upon farming operations" (pp. 213–14), a view which SCS officials describe as "extremely outdated" (letter to author, February 9, 1973). Some of these committees undoubtedly do have broader representation now, especially in the more urban Northeast; but in other areas such as the Southeast where many of the most extensive and damaging stream channelization projects are planned, SCS testimony confirms that the membership represents almost exclusively agricultural interests. See *Stream Channelization*, H. Rept. 93–530, p. 31, footnote 52.

Morgan also asserts that these state soil and water conservation committees generally maintain no technical staffs and frequently do not publicize the criteria upon which their screening of projects is based. It is thus not clear how such priorities are established; but the crucial point is that the SCS officially defers to this body with respect to priorities among projects in each state, while the Corps must simply obtain the unranked concurrence of the governor (or his designate) for each project. See Morgan, *Governing Soil Conservation*, pp. 213, 259, 368.

15. *Administration of NEPA*, Serial 91–41, Part 1, pp. 984–85, 995. The testimony of the Director of the SCS Watershed Planning Division is particularly instructive: "I don't believe you could construe [section 4 of P.L. 566] as cloaking the Secretary with authority to require the local organizations to carry out fish and wildlife enhancement measures, and if they did so, he would bear 50 percent of the cost . . . . we have held to the view that they could select their objectives and goals, so long as they developed a sound project . . . even though there may be a need for municipal water supply, or fish and wildlife enhancement, or recreation, or whatever, and the local people feel they do not have the finances necessary to carry out those needs, or to finance their share of those needs, and can carry out a sound project, we would provide the assistance . . . we can deny the assistance if in our judgment it would result in a significant loss of environmental or other values."

16. *Red Tape*, Serial 92–15, p. 217.

17. See Chapter 2.

18. See *Stream Channelization*, Hearings, Part 1, p. 211; Part 2, pp. 515, 516, 528, 529, 532. For instance, SCS testimony discounted the impacts of its projects on recreational values of streams, on ground water, on downstream hydrology (for instance, the possibility of higher flood peaks), and on timber resources. Clearing of bottomland hardwoods as a result of SCS projects was declared an "insignificant" environmental impact "when considered in relationship with clearing taking place irrespective of channel improvement"; private drainage of wetlands, which was made feasible by SCS channel projects, was similarly discounted. The SCS asserted that only "some adverse effects to the

fishery resource" had occurred on some streams and that "most" of the streams channelized were intermittent and provided "at best only poor to fair fisheries."

In answer to charges that extensive drainage of wetlands frequently resulted from its projects and that this was a significant environmental impact, SCS replied that it did not drain "historic" swamps. It cited a dissertation purporting to show that "supposed natural swamps" drained by the SCS "were actually well-defined channels and rocky streambeds as recently as the late 1800s," and on this basis defended its "rescue" of their capacity to carry water from the "influence of man's careless land use." Even if true (which has been disputed), such an argument was specious, since a central purpose of the environmental statement was to identify impacts of federal actions upon the functions currently performed by natural systems, not upon their historic origins.

Finally, the SCS ignored or minimized the secondary effects of its projects in making feasible further *private* drainage, especially in the pothole areas of the upper midwest which were important for the maintenance of migratory waterfowl populations, despite testimony to these effects by fish and wildlife agencies.

19. See Soil Conservation Service, *Watershed Protection Handbook*, Sections 113.11-5 and 113.09-18, -19, -20, and -21. Categories of impacts to be considered included flood prevention, erosion, and sedimentation; agricultural water management; water supply; fish and wildlife and recreation; archaeological, historic, and scientific; and economic and social. Water quality was mentioned only insofar as it related to "project needs"; as of 1972, the chapter of the *Handbook* dealing with water quality management (Chapter 10) had not yet even been issued. Other categories of impacts were mentioned only briefly if at all, in sharp contrast to the Corps' attempts to provide a far-ranging and thought-provoking list of illustrative sorts of impacts that should be considered.

20. *Supra*, Chapter 4.

21. Extensive testimony on this point is contained in *Stream Channelization*, Hearings. For scientific evidence, see, among others: William Alvord and J.C. Peters, *Channel Changes in 13 Montana Streams* Montana Fish and Game Commission, Fisheries Division, 1963; C.J. Barstow, *Fish and Wildlife Resources, Obion-Forked Deer River Basin, Tennessee*, unpublished report, Tennessee Game and Fish Commission, 1970 (synopsis published in *Stream Channelization*, Hearings, Part 1, pp. 323-30); Jack Bayless and William B. Smith, *The Effects of Channelization Upon the Fish Population of Lotic Waters in Eastern North Carolina*, North Carolina Wildlife Resources Commission, 1964; Allen A. Elser, "Fish Populations of a Trout Stream in Relation to a Major Habitat Zones and Channel Alterations," *Transactions of the American Fisheries Society* XCVII (1968), pp. 389-97; Trusten H. Holder, *Disappearing Wetlands in Eastern Arkansas*, Arkansas Planning Commission, 1970; Larry A. Morris, R.N. Lengemeier, T.R. Russell, and A.C. Witt, Jr., "Effects of Main Stem Impoundments and Channelization Upon Limnology of the Missouri River, Nebraska," *Transactions of the American Fisheries Society* XCVII (1968), pp. 380-88; and William H.

Tarplee, Jr., Darrell E. Lauder, and Andrew J. Weber, *Evaluation of the Effects of Channelization on Fish Populations in North Carolina's Coastal Plain Streams*, North Carolina Wildlife Resources Commission, 1971 (also printed in *Stream Channelization*, Hearings, Part 1, pp. 188-210).

22. *Administration of NEPA*, Serial 91-41, Part 1, pp. 970, 993.

23. See especially U.S. Congress, Senate Committee on Public Works, *The Effect of Channelization on the Environment*, Hearings, July 1971, Serial 91-H24, Washington, D.C., 1971, p. 111, and also *Administration of NEPA*, Serial 91-41, Part 1, p. 971, 988-95. For example, even though responsibility for the channelization review and classification under *Watersheds Memorandum 108* had been assigned to the State Conservationists (to be carried out by an interdisciplinary team of professionals), at least one State Conservationist replied to a request for classification of a project in Group 3 merely that the request would be "called to the attention of the sponsors"—rather than considered on its merits by the agency's review team. (Letter of September 13, 1971, from David N. Grimwood, SCS State Conservationist for the State of Virginia, to Ernest C. Martin, Acting Regional Director, U.S. Bureau of Sport Fisheries and Wildlife. Printed in *Stream Channelization, Hearings*, Part 4, p. 2721).

24. Executive Order 11514, concerning the implementation of NEPA (March 5, 1970), directed that federal agencies' procedures include "whenever appropriate, provision for public hearings." In addition, Executive Order 10584 (December 18, 1954), as amended by Executive Order 10913 (January 18, 1961) authorized the Secretary of Agriculture to hold "public hearings at suitable times and places when he determines that such action will further the purposes of Public Law 566." See *Stream Channelization*, H.R. 93-530, pp. 33-34.

25. U.S. Department of Agriculture, Soil Conservation Service, *Watershed Protection Handbook, Notice 1-17*, April 7, 1971, Section 113.1331. Section 113.1332 did permit field review and comment on preliminary draft statements for *administratively* authorized projects, as opposed to those that must be authorized by the Congress.

In contrast to this SCS norm, an unusually specific requirement for public information about proposed water resource projects was enacted by the State of North Carolina in 1971. This law required a public hearing for every water resource project proposed by either the Corps of Engineers, the Soil Conservation Service, or the Tennessee Valley Authority that would involve stream channel excavation. The hearing was to be conducted by the State Board of Water and Air Resources or its designee in the county or counties where the project would be located; and no such project could be constructed without the approval of that Board, under penalty of injunction. The hearing was to be held at the preliminary project investigation stage of the SCS process (or recommended report stage of the TVA process); and it was to be preceded by public notice in local newspapers including a quarter-page map of the entire project showing all proposed "works of improvement," no less than two and no more than four weeks prior to the hearing (General Statutes of North Carolina, 1971 Cumulative Supplement, section 139–47).

26. *Notice 1-17*, Section 113.3112. In this context it is hardly surprising that the Assistant Secretary of the Interior testified in June 1971 that "Our problem is under the Environmental Policy Act; it is late in the game. It is a review of what has already been decided upon, and under the [Fish and Wildlife] Coordination Act our recommendations need not be followed." See *Stream Channelization*, Hearings, Part 2, p. 424.

27. See *Stream Channelization*, H. Rept. 93-530, pp. 13, 50, 73. It is worth recalling that NEPA was sponsored and overseen in the House of Representatives by the Subcommittee on Fish and Wildlife Conservation of the Committee on Merchant Marine and Fisheries, one of the two committees (along with the Subcommittee on Conservation and Natural Resources of the Committee on Government Operations) that most regularly attacked the SCS for the impacts of stream channelization on fish and wildlife resources.

28. For a list of "actions taken by SCS to implement Public Law 91-190," see *Stream Channelization*, Hearings, Part 2, p. 534. Initial directives included *Advisory Leg-1*, January 29, 1970; *Advisory Intera-4*, April 1, 1970; *Watersheds Memorandum 102*, May 1, 1970; *Watersheds Memorandum 103*, May 1, 1970; *Watersheds Memorandum 104*, May 1, 1970; and *Advisory WS-13*, May 1, 1970. The first two of these were merely informational; *Memorandum 101* directed stronger involvement by SCS state biologists in watershed investigations and planning; *Memorandum 102* required minimization of damage to fish and wildlife habitat and inclusion of mitigation measures (in addition to land treatment) in work plans; and *Memorandum 104* directed that at least two public meetings be held by the sponsors during watershed planning and that the sponsors take leadership in developing public information programs.

29. See *Watersheds Memorandum 102*, which is illustrative. It opens with the statement that "This memorandum re-emphasizes policies of the Soil Conservation Service . . . ."

30. *Watersheds Memorandum 103*.

31. U.S. Department of Agriculture, Soil Conservation Service, *Advisory EVT-5*, September 11, 1970. This communication transmitted *Secretary's Memorandum No. 1695*, issued May 29, 1970, and *Supplements 1, 2, and 3*, issued August 3, 1970. *Supplements 4 and 5* were issued December 1, 1970, and not transmitted to the field by SCS until sometime thereafter. Note that a draft of the SCS *Watersheds Memorandum 108* (discussed further below) was also circulated on this date, perhaps stimulated in part by a desire to build a good record prior to the Dingell oversight hearings.

32. See Table 5-1.

33. U.S. Department of Agriculture, Soil Conservation Service, *Watersheds Memorandum 108*, February 4, 1971. According to this memorandum: "Chan-

nel improvement is to be placed in Group 1 if it meets all the Group 1 criteria [minor or no known adverse effects; clearly conforms or can easily be modified to conform to enumerated guidelines; benefit-cost ratio clearly favorable] ; in Group 3 if it meets any Group 3 criteria [serious adverse effect; major modifications needed to reduce adverse effects to an acceptable level; benefit-cost ratio less than unity] ; and in Group 2 if it meets any or all Group 2 criteria and none of Group 3 [some adverse effect; some modifications needed; benefit-cost ratio near unity but appears to be favorable] . . . . any channel improvement that is on the borderline between two groups should be placed in the more critical group, subject to change with more detailed analysis."

34. Ibid.: "Channel improvement is to be planned and carried out with minimum losses to fish and wildlife habitat (WS Memo—102) . . . . Channel improvement is supplementary to floodwater retardation, not an alternative for achieving an adequate level of flood protection . . . . Channel improvement is not to be used where its primary purpose is to bring new land into agricultural production . . . . In agricultural flood plains, the level of flood protection should be only high enough to permit profitable use of such land within its capabilities for sustained agricultural production . . . . In non-agricultural flood plains . . . except in unusual cases channel improvement should not be used if its primary purpose is to make land suitable for non-agricultural development . . . . Channels must be stable immediately after construction as well as after aging . . . . improved channels should follow existing alignment approximately . . . . Even though they may increase costs, the least destructive construction techniques are to be used . . . ."

35. See for instance *The Effect of Channelization*, Hearings, especially pp. 201–02; also *Stream Channelization*, Hearings, Part 1, especially pp. 11, 159, 408–09.

36. *Watersheds Memorandum 108*: "Much of the channel improvement work that is not yet installed was planned before the enactment of P.L. 91-190 and the recent changes in our planning policies and criteria. The purpose of this review is to determine what changes in work plans or engineering design are needed to further national policy and goals for the environment . . . . The channel improvement in the [sic] Group 1 can be implemented without further action except for minor changes of design and specifications and of construction drawings already prepared. Work plans with channel improvement in Group 2 are to be supplemented or revised before scheduling or proceeding with additional construction. Plans in Group 3 are to be set aside for complete restudy and reformulation before further construction."

37. See *Stream Channelization*, H. Rept. 93-530, pp. 92-93. This uncertainty was clarified in April 1972 by *Advisory WS-12*, which directed that environmental statements be prepared for fiscal year 1973 channelization projects, *if* they had been placed in Group 2 or Group 3 under the 108 review, "unless agreement has been reached that plans for structural measures, as revised, do not

have significant adverse impacts." The memorandum stressed, however, that this "agreement" was also a "determination" within the sole responsibility of the SCS, which was "not to be relegated to another agency." In short, application of NEPA's requirements was to be based upon the 108 review, and even projects that had been identified as having significant environmental impacts by this process might not have environmental statements prepared if modifications were made to mitigate those sorts of impacts.

38. *Stream Channelization*, Hearings, Part 2, p. 530. The testimony of the SCS Administrator in mid-1971, four months after *Watersheds Memorandum 108* was issued and approximately at the time the review was due to be completed, is particularly instructive: "The extent of channel improvement in a watershed is determined by the intensity of development and the planned use of the adjacent flood plain and the magnitude and frequency of flooding expected after other feasible measures have been installed. The decision to provide a specific level of protection is based on existing investments in the flood plain, its productivity in comparison to available alternative land . . . . the type of farm enterprise . . . . availability of alternative development sites for future growth, and impact of lack of development on the community." Conspicuously absent from this set of criteria was any reference to nonagricultural ecological productivity, to the noneconomic functions and "best uses" of flood plains in a broad sense, or to the environmental policy goals and mandate of NEPA. The Administrator's statement shows no evidence of any change in the economically dominated objectives and criteria by which channelization projects had traditionally been justified.

39. Ibid., Part 1, pp. 11, 152; Part 2, p. 518.

40. Ibid., Part 2, p. 485.

41. For fuller discussion, see *Stream Channelization*, H. Rept. 93–530, pp. 82, 86, 92–95.

42. U.S. Department of Agriculture, Soil Conservation Service, *Environment Memorandum 1*, March 19, 1971.

43. Ibid.: "The National Environmental Policy Act and its requirements for environmental statements reinforces the mission of the Soil Conservation Service. The Service mission *is* concerned with the environment and all its complex interrelationships . . . . It *is* SCS policy to assist public and private institutions, organizations and individuals in improving the quality of man's environment . . . In providing technical assistance, it *is* SCS policy to use a systematic interdisciplinary approach" [emphasis added].

44. Ibid.: Section 102 (2)(C) procedure is to be applied to those major federal actions having a significant effect on the environment even though stemming from projects initiated prior to enactment of the Act on January 1, 1970. *Major federal actions in these older projects are to be handled on a case-by-case basis*" [emphasis added].

45. See for instance *Stream Channelization*, Hearings, Part 1, pp. 9-10, 35-36, 110, 112, 164-65. This is not intended to suggest, however, that the other activities of the agency were necessarily free of potentially adverse environmental impacts (for instance, from fertilizer and herbicide usage in land treatment).

46. *Watershed Protection Handbook Notice 1-17*, April 7, 1971.

47. In the words of *Notice 1-17* (Section 101.313): "To satisfy the Act . . . it is necessary that all appropriate disciplines be consulted and that their multiple judgment be seriously and objectively considered. The State Conservationist is to establish operating procedures which will assure that all appropriate disciplines, including those outside the watershed planning staff, are consulted frequently throughout the planning process and early enough for their views to be given meaningful consideration. Alternatives . . . and recommendations given are to be based on interdisciplinary judgment and not prejudiced by the views of a singular technical background." In *Notice 1-17*, the SCS also stated, finally, a policy that environmental quality was to be considered an objective of all watershed projects, thus apparently bringing it to the official position that the Corps had taken a year previously. A later revision of *Environment Memorandum 1* (November 1971), however, reiterated the previous assertion that NEPA merely reinforced prior policy of the agency.

48. Ibid., Section 113.133.

49. *Supra*, note 25.

50. *Supra*, note 26.

51. Ibid., Section 113.42.

52. *Supra*, Chapter 4, note 41 and footnote f.

53. *Notice 1-17*, Section 113.42-43. Measures such as acres and stream miles reveal nothing about the values or functions of those areas that would be damaged by a proposed project. They thus provide little new information that would have value for decisionmaking, in the absence of more detailed measures of effects on conditions and biological communities in the acres and miles affected.

54. U.S. Department of Agriculture, Soil Conservation Service, *Environment Memorandum 6*, September 9, 1971.

55. See U.S. Congress, *Agriculture-Environmental and Consumer Protection Appropriations, Fiscal Year 1972*, Conference Report 92-376, Washington, D.C., 1971.

56. See Chapter 4.

57. U.S. Department of Agriculture, Soil Conservation Service, *Watershed Protection Handbook Notice 1-18*, October 22, 1971.

58. Ibid., Section 108.05.

59. U.S. Department of Agriculture, Soil Conservation Service, *Environ-

ment Memorandum 1 (Revised), Federal Register XXXVI (December 11, 1971), p. 23674. One important new policy that was established by this memorandum was that *private land treatment measures* associated with SCS watershed projects were to be considered part of the "major federal action" whose environmental impacts must be considered. This change seems consistent with judicial decisions applying NEPA to other federal assistance programs, such as a ruling blocking the State of Texas from "piecemealing" a highway project in order to build one link through a park with state funds and thus avoid compliance with NEPA and other federal laws (see *San Antonio Conservation Society v. Texas Highway Department*, 2 ERC 1872, 1 ELR 20379, 5th Circuit 1971). It was also consistent with the philosophy of applying NEPA to the whole set of impacts that might be triggered by a federal action.

An important practical consequence of it, however, was to weaken the policy of *Watersheds Memorandum 102* that "SCS does not consider land treatment measures installed by land owners and operators as adequate mitigation for damages caused by structural measures." While it did not directly supersede this policy (and may not have been intended to), the effect of it was obvious in the revised draft environmental statement for the controversial Chicod Creek (North Carolina) project, in which heavy emphasis was placed upon the "beneficial" impacts of land treatment in order to blanket the potential damage of the structural measures. See Soil Conservation Service, *Revised Draft Environmental Impact Statement, Chicod Creek Watershed, North Carolona, May 1974.*

One additional point about this new memorandum was that it was the first to be published in the *Federal Register* for general information. The SCS had been under considerable pressure from the Council on Environmental Quality and other sources to begin publishing its regulations in this fashion.

60. *Environment Memorandum 1 (Revised)*: "The National Environmental Policy Act . . . reinforces the mission of the Soil Conservation Service. The Service mission is concerned with the environment and all its complex interrelationships. Program activities focus on conserving, developing, and productively using the Nation's soil, water, and related resources within the concept of balanced growth—quantity with quality . . . The goal is to help meet man's requirements for goods and services while the natural environment is maintained in a quality condition . . . . SCS resources are to be used in ways that contribute to the prudent use of natural resources and the improvement of the environment."

61. U.S. Department of Agriculture, Soil Conservation Service, "Questions and Answers with respect to Watershed Program Activities prepared by SCS Watersheds Group," August 1971. It *was* circulated to SCS staff one and a half years later as an informational item: see SCS, *Advisory WS-5*, January 30, 1973, reprinted in *Agriculture . . . Appropriations for 1974*, Hearings, Part 2, pp. 344–80.

62. Ibid., p. 347 and others following.

63. See ibid., pp. 347–48 and others following.

64. See, for instance, ibid., p. 350.

65. See, for instance, ibid., page 371.

66. Ibid., p. 349.

67. Survey by author, October 1971. See also footnote b and Chapter 4, notes 64 and 65.

68. See U.S. Congress, Senate Committee on Public Works, *Small Watershed Program*, Hearing, April 22, 1970. Washington, D.C., 1970. The texts of these statements and comments on them may be found in *Stream Channelization*, Hearings, Part 2, p. 618-722.

69. *Stream Channelization*, Hearings, Part 2. For instance, two-thirds of these statements contained no description of the setting of the project at all, and the remainder contained only brief descriptions mentioning some major indicators (for instance, total acreage, percentages of major land uses, and general mention of environmental resources and "watershed problems"). All contained little or no detailed or quantified discussion of potentially adverse environmental impacts: at most, acreage of wildlife habitat destroyed might be mentioned. Several stated categorically that the project would have "no known adverse impacts," despite comments to the contrary by other federal agencies. None of the statements provided any detailed discussion of alternatives to the proposed projects. One stated without explanation that there were "no alternatives . . . which would also accomplish the desired objectives" (p. 693).

Eleven stated that several alternatives had been considered, but failed to discuss their content, their relative merits, or the reasons for their rejection. Only three mentioned the alternative of inaction, and only five went even so far as to specifically *identify* any other alternatives that had been considered. In four statements in which problems raised by other agencies were mentioned, no response to these problems or disposition of them by the SCS was included; and four of the five statements among these fifteen which had been commented upon by other federal agencies misrepresented the comments that were made (see pp. 621-79).

70. *Administration of NEPA*, Serial 91-41, Part 1, p. 985. Agency witnesses testified that these statements did not "fully meet our current standards for environmental statements," but that they ". . . have not been revised for a number of reasons including the fact that these plans have now been approved by the Committees of Congress and Federal assistance for their implementation has been authorized."

71. *Stream Channelization*, Hearings, pp. 713-16, 735-47, 766-85, 798-809, 825-34, 863-74. SCS Environmental Statements for the Little Bigby Creek Watershed, Tennessee; Cedar Creek Watershed, Georgia; Clarence Cannon Memorial Watershed, Missouri; Middle-South Branch Forest River Watershed, North

Dakota; Yantic River Watershed, Oklahoma; and Sweetwater Creek Watershed, Tennessee. These averaged 4.7 pages per statement, and 7.6 miles of channelization per project.

72. Ibid. As noted above (note 69), at least four earlier statements had overtly misrepresented the comments made by other agencies. In three of these statements, the SCS concluded its text with the categorical statement that "comments from all reviewing agencies were favorable toward the project" (pp. 623, 634, 671), failing to mention adverse impacts and criticisms included in these comments that had not been discussed in the environmental statements themselves (pp. 628, 631, 640, 677, 678). In the fourth statement, on North Dakota's Upper Turtle River Watershed, the SCS quoted comments favorable to its activities and ignored other portions of the same comments citing environmental damage that would be caused by the project (pp. 647–652). Finally, also on the Turtle River statement, the SCS failed even to mention comments received from the U.S. Bureau of Sport Fisheries and Wildlife, whose reconnaissance report of June 1966—twelve pages long and submitted as a portion of that agency's comment on the SCS' environmental statement—amounted to a far more detailed statement of many of the project's environmental impacts than the environmental statement itself (pp. 665–66).

73. Ibid., pp. 801, 828. One statement mentioned the alternative of purchasing the endangered lands and dedicating them to wildlife management or other flood-compatible uses; this was immediately ruled out as too expensive, however, without mention of the intermediate alternative—possibly cheaper, though not necessarily—of purchasing easements for the same purpose. Two statements said simply that "no other means of development and use of the area had been *suggested*" (emphasis added), ignoring the agency's responsibility to suggest and consider such alternative means itself.

74. Letter dated December 15, 1970, from Mr. Timothy Atkeson, General Counsel, Council on Environmental Quality, to Dr. T.C. Byerly, Assistant Director, Science and Education, Department of Agriculture. Quoted in *Stream Channelization*, Hearings, Part 2, p. 392. In Mr. Atkeson's words: "... the SCS appears to be going through the motions in their preparation. They are almost identical in form and appear to have been prepared in Washington from a standard form system rather than in the field. Most SCS statements fail to mention esthetics. Only one mentions how many miles would be channelized. Only two mention the number of acres of swamp or wetlands to be drained. None of them include Department of Interior Fish and Wildlife Service comments on environmental impact. A change in the method of preparation of SCS 102 (2) (C) statements is clearly needed. The discussion of them in last week's hearings in the House Committee on Merchant Marine and Fisheries is indicative of the criticism outside of the Council on Environmental Quality upon SCS procedures."

75. All statements submitted prior to May 1971 on projects involving channelization may be found in *Stream Channelization*, Hearings, pp. 723–34,

748–65, 786–97, 810–24, and 835–61. Later statements must be obtained individually through the agency or other sources.

76. See ibid., pp. 726, 752, 789, 846, 858–59. Each statement, for instance, typically asserted that "continuation of the present trend in the use of the flood plain is in harmony with local desires"; it then mentioned the alternative of less intensive development of the flood plain, but then immediately dismissed it on the grounds that it "would not fit into the economic enterprises to which most of the present landowners are committed." Such phraseology gave the appearance of rational decision making while actually communicating no factual information about the proposed project: it substituted undefended assumptions and judgments for the factual information that must either support or belie them. Even if true, such assertions did not fulfill the law's intent that the statements be useful for independent review.

77. Ibid., pp. 690, 867. For instance, one statement counted the following as separate "favorable impacts":

1. Reduce the rates of erosion and sediment production.
2. Protect 4,800 acres of upland from land destruction or depreciation by gully head advancement.
3. Reduce sediment entering the Big Sioux River from this project area by about 80 percent.
4. Reduce sediment entering Lake Nixon from 22,500 tons to about 3,800 tons annually.

78. See ibid., for the following examples:

Reduction of groundwater recharge.
Reduction in benefits of periodic flooding (for instance, benefits in maintenance of certain species of bottomland hardwoods).
Effects on stream velocity (and the implications of such effects for both water quality and fish habitat).
Effects on stream temperature (and similar implications).
Effects on river bottom substrata.
Specific increases or decreases likely in fish and wildlife populations (for instance, pounds or numbers of each species of fish expected per unit area before and after channelization, and the basis for the expectation).
Secondary impacts: for instance, environmental impacts of private lateral drainage made feasible by presence of the SCS project.
Implications of various *combinations* of actions.

79. See ibid., p. 547–51. The SCS Administrator explained the fact that no projects had been cancelled by saying: ". . . we haven't turned them down, because when you make the 102 study and you find that you have problems, we are then back in the process of attempting to modify or change or adjust or make a determination on those projects." He conceded that no project had ever been turned down as a result of such a determination.

80. *The Effect of Channelization*, Hearings, pp. 120–21.

81. *Administration of NEPA*, Serial 91–41, Part 1, p. 1002, and *Agriculture . . . Appropriations for 1972*, Hearings, p. 498.

82. See *Administration of NEPA*, Serial 91–41, pp. 1001-02. According to testimony of Agriculture Department witnesses: ". . . under our organization the preparation of 102 (2)(C) statements and other costs directly attributable to the National Environmental Policy Act will be absorbed by the agencies. There has been no special request, none that I know of, for additional funds to implement the act. That does not mean that there are no costs, but that they would be absorbed within our present means, those directly attributable to this act."

83. *Watersheds Memorandum 108*. The proposed committee would also have been authorized to provide consultation and guidance on the review of all watershed work plans, to review the state reports and make action recommendations to the Administrator, and to "review the need for and place of channel improvement in the watershed program."

84. *Stream Channelization*, H. Rept. 93-530, pp. 82-83; also Hearings, Part 4, p. 2704.

85. See David Braybrooke and Charles E. Lindblom, *A Strategy of Decision* (New York: Free Press, 1963); also Charles E. Lindblom, "The Science of Muddling Through," *Public Administration Review*, XIX (Spring 1959), pp. 70-88. "Disjointed incrementalism" is the term coined by Charles Lindblom to describe the routine behavior of bureaucratic organizations. Its principal characteristics include jurisdictional fragmentation (as a means of breaking down complex problems into manageable units), incremental rather than radical actions, sequential planning (or reliance on later incremental actions to correct any errors in present decisions), and "partisan mutual adjustment" or bargaining and compromise among conflicting organizations.

86. See *Stream Channelization*, H. Rept. 93-530, pp. 83-96. On page 86, the report concludes flatly that "The Soil Conservation Service's level of compliance with NEPA has been so low as to verge on deliberate evasion of the law."

87. *Natural Resources Defense Council v. Grant*, 341 F. Supp. 356, 2 ELR 20185 (E.D.N. Carolina, March 16, 1972).

88. Ibid., at 3 ELR 20176 (E.D. N. Carolina, February 3, 1973). For mid-1973 status report, see U.S. Congress, House Committee on Appropriations, *Agriculture-Environmental and Consumer Protection Appropriations for 1974*, Hearings, Washington, D.C., 1973, Part 2, p. 343.

89. For the 1972 revisions see U.S. Congress, House Committee on Merchant Marine and Fisheries, *Administration of the National Environmental Policy Act-1972*, Hearings, Serial 92-24 Washington, D.C., 1972, pp. 488-97. For the later revisions see *Federal Register* XXXVIII (November 19, 1973), p. 20549, and *Federal Register* XXXIX (May 29, 1974), p. 18678.

90. U.S. Council on Environmental Quality, *Report on Channel Modifica-*

tions, by Arthur D. Little, Inc. (Washington: U.S. Government Printing Office, 1973).

91. For this conclusion as well as more detailed history of the evolution of this report, see *Stream Channelization*, H. Rept. 93-530, pp. 97-109.

92. Reprinted in *Stream Channelization*, Hearings, Part 5, pp. 3238-69. For a chronology of these and other events bearing upon the channelization issue, see *Stream Channelization*, H. Rept. 93-530, pp. 8-9.

93. U.S. General Accounting Office, *Adequacy of Selected Environmental Statements*, Report B-170186 (November 27, 1972).

94. U.S. National Water Commission, *Water Policies for the Future*, Washington, D.C., June 1973, pp. 32, 34-36.

95. *Stream Channelization*, H. Rept. 93-530.

96. *Federal Register* XXXVIII (September 10, 1973), pp. 24778-869.

97. The Water Resource Development Act of 1973, Public Law 93-251, Section 73. See Chapter 4, text at note 107.

98. See *Agriculture . . . Appropriations for 1974*, Hearings, Part 5, p. 944.

99. For this latter codification, see *Federal Register* XXXIX (May 2, 1974), pp. 15284-94. This codification appears to have resulted at least in part from one of the recommendations of the Reuss Committee the previous September (*Stream Channelization*, H. Rept. 93-530).

100. Above, note 89.

101. Ibid., p. 490.

102. U.S. Department of Agriculture, Soil Conservation Service, *Watershed Protection Handbook Notice 1-19*, May 24, 1972. Subsequently *Notice 1-20* (September 1, 1972) directed additional changes, but these appeared to be strictly technical rather than substantive in nature.

103. U.S. Department of Agriculture, Soil Conservation Service, *Advisory WS-17*, June 7, 1972.

104. U.S. Department of Agriculture, Soil Conservation Service, *Watersheds Memorandum 121*, September 1, 1972.

105. *Environment Memorandum-12.* The memorandum listed twelve issues that the SCS defined as being within its "jurisdiction or special expertise," upon which its reviewers should comment in the statements of other agencies, including land suitability and limitations for the proposed actions, erosion control and water management, effects on drainage patterns, commitments of prime farmland and other land and water resources, and changes in the well-being of rural communities.

106. *Environment Memorandum-9* was dated June 20, 1972; EM-10, July 14, 1972; EM-12, September 15, 1972; and EM-13, November 6, 1972.

107. U.S. Department of Agriculture, Soil Conservation Service, *Advisory*

WS–26, June 25, 1973: "Guidelines for Improving Soil Conservation Service Environmental Statements for Watershed Projects."

108. Ibid., p. 8 and Appendices B, C and E.

109. Ibid., p. 6.

110. Above, note 74 and accompanying text.

111. *Federal Register* XXXIX (June 3, 1974), pp. 19646-60.

112. Ibid., p. 19648, section 650.3.

113. Ibid., pp. 19650-51 (section 650.8) and pp. 19659-60.

114. Ibid., pp. 19660.

115. Ibid., pp. 19649-50, section 650.7.

116. Ibid., section 650.7 (a)(2).

117. According to SCS officials interviewed by the author.

118. U.S. Department of Agriculture, Soil Conservation Service, *Environmental Assessment Procedure*, May 1974.

119. U.S. Department of Agriculture, Soil Conservation Service, *USDA Procedures for Planning Water and Related Land Resources In Programs Administered by the Soil Conservation Service*, March 1974.

120. *Federal Register* XXXIX (June 3, 1974), p. 19651, section 650.8(b)(3).

121. Ibid., pp. 19650-51, section 650.8(b)(2).

122. See U.S. Congress, House Committee on Appropriations, *Agriculture-Environmental and Consumer Protection Appropriations for 1975*, Hearings, Washington, D.C., 1974, Part 2, p. 361. In a letter dated the preceding August, SCS Deputy Administrator William Davey also informed Subcommittee Chairman Whitten that 618 previously approved watershed projects would be subject to NEPA requirements and that 79 of these were being directly delayed. This letter is also reprinted in the hearings (p. 372).

123. *Agriculture . . . Appropriations for 1975*, Hearings, Part 2, p. 430.

124. SCS staff estimate.

125. SCS staff interview, October 1971.

126. *Agriculture . . . Appropriations for 1974*, Part 2, pp. 392-93.

127. Ibid., Part 2, pp. 278-79, 290, 295, 328.

128. *Agriculture . . . Appropriations for 1975*, Hearings, Part 2, p. 430.

129. *Agriculture . . . Appropriations for 1974*, Hearings, Part 2, p. 278.

130. *Agriculture . . . Appropriations for 1975*, Hearings, Part 2, p. 360.

131. *Agriculture . . . Appropriations for 1974*, Hearings, Part 2, p. 192.

132. Ibid., Part 2, e.g. pp. 328 and 419.

133. See ibid. During the SCS' appropriations hearings for Fiscal Year 1974, for instance, Congressman Whitten opened the session with a long soliloquy about the value and accomplishments of the SCS watersheds program,

followed by a heated denunciation of the Environmental Protection Agency for alleged ignorance of traditional environmental programs, failure to spend funds appropriated to clean up the Great Lakes, and delaying SCS programs by imposing environmental requirements (pp. 143–45). At two later points in the hearings he returned to this theme, pressing SCS witnesses to furnish evidence of EPA interference in SCS programs and to tell him "what the Subcommittee needs to do to get the Environmental Protection Agency off your neck to the point of letting you go on with your business" (pp. 288–305, 419–20). The testimony of SCS officials indicates their recognition that they would save themselves time and effort by complying with NEPA's procedures rather than being sued, but Whitten's line of questioning suggested not only irritation with bureaucratic delays, but also personal pique at the new political effectiveness of environmental advocates and a desire to intimidate the EPA out of any strong pressure on previously approved SCS projects (pp. 279, 290, 295, 328, 420).

Other subcommittee actions bear out these conclusions and particularly show its determination to reduce pressures from EPA and the Council on Environmental Quality on the public works and agriculture agencies. During the Fiscal Year 1975 hearings on the EPA budget, for instance, Chairman Whitten staged a patronizing political "stunt" at the expense of new EPA Administrator (and former CEQ Chairman) Russell Train (*Agriculture . . . Appropriations for 1975*, Hearings, Part 5, pp. 145–49). He opened the hearings with a speech to the effect that the EPA was "putting the undesirable ahead of the dangerous," referring particularly to the substitution of organo-phosphate pesticides for the banned DDT but also to EPA delays of flood control projects, a theme which he reiterated throughout the hearings. Following this speech, he directed the showing of a slide show and a movie for Mr. Train's benefit. The slide show was a promotional briefing by a lieutenant colonel from the Corps of Engineers, touting the benefits of the Corps' Mississippi River and Tributaries flood control project and showing scenes of flooding and destruction during a 1973 flood in areas where Corps projects had not yet been constructed. Whitten's "moral" from this show was that "not only should the Corps make an environmental impact statement as to what their projects may mean, but the Environmental Protection Agency, before it becomes a party in any way toward holding up any of these projects that are badly needed, should have a study so that they can see what the effect might be in advance" (p. 149). In other words, the EPA should stop taking actions whose effect might be to slow down the construction of water projects. The movie, which followed the slide show, appeared from Whitten's introductory remarks to show the "environmental backlash" that was allegedly developing in areas "where all the forested areas . . . are at present being destroyed because of EPA's refusal to let them use DDT."

The showing of these films was at the least a condescending put-down of Mr. Train, who had been actively concerned with the policy decisions between environmental quality and both these issues, water projects and DDT, for some years. It was a deliberate "jerking of his chain," bluntly reminding him of his subservience to the committee that must approve his agency's annual budget. More than that, however, it interjected Whitten into the role of refereeing the policy disagreements between the EPA and the water development agencies (most directly the Corps), and refereeing them from the viewpoint of the most conservative forces in those agencies.

The subcommittee supplemented its oratorical tactics with several tangible measures. It added fourteen new positions and $250,000 to the budget of the EPA, earmarked for additional environmental staff to conduct early and authoritative field liaison with public works agencies—specifically the Corps, SCS, Tennessee Valley Authority, and Department of Transportation (p. 369). The "string" attached to this gift was the implication that the EPA had better stop delaying those agencies' projects: in the Committee's words, "With this procedure the Committee would expect the Environmental Protection Agency to reduce the formal review process from months down to days" (H. Rept. 93-275, June 12, 1973, p. 57). Moreover, despite the likelihood that such a procedure would make the review process more "efficient," it amounted to a subtle means of circumventing the openness of the review and comment process created by NEPA, by directing that these field liaison officials approve projects on behalf of the EPA "during the initial planning stages of a project when mutually agreeable with and requested by the initiating agency." (p. 56). It also carried an almost certain risk that these individuals would quickly be co-opted by the initiating agencies or their own departmental officials into poor bargains: the experience of the Bureau of Sport Fisheries and Wildlife in commenting on SCS projects prior to NEPA is instructive on this point. (cf. *Stream Channelization*, H. Rept. 93-530, pp. 57-61; also cf. Gilbert F. White, "Environmental Impact Statements," *The Professional Geographer* XXIV, November 1972, pp. 302-09).

The subcommittee also established two new criteria for environmental review of projects that were already under construction. The Committee Report for Fiscal Year 1974 directed that in reviewing such projects, the project's total benefits be weighed against only the *remaining* costs, rather than against the total costs; and second, that the review of impact statements prepared for ongoing projects "should in no case exceed ten working days" (H. Rept. 93-275, p. 57). The first of these criteria was reasonable, since costs already incurred were "sunk"; the second, however, reduced the review process for such projects to a charade. The obviously intended effect of both provisions was to take the environmentalists' heat off of ongoing projects, regardless of the magnitude of environmental impacts that might be caused by federal actions to complete them.

The subcommittee also directed its staff to undertake an investigation of the practices of the Council on Environmental Quality and the Environmental Protection Agency in reviewing environmental impact statements; and it directed

the EPA to contract for a $5 million study of its own structure and perform-
ance, to be conducted by the National Academy of Science with periodic progress reports to the subcommittee (see *Agriculture . . . Appropriations for 1975*,
Hearings, Part 5, pp. 917-54; Part 8, pp. 505-18; and H. Rept. 93-295, p. 59).

Finally, in the second House Report on EPA's appropriations for Fiscal
Year 1975 (after a Presidential veto), Whitten's committee directed that "none
of these funds are appropriated for the purpose of administering any program
that reduces the supply or increases the cost of electricity or food to the consumer." (H. Rept. 93-1379, September 25, 1974). This language did not pass
the Senate, but it was clearly the most direct attack yet by Whitten on any effective EPA action involving agricultural or energy programs (or indeed involving
any of the multitude of energy and food processing industries).

134. The origin of this policy was EPA's preference of a standards-and-
enforcement approach to water quality management over an approach that in
effect provided federal subsidies to polluters by regulating streamflow for their
benefit. The streamflow-regulation approach is also known as the "low-flow
augmentation" approach to water quality management.

135. House Report 93-1120, June 18, 1974, p. 72. Final action had not
yet been completed on this legislation as of this writing, however, following a
Presidential veto in August 1974.

136. See for instance H. R. 93-275, p. 76 and pp. 78-79; also House Report 93-520, September 20, 1974 (conference report). The broader history of
this issue is a story in itself of the perennial struggle between successive Administrations and Congresses over the Rural Environmental Assistance Program
(REAP), originally named the Agricultural Conservation Program. This program allowed each farmer to propose agricultural conservation projects for his
lands and to receive federal assistance for implementation of those projects if
they were approved by the local Soil and Water Conservation Committee and the
Agricultural Stabilization and Conservation Service. It was linked to SCS activities in part by similar programs and objectives and more tangibly by the fact that
up to 5 percent of the ACP funds were "passed through" to support SCS technical assistance.

According to Congressman Whitten, this program was created in 1936, and
had been cut from Administration budget requests 18 times in the past 36 years.
Each time, however, the funds were restored by Congressman Whitten's Agricultural Appropriations Subcommittee (*Congressional Record* CXX, June 21,
1974, p. H5517). The Nixon Administration made its own attempt to eliminate
this program in December 1972, and the program's congressional supporters
immediately attempted to require its reinstatement by legislation; but this drive
failed when Senate and House conferees were unable to agree (see U.S. Congress,
House Committee on Agriculture, *Rural Environmental Assistance Program*,
Hearing, January 1973; H. Rept. 93-6, February 5, 1973; and H. Rept. 93-107,

April 2, 1973). Failing this, Whitten refused to fund the Administration's proposed Land Inventory and Monitoring Program and included funds in the budget for REAP despite the Administration's termination of the program; he angrily criticized the Council on Environmental Quality for not requiring preparation of an environmental statement on the Administration's action in terminating the program (*Agriculture . . . Appropriations for 1974*, Hearings, Part 5, pp. 4-5, and H. Rept. 93-275, pp. 78-79). In the conference report on the appropriations bill, both Senate and House conferees denounced the Administration's promotion of the Rural Development Act programs while cutting previous ones, arguing that the Act was supposed to amplify rather than replace past programs (H. Rept. 93-520, September 20, 1973). In December 1973, a judicial decision held that the Administration's termination of the program had been illegal and directed that the funds appropriated for it be expended (*Guadamuz v. Ash*, D D.C. Civ. No. 155-73). The Administration's response was to propose a consolidation of various agricultural conservation programs under a new label, the Rural Environmental Program (REP), to be administered by the ASCS, ostensibly to increase administrative efficiency and to permit farmers to come to one place for all their federal assistance needs. An additional result, however, would have been to permit more administrative discretion as to how the funds would be spent, and Whitten's committee therefore refused to fund the new program and funded the old REAP instead. The crux of Whitten's argument was that ACP/REAP was a successful program and therefore should not be disturbed (*Agriculture . . . Appropriations for 1975*, Hearings, Part 2, p. 407). The Administration would probably argue in response that it was indeed a successful "pork barrel" for farmers; but whatever its merits, it was a focal point of congressional opposition to the Nixon Administration's agricultural policies, to which the implementation of the Rural Development Act was held hostage.

This incident also provides additional insight into the long history of Whitten's subcommittee in defending agricultural programs against external pressures for change and its record of effectiveness in doing so. The demands of environmental advocates in the 1970s were different in their substance than many previous pressures on the agricultural agencies, but they had no greater means for effecting those demands than did the Presidents who had eighteen times sought to alter or abolish the Agricultural Conservation Program.

137. Public Law 93-251, Section 73.

138. SCS staff interview, October 1971.

Chapter 6
A Comparative Evaluation

1. SCS staff interview, October 1971.

2. U.S. Congress, House Committee on Appropriations, *Agriculture-*

Environmental and Consumer Protection Appropriations for 1975, Hearings, Washington, D.C., 1974, Part 2, pp. 355, 361; also SCS staff interviews.

3. See Chapter 5, note 75. For instance, during the spring of 1971 the SCS submitted environmental statements on six channelization projects averaging just under six miles of channel excavation per project; in no case was more than fourteen miles of channelization involved. During the same period, however, it entered new contracts—a major decision point—for at least nine channelization projects averaging nearly eleven miles of channelization per project, and in one case as much as twenty-three miles, none of which were preceded by environmental statements. See also U.S. Congress, House Committee on Government Operations, Subcommittee on Conservation and Natural Resources, *Stream Channelization*, Hearings, Washington, D.C., 1971, Part 2, pp. 545–47. Thirteen new contracts are listed, of which nine mention the number of miles of channelization proposed.

4. See *Stream Channelization*, Hearings, Part 2, p. 545. This conclusion is supported by testimony of SCS officials: "Projects that were underway are going ahead on the determination that they would not create a serious environmental concern. In other words, if we and the sponsors recognized that we had a serious problem or one that needed to be looked at, we would not be proceeding."

5. See, for instance, Leonard Ortolano and William W. Hill, *An Analysis of Environmental Statements for Corps of Engineers Water Projects* (Fort Belvoir, Va.: U.S. Army Engineer Institute for Water Resources, 1972).

6. U.S. Congress, House Committee on Government Operations, *Stream Channelization*, House Report 93–530, Washington, D.C., 1973, p. 95; see also *Stream Channelization*, Hearings, Part 5, p. 2806.

7. Id.

8. U.S. Water Resources Council, *Initial Report to the Water Resources Council by the Special Task Force*, Washington, D.C., June 1969; see also *Report to the Water Resources Council by the Special Task Force*, Washington, D.C., July 1970.

9. See Chapter 4, note 104.

10. See U.S. Congress, House Committee on Appropriations, *Agriculture–Environmental and Consumer Protection Appropriations for 1974*, Hearings, Washington, D.C., 1973, Part 2, pp. 295, 343. The best known of these was against the 66 miles of channelization planned in the Chicod Creek project, North Carolina (*Natural Resources Defense Council v. Grant*, E.D. North Carolina, complaint filed November 2, 1971). Two others were directed at the Blue Eye Creek project in Alabama (June 1971), and the Black Creek–Mason County project in Michigan (November 1971); the first of these was not a NEPA suit originally, but environmental issues were later added to it.

11. For these hearings, see U.S. Congress, House Committee on Merchant

Marine and Fisheries, Subcommittee on Fisheries and Wildlife Conservation, *Administration of the National Environmental Policy Act*, Hearings, December 1970, Serial 91-41, Washington, D.C., 1970; *Stream Channelization*, Hearings; and U.S. Congress, Senate Committee on Public Works, *The Effect of Channelization on the Environment*, Hearings, July 1971, Serial 91-H24, Washington, D.C., 1971.

In the NEPA oversight hearings, subcommittee members questioned the SCS witnesses briefly on their interpretation of the applicability of NEPA to their watershed projects, but the bulk of their inquiry centered on two issues affected by NEPA whose history was far longer: objections to SCS watershed projects by state fish and wildlife agencies, and the extent of SCS' authority to deny assistance or require project modifications in order to protect fish and wildlife values. In all, thirty of the total forty-four pages of testimony on the implementation of NEPA by the entire Department of Agriculture were devoted to its implementation in the SCS watersheds program; and Chairman Dingell used the occasion to admonish the SCS sternly concerning its openness to public concerns, and to hold up innovations by the Corps as examples for SCS to follow. (*Administration of NEPA*, Serial 91-41, Part 1, pp. 987-88).

The hearings on stream channelization, and in the Senate on the effect of channelization, centered on the practice of stream channel excavation by federal agencies and the effects of this practice on environmental resources. Among the topics about which SCS witnesses were questioned were the agency's use of environmental impact statements, and the status of its channelization review under *Watersheds Memorandum 108*—both of which, as noted in the text, stemmed wholly or in part from NEPA.

While the questioning during these hearings does not appear to have been hostile, the obviously intended effect of them was to spread on the public record evidence of widespread and frequently well-documented opposition to the practice. This evidence in turn provided ammunition for Congressman Reuss' abortive effort to halt the funding of channelization in the Fiscal Year 1972 appropriations legislation. As chairman of the subcommittee, Reuss prepared for the hearings by soliciting statements from agencies in all fifty states, particularly from fish and wildlife agencies, which he then compiled as a part of the hearing record. The testimony of the agencies practicing channelization—principally the Corps of Engineers, SCS, and the Tennessee Valley Authority—was sandwiched between three volumes of testimony, letters, and other information submitted for the record by its opponents, which included both federal and state fish and wildlife officials as well as conservation interest groups and some of the new "environmentalist" groups.

12. See U.S. Congress, House Committee on Public Works, Subcommittee on Investigations and Oversight, *Red Tape—Inquiring Into Delays and Excessive Paperwork in Administration of Public Works Programs*, Hearing, June 1971, Serial 92-15, Washington, D.C., 1971.

The difference in testimony between the Corps and the SCS at these hearings was striking. The Corps took a relatively neutral, factual position in its presentation, devoid of histrionics about how much the requirements of NEPA and environmental litigation were delaying its projects, and it even pointed out that significant portions of the delays in its processing of projects were the fault of the Congress itself (*Red Tape*, Serial 92-15, pp. 313-38). In contrast, Hollis Williams of the SCS, the Deputy Administrator for Watersheds, used the occasion to complain strenuously about attacks on channelization by witnesses at the Reuss hearings and by "special interest groups." His obvious intent was to whip up visible Congressional support against the pressures raised by the Reuss hearings, in favor of his traditional program and practices. The following dialogue is illustrative (*Red Tape*, Serial 92-15, pp. 217-18):

MR. WILLIAMS: Mr. Henry Reuss, Chairman of the Subcommittee on Conservation and Natural Resources, Committee on Government Operations, has written to Mr. Mahon, Chairman of the Appropriations Committee, that he is going to propose an amendment on the floor through the Agriculture Act of 1972 that there be a moratorium on all channel work until study is made by the professionals.

MR. WRIGHT: Who would he regard as being professional, if the Soil Conservation Service with all the years of background is not regarded as professional?

MR. WILLIAMS: I believe he would have to answer that, Mr. Chairman. The point is, he has openly and notoriously served notice on the chairman of the Appropriations Committee of the House that he intends to do this, and Mr. Whitten and others have been in contact with us regarding this issue . . . .

MR. WRIGHT: . . . I am certain that the Congress in passing requirements for the interagency review process never intended to create an adversary situation in which one agency of the Government would assume the almighty wisdom to try to block all the activities of another agency of the Government . . . . I think it is a travesty that certain agencies have abrogated to themselves the right to pass almighty judgment on the work of other agencies, and obviously it has slowed down a great many worthwhile public activities.

13. See U.S. Congress, *Agriculture-Environmental and Consumer Protection Programs, Fiscal Year 1972*, Conference Report, House Report 92-376, Washington, D.C., 1971, Amendment No. 22.

14. U.S. Congress, Senate Committee on Public Works, *Small Watershed Program*, Hearing, April 1970, Washington, D.C., 1970. See also *Administration of NEPA*, Serial 91-41, Part 1, p. 985.

15. One important example of this publicity was a 1972 article entitled "Stream Channelization: Conflict Between Ditchers, Conservationists," *Science* CLXXVI (May 26, 1972), pp. 892-93).

16. See Frederick R. Anderson, *NEPA in the Courts* (Baltimore: Johns Hopkins Press, 1973), especially pp. 286-89.

Chapter 7
Values and Limitations of the NEPA Mechanism

1. U.S. Congress, *National Environmental Policy Act of 1969*, Senate Report 91-296, July 9, 1969, Washington, D.C., 1969, p. 13.

2. Id.

3. Ibid., p. 6, note 2.

4. See Chapter 2; recall especially Professor Caldwell's testimony that "A statement of policy by the Congress should at least consider measures to require the Federal agencies, in submitting proposals, to contain within the proposals an evaluation of the effect of these proposals upon the state of the environment" (U.S. Congress, Senate Committee on Interior and Insular Affairs, *National Environmental Policy*, Hearing, April 16, 1969, p. 116). See also Joseph L. Sax, "The (Unhappy) Truth About NEPA", *Oklahoma Law Review* XXVI (May 1973), pp. 239-48.

5. For definitive discussion of the judicial treatment of NEPA through early 1973, see Frederick R. Anderson, *NEPA in the Courts* (Baltimore: Johns Hopkins Press, 1973).

6. Sax, "The (Unhappy) Truth," refers to this tendency as the "adhesion syndrome," the habit of agencies in trying to "stick together and tell the same story." See also Gilbert F. White, "Environmental Impact Statements," *The Professional Geographer* XXIV (1972), pp. 302-09. The Daddario report was titled *Managing the Environment*, discussed in Chapter 2.

7. Mancur Olson, *The Logic of Collective Action* (New York: Schenken Press, 1968).

8. The Administrative Procedures Act of 1946, 5 U.S. Code 551 *et seq.*; and the Freedom of Information Act, 5 U.S. Code 552 *et seq.*, as amended.

9. Cf. Joseph L. Sax, *Defending the Environment* (New York: Alfred Knopf, 1970).

10. Cf. David Braybrooke and Charles Lindblom, *A Strategy of Decision* (New York: Free Press, 1963).

Index

Index

About the Author

Richard N. L. Andrews is Associate Professor in the School of Natural Resources of The University of Michigan, where he teaches in the areas of natural resource and environmental policy, and urban and regional planning. He has been engaged in research on the National Environmental Policy Act since 1971, and his related experience includes employment on the professional staff of the Office of Management and Budget and as a consultant to three federal agencies and several private research and training organizations. Professor Andrews received the B.A. degree from Yale University in 1966, the Master of Regional Planning from the University of North Carolina in 1970, and the Ph.D. from the University of North Carolina in 1972. Portions of this research were carried out under a Resources Fellowship awarded by Resources for the Future, Inc., a private, nonprofit organization devoted to the study of natural resource policy issues.